A ghost A Day

A ghost A Day

365 TRUE TALES

of the Spectral, Supernatural, and …
Just Plain Scary!

MAUREEN WOOD and RON KOLEK

Avon, Massachusetts

Published by
Adams Media, a division of F+W Media, Inc.
57 Littlefield Street, Avon, MA 02322. U.S.A.
www.adamsmedia.com

ISBN 10: 1-4405-0608-6
ISBN 13: 978-1-4405-0608-6
eISBN 10: 1-4405-0862-3
eISBN 13: 978-1-4405-0862-2

Printed in the United States of America.

10   9   8   7   6   5   4   3   2

Library of Congress Cataloging-in-Publication Data
Wood, Maureen.
A ghost a day / Maureen Wood and Ron Kolek.
p. cm.
ISBN 978-1-4405-0608-6
1. Ghosts. I. Kolek, Ron. II. Title.
BF1461.W65 2010
133.109—dc22
2010019546

This publication is designed to provide accurate and authoritative information with regard to the subject matter covered. It is sold with the understanding that the publisher is not engaged in rendering legal, accounting, or other professional advice. If legal advice or other expert assistance is required, the services of a competent professional person should be sought.

—From a *Declaration of Principles* jointly adopted by a Committee of the American Bar Association and a Committee of Publishers and Associations

Many of the designations used by manufacturers and sellers to distinguish their product are claimed as trademarks. Where those designations appear in this book and Adams Media was aware of a trademark claim, the designations have been printed with initial capital letters.

This book is available at quantity discounts for bulk purchases.
For information, please call 1-800-289-0963.

DEDICATION

This book is dedicated to our significant others, Janet Kolek and Stephen Wood, without whose patience and continued support this book would never have made it to the shelf.

ACKNOWLEDGMENTS

Any book dealing with such a wide variety and number of entries requires a lot of support. To mention a few, we would like to thank Jeff Belanger of Ghostvillage.com and Jeremy D'Entremont and Richard Felix of *Most Haunted* for their inspiration and guidance.

In gathering supernatural accounts for this book, we would like to thank Bety Comerford, Rick Hines, Leigh Ross, Michele Nixon, and Ryan Dube for sharing their personal stories.

And, of course, we would like to thank our agent Deidre Knight, of the Knight Agency, for her unending faith and constant support.

We especially would like to thank Andrea Norville and Adams Media for providing us the opportunity to make this book a reality.

Last but certainly not least, we would like to thank our children, Ron Kolek Jr. and Sabrina and Joshua Wood for their belief in us and their encouragement to persevere.

FOREWORD:

Three Hundred and Sixty Five Ghosts

No matter how technologically advanced we become, ghost stories will always be a part of human existence. The Italian writer Italo Calvino said it well: "The more enlightened our houses are, the more their walls ooze ghosts." Everyone loves a good ghost story, and even the most hardened skeptic is likely to get a shiver or two from many of the tales in this book.

Ghost stories are compelling because they awaken a part of our brain that's usually dormant in our sunlit everyday lives. They suggest possibilities. Obviously, they suggest that there is life after death, something we all want to believe in, but more generally, ghost stories are a bridge from the world we understand to a world we can't fully know. They're a spark for the imagination.

There's a smorgasbord of hauntings here, from haunted houses to ships to airplanes to lighthouses—even a haunted cane that was sold on eBay. Many of the entries fall under the heading of folklore. Tales of that category should never be confused with factual history, but they do serve an important role as reflections of our cultural identity. Folklore, as a wise man once said, is history as it is remembered by the people.

Other stories contained here aren't so easy to explain away as folklore or tall tales. Some are firmly rooted in factual history. Those are the ones that may get deep under your skin.

I've had some interesting nights in my life, but I've had few as deeply affecting as the ones I've spent with Ron Kolek and Maureen Wood during paranormal investigations. I first met them in the summer of 2005, when the New England Ghost Project became the first organization to conduct a paranormal investigation at Portsmouth Harbor Lighthouse in New Castle, New Hampshire. I quickly learned that Ron and Maureen's approach to their work was careful and professional, but I also learned that they maintain a healthy sense of humor about it all. That seems to me to be a very human and healthy response to the strangeness they deal with on a regular basis.

Since then, I've come to know Ron and Maureen as friends, and as sincere explorers of an uncharted realm. They're the perfect guides for this year's worth of spooky tales. Enjoy!

—Jeremy D'Entremont, author of *Great Shipwrecks of the Maine Coast* and *The Lighthouse Handbook: New England*

INTRODUCTION

Within the pages of this book, we have captured numerous occurrences throughout history, dating back to the first recorded ghost hunter, Athenodoros Cananites, who encountered a ghostly apparition that guided him to its skeletal remains, to American troops encountering a ghostly child while fighting in Afghanistan.

Without even leaving the comfort of your chair, you'll journey across the globe, from the top of Mount Everest to a sunken wreck at the coldest depths of the ocean. You'll find that ghosts show up in innocent places, such as the school where a lost soul returns for a yearbook picture or the lonely lighthouse where a keeper continues his thankless duties, as well as in more terrifying locations, like the creepy cemetery where the dead have come back to taunt the living.

Although many of these stories are based on legend, others are eyewitness accounts. As you read this book, you'll find it's hard to separate the truth from the legends. Yet history tells us that even legends are based on fact. And truth is stranger than fiction!

JANUARY 1, 1745
THE BONES OF GENERAL
"MAD ANTHONY" WAYNE
Route 322, United States

General Anthony Wayne was one of George Washington's most brilliant commanders. Nicknamed "Mad Anthony" by his troops, he was at times quick tempered, but fearless and a brilliant tactician who was personally responsible for several key American victories. After the war, he retired to Pennsylvania and served in the state legislature. He later moved to Georgia and served in the U.S. Congress.

During the Northwest Indian war, he was recalled to duty. After a successful campaign, he grew ill on the way home from Detroit, and on December 15, 1796, he died from complications of gout. General Wayne was then buried beneath the flag in front of the blockhouse at Fort Presque Isle.

Thirteen years later his son, Isaac, returned to Fort Presque Isle to retrieve his father's body for burial in the family's plot. When they opened the coffin, they found that the body was in better shape than expected. Lacking adequate space in the surrey to transport the general's remains, they decided to bring just his bones home. With the help of a doctor, the flesh was removed by boiling the corpse in a big pot.

The flesh and water was then reburied at Fort Presque Isle and the bones were packed in a trunk. It has been rumored that on the way home some of the bones fell from the surrey and were lost. Today, if you drive along Route 322 on New Year's Day, Wayne's birthday, you might be lucky enough to spy the General's ghost wandering the road looking for his bones.

JANUARY 2, 1815
THE KEEPER OF GIBRALTAR
POINT LIGHTHOUSE
Toronto, Canada

Erected in 1808, Gibraltar Point Lighthouse is one of the oldest lighthouses in Canada. The lighthouse's first keeper was a man named John Paul Rademuller. It was well known that John was a bootlegger, often keeping a stash at the lighthouse to help pass the long, cold winter days and nights. On a dreary night in January, John heard a knock on the lighthouse door. When he opened the door he was confronted by three drunken soldiers from a nearby fort. They demanded some of his homemade brew. When he refused, they beat him to death, dragged his body up the stairs of the tower, and threw him off the top of the lighthouse. When sanity set in and they realized what they had done, they panicked. In order to cover up their crime, the soldiers decided to get rid of Rademuller's body. They dismembered him and buried the mutilated remains around the lighthouse, and as the legend goes, Rademuller was never seen again. At least not in corporal form.

In 1893, another lighthouse keeper, George Duman, found bones buried near the keeper's house. Believing they belonged to the legendary Rademuller, he continued his search. Unable to find a complete skeleton, Duman reburied the ones he had found. Unfortunately he never marked the grave, and to this day, no one knows where it is located.

Through the years, many have witnessed mysterious happenings at the lighthouse. Spectral images, unearthly groans, the sounds of "something" being dragged up the towers stairs, materializing blood spots, ethereal lights, and a strange mist swirling around the tower have all marked the return of Rademuller. Could he be reliving that cold winter night back in January 1815, or is he roaming about searching for his bones? We will never know until the day the dead can speak.

JANUARY 3, 1870
THE BOUNCER OF THE BRIDGE CAFÉ
New York, New York

Formerly named the Hole in the Wall, the Bridge Café, built in 1794, has changed hands several times. The building has been a brothel, a bar frequented by pirates, and a seafood restaurant to name a few of its incarnations. Throughout its history, there have been many unsavory characters associated with the building, most notably, Gallus Mag. Mag, who was nicknamed Gallus by the type of suspenders she wore, was a six-foot-tall Englishwoman who took her role as bouncer to a gruesome level. Brandishing a pistol and knife, she would clamp on to her unruly patrons with her teeth and drag them out of the bar. If they were too rowdy, this overzealous bouncer was known to bite off the offending patron's ear. As a warning to would-be troublemakers, the ear would be pickled and left atop the bar for all to see.

Today, patrons and employees of the Bridge Café have reported seeing shadows moving about the building. But that's not all; during the late-night hours disembodied voices have been heard. And the sounds of footsteps have reportedly echoed from the second floor when no one is upstairs. If the owners and patrons are correct, then Gallus Mag, the bouncer who ruled with an iron fist, is still on duty.

JANUARY 4, 2010
THE "E STREET UNWELCOMER"
Springfield, Oregon

According to the *Eugene Community Examiner*, a ghostly apparition has startled commuters heading west on E Street, toward Eugene. The majority of reports come from witnesses who have driven the patch of road during the evening hours. While driving, they've looked to the left side of the road and seen a ghostly figure dressed in black materialize before their eyes. Many have claimed to be overcome with fear. Some have reported that the dark figure advanced toward them and then disappeared before their eyes. Other locals have stated that they've come close to striking the specter. And even then, when the strange entity is close enough to reach out and touch, its features are indiscernible. Although no one knows why this ghostly visitor is haunting E Street, one thing is for certain. The "E Street Unwelcomer," as it has become known, is not only a distraction, but also, a road hazard.

JANUARY 5, 2005
DEADLY SKIES
Inchon, South Korea

According to the Korean news outlet *Chosun Ilbo*, a thirty-six-year-old woman committed suicide onboard a Korean Airline flight in January 2005. Flight attendants became worried when one of the passengers did not return to her seat. Upon investigating the plane's lavatory, they discovered that the woman had hanged herself with her scarf. Attempts to revive her failed.

Over the next few months, the plane was plagued by a series of odd occurrences. The crew noticed peculiar cold spots and heard unworldly voices. On one occasion a Buddhist monk, the lone passenger in the first-class section, began chanting. When the flight attendant asked if anything was wrong, the monk replied, "There are dead people sitting in each of the empty seats." On another occasion, a member of the crew was taking a nap when he felt someone tuck the blanket in around him. When he opened his eyes he saw a hand coming out from the wall. In an attempt to free the plane of the spirits, the crew secretly blessed the bathroom with sacred liquor. But it was unsuccessful. To quell the increasing complaints by the crew, the airline reportedly took the plane out of service.

In May 2008, on a Korean Airline flight, another passenger, like the first, committed suicide in the bathroom by hanging herself with a scarf. Was this the same plane that was secretly put back in service or just some macabre coincidence?

TERRIFYING TIDBIT

Cold spots are an indication that spirits are at hand because they are thought to draw the energy (heat) out of the air.

JANUARY 6, 2003
HAUNTED DERBY
Derby, England

As reported on the BBC's website, Derby, England, with over 1,000 documented ghostly sightings, has been named the ghost capital of England. Just ask Terry, the landlord of the Dolphin Pub, about the

spirits that frequent his establishment. And by spirits, he's not refer-
ring to the liquid gold behind the bar.

The 500-year-old pub is haunted by at least four spirits. In fact,
Terry's wife once felt a strong presence in the bathroom. And on
another occasion was shocked when her pants suddenly levitated
off of the bathroom floor! Despite this bizarre incident, it appears
that Terry has little to worry about. A psychic who was called in to
investigate stated that the spirits were attracted to her kind, spiritual
nature.

JANUARY 7, 1870
VIVIA THOMAS'S REVENGE
Fort Gibson, Oklahoma

Vivia Thomas was the daughter of a wealthy Boston businessman and
attended the finest schools. One day, at a social gathering, she met a
handsome army officer. After a whirlwind courtship, they announced
their engagement. But shortly before the wedding, the young officer disappeared, leaving a note stating that he was going out west in
search of adventure. Vivia was enraged and embarrassed by this turn
of events, and she swore revenge.

Discovering that he had been stationed at Fort Gibson in Indian
Territory, Vivia devised a plan; she cut off her hair, put on men's
clothes, and departed for Fort Gibson to enlist in the army. Careful not to get caught, she watched the young officer and waited
for her chance. Finally, on a cold day in December an opportunity
presented itself. She stationed herself with a gun behind a rock she
knew her ex-fiancé would ride by, and as he did, she shot and killed

him. When they found him, they assumed he had died at the hands of the Indians and brought his body back to the fort to be buried.

At first Vivia was delighted. Then guilt set in. Each night she would go to his grave and weep. On a frigid January night in 1870, she wept no more. Overcome by grief, she lay down on the grave and cried herself to sleep. The next morning, they discovered her frozen body. The fort's doctor examined her corpse and found that the young soldier was actually a woman. A priest in whom she had confided then came forward, and her whole tragic story unfolded.

Today, you can find Vivia buried at Fort Gibson National Cemetery in a place called the Circle of Honor. But it seems the Circle of Honor does little to quiet her restless soul, as many have claimed to see Vivia's apparition still in soldier's garb weeping for her young officer.

JANUARY 8, 1851
THE BLOODY PIT
North Adams, Massachusetts

In 1851, the construction of the Hoosac railroad tunnel, which cut through the side of a mountain, was a gigantic feat and one that would be the cause of over 200 deaths by the time it was completed. In fact, many of the crew had nicknamed the five-mile long tunnel, "The Bloody Pit."

During its construction, there was an explosion at the site that left two miners dead. The third man involved, the one who accidentally caused the blast, Kelly Ringo, walked away unharmed. Not more than a year later, Kelly entered the tunnel to begin his workday. He was later found dead of strangulation. No living person was ever apprehended for his murder. In fact, many of the locals believed that the spirits of the two minors had returned to exact their revenge.

Over the years there have been numerous supernatural events reported at the site. Swaying spectral lanterns have been seen in the otherwise dark tunnel. And many have heard the tortured cries of lost souls emanating from within.

There are those that believe the men who lost their lives to the development of this railroad pass still linger in its dark cavern. And although entering on foot is not allowed, many a grown man would refuse to go in anyway, under any circumstances.

JANUARY 9, 1979
THE RIDGES
Athens, Ohio

The Ridges, an asylum for the criminally insane, opened its doors in 1874. Also referred to as the Athens Mental Health Center, this 1,000-acre facility in its heyday was considered to be one of the more humane psychiatric centers. Evidently, the popularity of the Ridges grew, because during the early 1900s overcrowding issues began, causing patient care to quickly deteriorate. Rather than maintaining their stance on therapeutic treatments, the doctors and staff brought back older methods. Eventually, patients were subjected to bouts of shock and water therapy, as well as lobotomies. Physical abuse ensued. By 1993 the asylum closed its doors for good.

It is said that all patients were accounted for except for one, Margaret Schillings, who disappeared on December 1, 1978. Although the facility was searched, she could not be found—not until forty-two days later when, on January 9, 1979, a maintenance man discovered her naked, decaying remains on one of the abandoned floors. Her mysterious death was ruled to be of natural causes. However, since then, people have heard the cries of a disembodied female voice. Shadows have been reported to linger in the empty halls. The unexplainable squeaking sound of gurneys in motion has been heard. Some have seen the ghostly image of a woman peering out one of the windows. But the oddest anomaly of all is the irremovable stain shaped like a human body on the floor in the exact spot where Margaret Schillings's remains were discovered that fateful day in January 1979.

JANUARY 10, 2000
PHANTOM WARRIORS
Nuwokat, Nepal

Maoist insurgents launched a nighttime attack on a police outpost just outside of Bidur, the capital of the district. Three policemen were killed in the brutal invasion, and the station was heavily damaged. Several months later, the police station was restored and reopened. But the terror of that night still remains.

According to the *Nepali Times*, since the post was reopened, it has been plagued by frightening events. Constable Tikaram Thapa told reporters that an unseen force enters the station at midnight and assaults the policemen stationed there. The men feel as if they are being strangled, and some have even fallen unconscious. Consensus among the department is that the spectral attackers are those who died in the invasion, who have come back to haunt the living. Many of the policemen are so terrified they've requested a transfer, but their requests have been denied.

Superintendent of Police Dhiraj Pratap Singh said that all "necessary steps" would be taken to end the assaults. He went on to say that either a puja (an appeasement ceremony) would be performed or, if all else failed, "the station will be moved somewhere else." But will the phantom warriors move with them? Only time will tell.

JANUARY 11, 2010
TAN HILL INN
North Yorkshire, England

Tan Hill Inn, the highest pub in England, is located 1,732 feet above sea level. Maybe the fact that this stone structure sits closer to heaven has something to do with the reports of paranormal activity. The unexplained sweet aroma of pipe smoke lingers in the air near the kitchen, the cellar, and the rear entrance to the building. Angie McKinnell, the manager of the inn, believes the pipe smoke is connected to three cattlemen from over several hundred years ago who had smoked heavily within the pub walls. The ghostly apparition of a young boy about ten years old wearing a brown jacket and shorts has been seen several times in the bunkroom area. Each time he is seen, he waits several seconds, makes eye contact, and then vanishes into thin air. Ellen, another worker for the inn, described her encounter with the spirit of a man just outside the rear of the building. He appeared just as she began to cut up cardboard boxes. The phantom specter was there so long, she even pointed out his unwillingness to help. Seemingly unaffected by her words, he just stood there, watching. Yet, just like the young boy, the ghost disappeared in a matter of moments. Ellen's encounter only proves that even death is no cure for laziness.

JANUARY 12, 2010
THE LOST MOTHER
AT THE SKIRVIN HOTEL
Oklahoma City, Oklahoma

Once a speakeasy during Prohibition, this grand hotel built in 1910 has such a tale of suicide and death that it has even its most skeptical visitors shaking in their boots. Rumor has it that the owner, W. B. Skirvin, impregnated Effie, one of his chambermaids. In an attempt to avoid a scandal, he locked the woman in a room on the fourteenth floor, where she remained throughout her pregnancy and after. The woman became so distraught that while holding her baby, she jumped from the window.

Since the hotel's reopening in 2007, reports of paranormal activity have flourished.

Many male visitors have claimed to have witnessed the ghostly apparition of a female who frequents their rooms and lingers in the bathroom while they shower. Other visitors of the hotel have heard the screams and cries of a mother and baby. Some have even seen the spirit of a woman who looks lost and distracted as she wanders the halls with her child in her arms.

As reported in *USA Today*, certain players of the New York Knicks, after staying in the hotel, were more than happy to return home. Apparently the rumors of the hotel's ghostly inhabitants affected them so much they barely got a night's sleep, to which the Knicks attributed their defeat at the hands of the Thunder.

JANUARY 13, 2010
THE DEMON
Buffalo, New York

Something strange was going on in Lisa's Buffalo, New York, apartment. Something nasty. Disembodied voices, frightening whispers, and eerie sounds struck a chord of horror within her. Although not a religious person, when her granddaughter claimed she'd seen a dark man roaming throughout the house, she knew she had to do something. That's when she called the Western New York Ghost Hunters. In order to find a source for the haunting, they launched an investigation. It wasn't long before they made contact with the entity. Using an electronic device called the "Shack Hack," they learned its name was "Melchom," a taker of souls. The team of investigators, realizing they needed help, contacted exorcists, Cassidy O'Conner and Michael Rambacher.

According to Examiner.com, Cassidy and Michael had set up their equipment and had begun to chat with Lisa when Lisa's dogs became uneasy. Michael opened a bag he was carrying and placed a statue of Michael the Archangel on the table. Cassidy said that she became dizzy. She told the *Examiner*, "It did not like us there, and in my opinion was packing its bags when we walked through the door; for the demonic do not seem to appreciate us very much." Burning sage in a Mayan bowl, they blessed every room and every corner of the house. Almost immediately the atmosphere lightened and the demon was gone. For the first time in a long time, Lisa was able to get a good night's sleep.

TERRIFYING TIDBIT

A Shack Hack is a modified AM FM radio used by ghost hunters to communicate with the dead. The scanner is disengaged so that it continuously scans the airways. The spirits then answer questions by pulling in words spoken from various radio stations.

JANUARY 14, 1599
THE SCREAMING SKULL OF BURTON AGNES HALL
Burton Agnes, Yorkshire, England

Anne was the youngest of Sir Henry Griffith's three daughters. One day while returning from the village of Driffield, Anne was set upon by a band of thugs who beat her and left her for dead. Some of the townspeople found her and took her home to her family. Knowing that she was dying, she asked her sisters to promise that after her death, her head would be kept in the manor. But after she died, her sisters failed to fulfill their promise. Instead, they had her body interred in the family crypt. That night, the sound of bloodcurdling screams, slamming doors, and crashing objects echoed through the halls of the mansion. The next day, they exhumed her body and found her head detached and the flesh gone. Removing her skull, they brought it back to the Hall. Immediately all of the horrible sounds and screams ceased. Anne's will had been fulfilled. However, some of the servants grew tired of the grisly relic. One of the maids even threw the skull into a horse-drawn trash cart. As she did, the horse reeled and would not move until the skull was removed.

Through the years, several other attempts have been made to rid the Hall of the skull and all have failed. Finally, her skull was walled up somewhere in the manor, but that was not the last of Anne. Today her ghost can be seen roaming the halls, keeping constant vigil over her skull.

JANUARY 15, 1847
THE BLACK DAHLIA AT THE BILTMORE HOTEL
Los Angeles, California

Elizabeth Short was a stunning woman. She had come to the West Coast looking for fame and fortune, but it didn't quite work out that way. Her friends nicknamed her "The Black Dahlia," because she had black hair and loved to wear black clothes. But even her beauty couldn't help make her a star. Stuck in an ordinary job, she finally gave up and decided to move back home.

Her boyfriend, Red Manley, dropped her off at the Biltmore Hotel to meet her sister and left her in the lobby to make a phone call. That was the last time Elizabeth was seen alive. Six days later her body was found in a vacant lot posed in a seductive position, her mouth cut from ear to ear, and her torso sliced in two. The grisly crime became known as the "Black Dahlia Murder." To this day, it has never been solved.

Elizabeth never returned home, and it appears her spirit hasn't either. Guests and staff of the Biltmore have seen the ghostly apparition of a woman dressed in black. Each time, she appears agitated, pacing back and forth, waiting by the phones. She has also been spotted in the elevator and in the halls. Is Elizabeth looking for help or trying to find her killer? We will never know. But what we do know is that she came to California to become famous. Sadly for Elizabeth, she will forever be remembered, as the victim of the infamous Black Dahlia Murder.

TERRIFYING TIDBIT

If the lobby of the Biltmore looks familiar, it is because it was used in the hotel scene in the filming of the 1984 movie *Ghostbusters*. Who you gonna call? The Biltmore evidently.

JANUARY 16, 1881
THE FRANKLIN CASTLE HORROR
Cleveland, Ohio

Hannes Tiedemann built Franklin Castle in 1865. The first of a series of tragic events to befall his family was the death of the Tiedemann's fifteen-year-old daughter, Emma. To distract his distraught wife, Luise, he began renovating their home. While he was at it, he installed numerous hidden rooms and passageways beneath this Gothic mansion.

Within a span of three years, three more of the Tiedemann children died. Soon, Tiedemann became the subject of rumors. Was there something more sinister taking place? No one could be sure. At age fifty-seven, Luise died of liver failure, and in 1908, the heirless Hannes Tiedemann, too, met his maker. By that time, the reputation of the castle was already stained in blood, sexual depravity, and murder.

The castle remained abandoned for some time until eventually being sold to the Romano family. Soon after moving in, they reported hearing disembodied voices and organ music, and the light fixtures would violently shake. An exorcism was performed, but it was unsuccessful. Finally, tiring of it all, in 1974, the Romano family moved out.

Subsequent owners made gruesome discoveries. Dozens of human baby skeletons were uncovered in one of the hidden passageways. Although no proof could be found, some believe that they were the result of medical experiments. In 2003, a local land developer purchased the castle, which is now a private club to the elite. But one can only wonder if their membership includes its ghostly inhabitants.

JANUARY 17, 1892
MERCY BROWN, THE RHODE ISLAND VAMPIRE
Exeter, Rhode Island

The Brown family of Rhode Island endured tragedy after tragedy when the family contracted tuberculosis. A total of three family members perished. The last to die was nineteen-year-old Mercy Brown. According to her epitaph, Mercy was laid to rest on January 17, 1892. But she wouldn't stay that way for long. After her brother Edwin contracted the disease, the townspeople grew nervous. Rumors of Mercy being a vampire surfaced after her father, George, proclaimed her ghost visited his dreams each night and she would tell him how hungry she was. Not more than a month after Mercy was buried, George's madness took over. He, along with neighbors and friends, dug up her remains. Not surprisingly, due to the time of the year, Mercy's body was barely decomposed. They took it as a sign that she was among the undead; a vampire. At George's request, a doctor drained Mercy's organs of the remaining blood. Truly believing her plight was somehow afflicting

Edwin, her heart was removed from her body, burned, then used as an elixir and fed to her brother. Edwin died two months later. Today, visitors to Mercy Brown's "resting" place have reported seeing her ghost. The apparition of a young woman draped in black tattered clothing has often been seen roaming round her grave in Chestnut Hill cemetery. Perhaps she doesn't have the heart to leave.

TERRIFYING TIDBIT

Vampires were thought to despise mirrors, as they were not able to see their own reflection.

JANUARY 18, 1532
ROMANIAN POLICE POINT
FINGER AT GHOSTS
Lilieci, Romania

As reported in Ananova, Romanian police cited ghosts as the source of the vandalism and havoc that have plagued the village of Lilieci. When the first reports of the ghost attack came in, the police only laughed. However, when they went to investigate, they too were assaulted with cups that sailed through the air. It appears multiple homes were involved, because scores of families living in Lilieci spoke of bicycles flying through the air, windowpanes breaking one by one, and dinnerware thrown haphazardly about the rooms.

Two witnesses spoke of putting a match to a candle, only to have it blown out before it could be lit. One villager, sixty-eight-year-old Mircea Hadimbu, had seen severe damage done to his home.

A spokesperson for the police was quoted as saying, "There were bottles and things flying around. I did not know what to dodge first. We can find nothing to suggest it was anything other than what the people claim."

And since ghosts can't be prosecuted, the vandalism case was closed. However, the police have not abandoned the people of Lilieci. The services of a local priest have been obtained and an exorcism will be performed on the houses afflicted by the spectral being, with hopes that the attacks will cease and desist.

JANUARY 19, 1875
THE FINAL DECISION
Shanghai, China

Sir Edmund Hornby was chief judge of the Supreme Consular of China and Japan. Each of the judge's decisions was extremely crucial to the citizens of Shanghai. He would render them the night before and then pass them off to a local reporter for morning publication.

On one such night, he wrote his decision down, placed it in an envelope, and before retiring early, gave it to his butler. Later that night, a knocking on the bedroom door startled the judge. It was the reporter. Angry for the disturbance, he informed the reporter that the butler had his decision. The reporter said he was unable to find the butler and pressed the judge for his verdict. Furious, Sir Edmund told him to go away, but the reporter persisted. Afraid his wife would awaken, the judge gave in. As Sir Edmund spoke, the reporter scribbled shorthand. Finished, the reporter left, promising not to bother him again. It was 1:30 A.M.

The next morning the judge was informed that the reporter had died. Shocked, he inquired of his death. It seems the reporter had been working at his home when his wife asked him to come to bed. He replied that he was just waiting for the judge's decision. At 1:30 A.M., she found him dead on the floor, notebook in hand. The coroner placed the time of death at 1:00 A.M., a half hour before he had visited the judge. Yet, the judge's decision was in his notebook. At least the reporter was true to his word—he never bothered the judge again.

JANUARY 20, 1921
THE GLENWOOD AMBUSH
Kilkishen, Ireland

The Irish War of Independence (1919–1921) began with an unauthorized ambush of two RIC (Royal Irish Constabulary) by IRA (Irish Republican Army) volunteers under the command of Daniel Breen. This set the tone of the war, which primarily became a guerilla conflict with ambushes and reprisals.

In January 1921, thirty-seven members of the IRA under the command of Michael Brennan ambushed an RIC patrol in the Glenwood area just outside of the town of Kilkishen. The members of the IRA lay in wait for the patrol truck to enter the killing zone and then opened fired with rifles, shotguns, and revolvers. It was over in two minutes. The IRA fire was deadly. None of the RIC was even able to get a shot off. All but two of the patrol were either killed or mortally wounded. The IRA volunteers captured eight rifles, seven pistols, and 1,000 rounds of ammunition. This was a day they would never forget. And it seems the ghosts of their victims won't let them either. For years after the ambush, inhabitants of the area have been haunted by the horrific screams of the men who died that day.

JANUARY 21, 2010
CHILDREN OF ST. MARK'S CEMETERY
Picton, Australia

Saint Mark's Cemetery in Picton is reported to be haunted by two children who died nearly sixty years apart. David Shaw, the son of a preacher, died from polio in 1946. And Blanche Moon died in 1886 when she was accidentally crushed to death while playing on a pile of railroad ties. Renee English was on a local ghost tour when something extraordinary happened. She was a skeptic, who had just gone on the tour for a lark. While teasing the guide and asking when the ghosts were going to come out, she snapped a picture with her camera of the empty cemetery.

That night when she uploaded the photos, she couldn't believe her eyes. There in the photo were two children, a little girl and a little boy. Astonished, she called the local newspaper, *Courier Mail*, who published the photograph. When the reporter asked Renee to comment on the picture, she said, "I wasn't a believer in ghosts, but now I'm intrigued." She went on to comment, "I'm never watching a scary movie again."

TERRIFYING TIDBIT

Many paranormal experts believe most children are susceptible to seeing spirits prior to the age of seven.

JANUARY 22, 1906
THE SS *VALENCIA*
Beale Point, Vancouver Island

When the SS *Valencia* set out on that day in 1906 it wasn't on its normal run. The ship had been assigned the route from San Francisco to Seattle because the SS *City of Puebla* was laid up for repairs. But nevertheless, the *Valencia* was a sturdy ship with a fine captain, so few had any fears.

Soon the weather turned foul, with high winds and low visibility. The *Valencia* was forced to navigate by dead reckoning (using a compass and determining the distance traveled). Just before midnight, after passing the entrance of the Strait of Jaun de Fuca, the ship struck a rock ledge and ruptured it's hull. Dead reckoning had become deadly.

For thirty-six long grueling hours the crew and passengers of the *Valencia* fought for their lives. Lifeboats capsized; men were swept from her decks, thrashed on the rocks, or swept out to sea. In a moment of irony, a giant wave destroyed the last remnants of the vessel just as rescuers had reached the ship. There were only thirty-seven survivors.

TERRIFYING TIDBIT
The four popular reasons a ghost stays on this earthly plane: unaware of its death; unfinished business; desire to say goodbye; and last but not least, guidance to a loved one.

Five months later, a fisherman found a lifeboat from the *Valencia* and eight skeletons. Twenty-seven years later, another lifeboat in almost pristine condition was found floating in the sea. Over the next few years, many a sailor reported seeing the spectral image of the *Valencia* near the reef. It seems the spirits of the *Valencia*, those who lost their lives on that tragic day, were reaching out from the other side, refusing to be forgotten.

JANUARY 23, 1897
WITNESS FROM THE GRAVE
Greenbrier, West Virginia

Eva Zona Heaster married a drifter named Erasmus (Edward) Stribbling Trout Shue.

Mere months after their wedding, under mysterious circumstances, Zona was found dead. When the coroner, Dr. George W. Knapp arrived, Shue appeared so distraught by his wife's death that the doctor dismissed the possibility of foul play, listing it as "everlasting faint."

Zona's mother never trusted Shue, and upon hearing of her daughter's demise, she knew immediately that Zona had been murdered and Edward had done it. With no proof, she prayed for answers, and apparently, her words were heard. Over a span of four nights, Zona's ghost came calling. The spirit relayed all to her mother: the beatings, the brutality, and finally her murder. During one visitation, the ghost spun her head around indicating her neck had been broken.

Horrified, Zona's mother sought out the local prosecutor and told him of her daughter's visit. The prosecutor, in turn, interviewed the coroner, who admitted that the body of Zona had not been examined fully. The case was reopened, and Zona's body was exhumed. During the autopsy it was discovered that her neck had indeed been broken and her windpipe crushed. Bruising in the shape of fingers was now evident and Shue was arrested. He was tried in a court of law where the defense attempted to make Zona's mother appear crazy. Much to his dismay, the jury took the ghost's side and Edward was convicted and sentenced to life in prison.

JANUARY 24, 2005
SIR ERNEST SHACKLETON
Cape Royds, Antarctica

Ernest Shackleton was one of Britain's most famous Antarctic explorers. From 1901 to his death in 1922 he participated and led several expeditions to the Antarctic, earning him knighthood from King Edward VII. On the Nimrod Expedition in 1907 (named after the vessel that took him there) he brought a special prefabricated hut with him. It was erected at Cape Royds and served as his base of operations. On his last expedition to the Antarctic, Shackleton died of a heart attack. Despite his death, the one-hundred-year-old hut still remains, frozen in time.

On January 24, 2005, famed climber of Mount Everest, Sir Edmund Hillary, was visiting the hut as part of an effort to preserve it for the Antarctic Heritage Trust. When he opened the door to the hut, he had an eerie encounter.

Hillary said of this encounter, "I'm not a person who really sees things very much but when I opened the door I distinctly saw Shackleton walking toward me and welcoming me. It's the only time I can ever remember something like that, so I have a very warm feeling indeed for Shackleton and for his hut and I really believe Shackleton's hut must be preserved."

If this really was the ghost of Ernest Shackleton, it appears that his fascination with Antarctica is truly eternal.

JANUARY 25, 1998
THE MacKENZIE POLTERGEIST
Edinburgh, Scotland

Greyfriar Cemetery is said to be the most haunted, if not the most dangerous, location in all of Scotland. But who is buried in Greyfriar that could be creating such a stir? George MacKenzie, the man who persecuted and hanged hundreds of Presbyterian Covenanters. During the 1600s it was the Covenanters' mission to keep Scotland a Presbyterian nation. Unfortunately for them, King Charles II, had a different plan. Members of the political group were imprisoned, tried, hanged and beheaded. Judge MacKenzie earned the name "Bloody MacKenzie" for his persecution and execution of over 18,000 Covenanters. His reign of terror only ended when he died on May 8, 1691. Ironically he was laid to rest in Greyfriars Kirkyard near the Covenanters prison. There he lay in peace until 1998, when a local man desecrated his grave.

Since that time, hundreds of visitors and tourists have felt the wrath of the MacKenzie poltergeist. Some have been bitten, scratched, or hit; others have blacked out. In 2000, a failed exorcism was performed by Colin Grant. Coincidently, Grant died several weeks later of a heart attack. In 2004, the cemetery was desecrated again by two youths who decapitated a corpse and used its head as a hand puppet. The cemetery was closed for a while by authorities but reopened shortly after. Ghost tours still make their way through the gates of the cemetery and into the prison. Often they are greeted with vicious attacks. Not surprisingly, the majority of the attacks take place at the black tomb, where the remains of MacKenzie reside.

JANUARY 26, 1923
THE *FLYING DUTCHMAN*
Cape of Good Hope

Perhaps the most famous ghost ship of all is the *Flying Dutchman*. As the story goes, in 1641, a Dutch captain by the name of Hendrik van der Decken was attempting to round the Cape of Good Hope when a brutal storm arose. Gales howled. Thunderous waves pounded the ship. The crew pleaded for him to turn back. Ignoring their cries, he pressed on. Gripped with fear, the crew mutinied. Hendrik murdered the leader of the mutineers, tossing him overboard. Just then, a dark silhouette of a man appeared and rebuked him.

Van der Decken drew his pistol and fired at the spectral visitor to no avail. The phantom raised his head, glared at the captain, then spoke, "For your deeds, you are condemned to sail the oceans for eternity with a crew of soulless men, bringing death to all who spy your spectral ship. . . . You will never know a moment's peace."

Through the centuries, sailors have reported many encounters with the *Dutchman*. Some ships have found their provisions spoiled after meeting the ghost ship, and the more unfortunate have been lured to their destruction on uncharted reefs. The best-documented account was that of the corvette HMS *Bacchante* in 1881. While cruising off the coast of Cape Town, a strange red light appeared, and with it the *Dutchman*. Thirteen seamen aboard the *Bacchante* including Prince George, the future King of England, reported seeing the *Dutchman*. According to his diary, the lookout that spotted the *Dutchman* fell from the mast and died. Since then the *Dutchman* has been spotted several more times across the seven seas. It seems Captain van der Decken of the *Flying Dutchman* is doomed to sail the seas for eternity.

JANUARY 27, 1918
LILLIAN COLLINS HOSPITAL
Turlock, California

This remodeled 1918 structure, now known as the Sierra building, is the old Lillian Collins Hospital. Since it only contained forty rooms, its usefulness as a hospital was soon outlived and it was abandoned, but not forgotten. Especially for the spirits that remain.

The building was purchased in 1994 and the first floor was completely renovated for its new tenants, Coldwell Banker Endsley & Associates. However, it appears that the upper levels have remained full of spirits. Apparently the second floor was so spooky that local charities used the space to run yearly haunted house tours. During these fundraising events strange experiences began to occur. Items used for the haunted house started to go missing. There were reports of cold breezes and unpleasant sensations being felt. Visual encounters occurred as well—sightings of dark, shadowy masses floating throughout the building, causing those who encounter them to feel ill, a feeling that persists until they return to the first floor.

The owner has even had motion detectors go off for no apparent reason. Curious for answers, he called in a paranormal investigation team, who found energy spikes, orbs, and light anomalies, as well as various electronic voice phenomena (EVPs). In one such example they reported capturing what sounded like a spirit singing a French lullaby. Was this the spirit of the hospital's maternity nurse still tending to some spectral child or patients who passed in childbirth? Perhaps further investigation will reveal the building's secrets.

TERRIFYING TIDBIT

EVP (electronic voice phenomenon), also known as voices of the dead, is the voice of a spirit manifested in the white noise of a recorder.

JANUARY 28, 1772
THE WITCH OF ROSE HALL MANSION
Montego Bay, Jamaica

Rose Hall mansion was once considered among the finest of homes in the West Indian Islands. This Georgian home, built in the late 1700s, now houses a restaurant where haunted tours are conducted. But how and why did the paranormal happenings begin? Possibly the answer lies in the legend of Annie Palmer.

It is said that Annie, the witch of Rose Hall, learned her voodoo practices as a child growing up in Haiti. It's also believed that she disposed of three husbands and various slaves. Because of her voracious sexual appetite, she quickly tired of them. One husband was done away with by poison, another stabbing, and the third by pouring boiling oil into his ears. Her third husband, Robert Rutherford, was foolish enough to have an affair with Millicent, the maid. But then again, it was this affair that led to Annie's own downfall.

Millicent's mother, Takoo, was known to be a fierce voodoo practitioner. When Annie learned of her husband's infidelity, she cursed Millicent with her black magic. Suddenly the maid became deathly ill. Apparently Takoo and a group of slaves, unwilling to allow Annie to continue on her path of evil, suffocated Annie in her sleep.

Is it the "witch of Rose Hall" lingering within the walls of the mansion? Or, perhaps the soul of a spirit that was unfortunate enough to cross paths with Annie Palmer. If you're really curious, and you decide to make a visit and see for yourself, you may not be disappointed. It's said that many a tourist captures the ghostly face on film.

JANUARY 29, 1829
NIDDRY STREET VAULTS
Edinburgh, Scotland

When William Hare's boarder fell behind on the rent, he asked William Burke to collect it from him. Arriving at his room, Burke found the tenant dead of natural causes. Furious that the tenant died owing money, the two men came up with a macabre solution. They would sell the body to Edinburgh's Medical College. The college was desperate for cadavers, and the only legitimate supply was the bodies of executed criminals. Because of a recent reduction in executions, universities began offering decent money for bodies, with few questions asked. It wasn't long before gangs began raiding local cemeteries and snatching bodies from graves.

Burke and Hare, pleased with their return on the body of the tenant, decided that collecting fresh bodies might be more profitable than collecting rent. Rather than waiting for someone to die, the two men began a string of fourteen murders that lasted from November 1827 to October 1828. Eventually their macabre business was discovered, and they were arrested. Hare escaped the gallows, but Burke was hanged. Ironically his body was given to the university for dissection. Today, you can find Burke's skeleton, death mask, and a variety of items made from his skin on display at the university's museum. However, his ghost prefers to hang around the Niddry Street Vaults.

Guests on the local ghost tours have reported extreme cold spots, dizziness, and the sighting of a spirit thought to be the ghost of William Burke. Why is he there? The vaults are where he was known to store his victims. Perhaps he is looking for a misplaced corpse. Or is he still searching for a "fresh kill"?

TERRIFYING TIDBIT

The term *graveyard shift* dates back to the sixteenth century. Occasionally, persons were mistakenly buried alive, so bells were attached to strings in the coffins. Workers would make the rounds through the cemeteries several times a night listening for the ringing of the undead.

JANUARY 30, 2009
HOSPITAL SPECTER
Derby, England

It appears that ghostly sightings at Derby City General hospital in England have its employees on edge. There have been repeated reports of a shadowy figure clad in a long black cape seen darting in and out of the hospital rooms, down the hallways, and always disappearing into the wall. However, the spirit apparently has a penchant for the dead as well as the living, since his presence is most often seen hovering about the morgue.

What could be the source of this paranormal phenomenon? It has been said that during construction of the hospital, ignoring recommendations for an alternate location, developers built a portion of the building over ancient Britain's old Roman Road. It is thought that perhaps the ghostly specter is the wandering spirit of a Roman soldier. The manager of the hospital, concerned for the well-being of her staff, placed a call to the bishop requesting assistance. In response, a paranormal advisor and exorcist from a local diocese promised to perform a blessing. It is hoped that this ceremonial cleansing will put the minds of the staff to rest, and hopefully the spirit as well.

JANUARY 31, 1979
RESURRECTION MARY
Chicago, Illinois

Resurrection Mary is believed to be a young woman who in the 1930s, after leaving her boyfriend at the O Henry Ballroom, hitchhiked down Archer Street in Chicago where she was run down and killed and left for dead. Adorned in her white party dress and shoes, the young blond was buried in Resurrection Cemetery. Although the first eyewitness account of Mary's ghostly apparition was in 1936, the most recent report came in an interview with a cab driver in the *Suburban Tribune* on January 31, 1979. While driving down Archer Street, Ralph said he came upon a young woman standing out in the cold without a coat. Thinking she had car trouble, he pulled over. Within moments, the young blond, dressed in a white party dress, hopped into the front seat of his cab. When he asked where to, the young woman said that she wanted to go home then nodded straight ahead down Archer Street. Mary barely uttered a word. As Ralph watched her out of the corner of his eye, she acted so strange he couldn't help wonder if she was under the influence of some drug. Then, just as they were passing the cemetery, she sprang up yelling, "Here! Here!" Confused, Ralph stopped the cab. He looked from his right to his left. When he turned back, Mary had vanished. And she hadn't even opened the door. Although there are skeptics who believe Resurrection Mary to be nothing more than an urban legend, ask Ralph the cab driver and he'll certainly disagree.

FEBRUARY 1, 1974
THIRTEEN LOST SOULS
São Paulo, Brazil

Early one February morning, an overheated air-conditioning unit on the twelfth floor of the Joelma Building caught fire. The flames spread quickly, turning the twenty-five-story skyscraper into an inferno with temperatures reaching nearly 1,300 degrees Fahrenheit. People panicked, and fearing that they would be burned alive, they jumped to their deaths from the roof and upper floors of the building. Before the fire was extinguished, 189 people had perished. Among the dead were thirteen unidentified bodies found in the building's elevator. They had escaped the fire, but not death. Their remains were removed and buried together in Saint Peter's Cemetery. But are their souls at rest?

The building was virtually destroyed, but after four years of heavy construction it was reopened and renamed the Plaza of the Flag. Many believe it is haunted because, since the fire, several people have witnessed apparitions. In an attempt to cleanse the building, numerous rituals and ceremonies have been performed, but all have failed. Even today, the spirits of the "thirteen lost souls" can still be seen roaming the corridors and offices of the Joelma Building in search of their bodies.

FEBRUARY 2, 2000
HAUNTED PAINTING
Los Angeles, California

Under the heading of Antiques and Art on eBay, was item number 251789217: Haunted Painting, titled, "Hands Resist Him." Along with it were several photos, a brief description of the painting, a warning and disclaimer, and a brief narrative on the current owner's relationship with it. The photos revealed a two-by-three-foot painting of a little boy and a doll standing in front of French doors with many small hands behind the glass. Definitely creepy enough, but was it haunted? According to the owner it was.

She had purchased it from a "picker" who found it behind an abandoned brewery. It hung in her daughter's room until "things" began to happen. One morning her daughter was quite distressed. When she inquired why, the four–year-old told her mother that the children in the painting were fighting and at night stepped out of the painting. Her husband set up a motion-activated camera to see if he could catch the phenomenon. For three consecutive nights, the infrared camera kept its vigil. While reviewing the photographs, the husband became horrified. To his astonishment, one of the shots revealed a boy stepping out of the painting. That's when he placed it on eBay. Thirteen thousand people viewed the site, and ten days later it sold for $1,025.00.

It is not known what the new owner did with the painting. However, the previous owners not only got rid of the painting haunting their daughter, but they made a tidy profit as well.

TERRIFYING TIDBIT

Bill Stoneham painted the picture "Hands Resist Him" in 1972. When he was asked how his artwork ended up on eBay, he was at a loss. What he did know was that the gallery owner and critic who reviewed it were both dead within a year of its showing.

FEBRUARY 3, 1953
YORK TREASURER'S HOUSE
York, England

York's Treasury building, which was built in 1419, is reportedly home to the ghosts of Roman soldiers.

One reported sighting came from an apprentice plumber, Harry Martindale. In 1953 he was standing on a ladder working in the cellar of the Treasury building when he began to hear the sound of a horn blowing. Startled, Harry stood still, afraid to move. Suddenly, to his shock, a horse and cart carrying an unkempt soldier materialized from the wall. Behind it marched a band of Roman soldiers armed with swords and spears. One disheveled soldier carried a horn. Evidently, it was this sad-looking specter that had been the source of the sound that had first startled Harry. Curiously, the ghostly legions were visible only from the knees up. Later investigation showed that the York Treasury building had been erected over an old Roman road which lay fifteen inches below its basement's floor. As it turns out, Harry was not the first to have seen the ghostly troop of Roman soldiers. Nor, it is believed, will he be the last.

FEBRUARY 4, 1987
LIBERACE
Palm Springs, California

As relayed by FlashNews, Michael Luckman, author of *Alien Rock: The Rock 'N' Roll Extraterrestrial Connection* (Pocket Books), stated that during a meeting with Michael Jackson he was informed of Michael's ability to communicate with the spirit of Liberace. Apparently the King of Pop had a "mirrored room" at the Neverland ranch where he and Liberace would frequently converse. Not only had Michael seen and spoken to Liberace, but also Jackson expressed his belief that Liberace was in fact his guardian angel. If that wasn't enough proof of their conversations, Jackson reported that once, during his ghostly communication with Liberace, "The Glitter Man" gave Jackson permission to sing his favorite song, "I'll Be Seeing You."

One can never be certain whether Michael Jackson did in fact communicate with the deceased Liberace. However, we can only hope that the King of Pop and the Glitter Man have been reunited in the afterlife and are performing their music for those lucky enough to hear it.

FEBRUARY 5, 1967
THE SPECTRAL USHER
Minneapolis, Minnesota

Young Richard never seemed to fit in. Growing up, he had been constantly tormented by his peers. But when he took a job as an usher at the Guthrie Theater, he found solace in the old opera house. In escaping the real world through the fantasy of the stage, he had finally found a place where he fit in. Unfortunately for Richard, that changed when he began attending the University of Minnesota. At first he hoped that, just like the old theater, he would come to be accepted among his peers. He wasn't. Richard soon became known as a nerd. And it wasn't long before the dark memories of high school came back to haunt him.

Unable to escape the torment, he drove to a local Sears store, purchased a rifle, returned to his car, and killed himself. Two days later, they discovered his body still wearing his usher's uniform. Shortly after Richard's suicide, the spectral usher began showing up at the theater. Dozens of employees and patrons reported his presence to the management, describing him to a tee. He was spotted on the catwalk, Row 18 (the section he had been assigned) and the VIP section called the Queen's Box. An exorcism was performed in the theater in 1994 to rid it of his ghost. Sadly, it seems that even in death, Richard is still not wanted.

FEBRUARY 6, 1838
BOARS HEAD PUB
Lancashire, England

Tracy Mappley, owner of the Boars Head on Preston Old Road, believes her pub is haunted. Not only is it haunted, but also the spirit has been helping itself to Tracy's jewelry. But did she call the authorities when her jewelry began to go missing? No. Together with the loud banging sounds that awakened her more nights than not, the missing jewelry convinced her that a supernatural prankster was at work. To verify the goings on, she reached out to a group of mediums. And soon the Third Eye Paranormal Investigators visited the Boars Head to see what they could dig up. During their night-time vigil, the team of mediums communicated with several spirits. As the session progressed, to Mappley's amazement, the table began to move of its own accord. The group also ran an experiment of sorts. Before locking up one of the cupboards, they placed a bag coated with talcum powder in it. Later, when they unlocked the cupboard, they found that someone had mysteriously drawn the initials M and A in the powder. But who are the spirits that haunt the Boars Head? The mediums believe it is the spirit of a former regular along with a local farmer named George, who passed in 1838, refusing to leave their favorite hangout. They also reported that a little boy named Sean, wanting nothing more than to play, is the prankster behind the missing jewelry.

And although Tracy continues to deal with the unexplainable events, she decidedly has come to terms with them. At least for now, she knows who is behind the odd goings-on, and that's all she needs to know.

FEBRUARY 7, 1862
THE LADY IN BLACK
Boston, Massachusetts

Fort Warren, located on George's Island in Boston Harbor, was once a jail for Confederate soldiers. Aware of her Confederate husband's incarceration there, Melanie Lanier, a lovesick newlywed, set about planning to break her husband Samuel out. Leaving her Southern home, she headed for Hull, Massachusetts, where she took refuge with a family of Southern sympathizers.

She then put her plan into motion. Chopping off her hair, she donned a uniform and boarded a boat bound for the island. With the help of a prisoner, Melanie was hauled up by a rope through a musketry opening in the fort's wall. After joyfully embracing her husband, she unpacked the tools she'd smuggled in for Samuel and the other prisoners. Rather than escaping, however, they concocted a plan to tunnel into the armory, taking over the fort for the Confederacy.

It was a futile plan, because soon their digging attracted attention and they were captured. Brought before the fort commander, Melanie took out an aged pistol she had hidden and fired. Unfortunately, the pistol exploded in her hands and a piece of the shrapnel embedded itself in Samuel's brain. Branded a traitor, she was given a black gown to wear for her execution, which was carried out on February 7, 1862.

Not long after her death, the ghost of "The Lady in Black" began to appear. One soldier guarding the fort felt hands strangling him from behind, and when he turned around, he saw Melanie's ghost. He was so terrified he ran off and was later sentenced to thirty days for leaving his post. Through the years, soldiers have been known to fire at the ghostly image only to have her vanish. Although there are no soldiers stationed there now, the Lady in Black still makes her presence known to tourists visiting George's Island.

FEBRUARY 8, 1879
ALTOONA RAILROAD
Altoona, PA

The Altoona Railroad Museum is one of the most popular destinations for history buffs, and it appears to attract not only the living, but the dead as well. One of the most visible spirits (so to speak) is a specter named Frank.

On numerous occasions, various employees and directors of the museum have sighted his ghostly apparition. On one occasion, one of the directors entered a seldom-used elevator to go to the fourth floor. Once inside, he noticed a man with black hair standing at the rear. When the doors closed, the man turned to look at him, shimmered, rose toward the ceiling, and vanished into thin air! When the director finally calmed down from what he'd seen, he took a good look at the old pictures of museum staff that adorned the first floor walls. Immediately, he recognized Frank as one of the men on the boiler crew during the 1920s.

Although Frank is a prankster, he's been spotted so many times that when he's seen climbing on the train engine located in the lobby, hardly anyone blinks an eye. It is said, however, that although the majority of the staff have accepted Frank's presence, the director still refuses to use the elevator.

FEBRUARY 9, 2004
HAUNTED DYBBUK BOX
Portland, Oregon

During World War II, a young Polish woman who had lost her parents, husband, and children in a Nazi concentration camp immigrated to America. One of the few items she brought with her was a wine cabinet. She was very protective of it. In fact, when asked about it, she would spit three times between her fingers and say, "a Dybbuk, a Keslim." When she became an old woman, she requested the box be buried with her. She died at age 103, but the Orthodox rabbi wouldn't permit the box to be buried with her. So the Dybbuk box was included in her estate sale, where a young man who owned a furniture refinishing business purchased it.

TERRIFYING TIDBIT

Dybbuk is the Polish translation of the Hebrew word that means demon or a demonic entity that has entered the soul of a living person.

Over a period of several weeks he tried to gift the box to different family members, but each time it was returned. Although none were aware of it, all their excuses for returning the box were eerily similar. The doors of the cabinet refused to stay closed. And an unbearable smell of cat urine and jasmine assailed their senses. Finally the owner of the box gathered his family to compare notes. They were shocked when they realized that each of them had had the same nightmare of a demonic old hag who beat them. Moreover, in the morning, they would awaken to find their bodies bruised and battered. And if that was not terrifying enough, they had all seen a dark loping creature out of the corner of their eye slithering throughout their home. Horrified and wanting nothing more than to be rid of it, the young man put the box up for sale on eBay.

Eventually a curator of a museum purchased the Dybbuk box. Just like those before him, he too began to experience similar, paranormal occurrences. So where is the box now? The story so mystified a Hollywood producer that plans are in the works to make a movie. Now that's terrifying.

FEBRUARY 10, 1973
THE MATERNITY WARD
OF GRACE HOSPITAL
Calgary, Alberta, Canada

Something strange is going on at the maternity unit of Grace Hospital. And it may not be of this world. A sullen woman with a newborn baby has been seen wandering around a delivery room. When the staff has approached her to see if she needs any help, the spectral entity vanishes into thin air. She has been known to open windows, and for some reason bang on the pipes. Women assigned to that room always seem to have difficult births. Some believe it is because of the phantom visitor. But who is she?

To find the answer, you need only cross the street. Opposite the hospital is a park with a monument bearing her name. She is Maudine Riley, and it is said that she once owned the land the hospital was built on. In fact, the delivery room may be exactly over what was once her bedroom. Maudine died giving birth in that room, and her newborn child died shortly thereafter. So perhaps she may be attempting to keep other women at the hospital from giving birth, lest they suffer the same fate.

FEBRUARY 11, 1979
THE SULTAN OF NEW ORLEANS
New Orleans, Louisiana

One of the most bizarre and horrific tales of murder in New Orleans history took place at the Sultan's Palace in the French Quarter in the mid to late 1800s. After nearly 200 years, the sordid details were recounted in 1979 by the *Times-Picayune*. The story goes that a man by the name of Jean Baptiste Le Pretre had built his lavish estate in 1836. However, suffering financial hardship, the property was rented to a foreigner. A self-proclaimed sultan, he, along with his extended family of numerous wives and children, moved into the house. It wasn't long before it looked more like a harem than a home. Steel bars were added to the windows and doors, and eunuchs were hired as armed guards. For two years the sultan reigned over his house in New Orleans. However, rumors began to surface regarding his evil doings. Many believed he kidnapped woman and children and tortured them into submission.

One morning, a neighbor walking past the house noted an eerie silence seconds before discovering blood pooling beneath the front door. The police were called in to investigate. Breaking down the door, they slid through blood soaked hallways, stumbling over the torsos and dissected limbs of all who had once lived there. All, that is, with the exception of the sultan. He was nowhere in sight. They later found his body in the garden; he'd been buried alive.

Today, many report seeing his ghost. One witness moved out of the estate after hearing torturous screams and the gurgling sound of someone choking to death. Others have awakened to find a turbaned specter peering down on them. Terrified, they turn on the light only to have the apparition vanish before their eyes.

FEBRUARY 12, 1965
HAMMOND CASTLE
Gloucester, Massachusetts

Hammond Castle, built in 1929, was the home of American inventor John Hays Hammond Jr. The castle also served as a laboratory for John, who was a pioneer in the development of remote control. He was an avid collector of Roman, Renaissance, and medieval artifacts. The castle housed his bizarre collection, including ancient tombstones, the sarcophagus of a Roman child, and a skull from one of Christopher Columbus's crewmembers.

Hammond and his wife also dabbled in the supernatural. They held séances and constructed a special Faraday cage for the medium to sit in while contacting the spirits. So enamored was he with the entombment of the pharaohs that in preparation for his future burial vault he had a number of cats embalmed. It was even rumored that Hammond experimented in necromancy—the raising of the dead.

Hammond died in 1965, and now the castle is a museum with a life of its own. Voices and eerie noises percolate through the castle walls. Unexplainable cold spots send chills up the spines of unsuspecting visitors. And a ghost or two has been known to make an appearance within the castle's halls and corridors. But what about Hammond?

In life, he always expressed interest in reincarnation, wishing to return as a cat. Oddly enough, since his death, a black cat has appeared. It roams freely throughout the castle and seems to prefer John's favorite haunts. One can only wonder if his wish has been fulfilled.

TERRIFYING TIDBIT

John Hays Hammond Jr. holds over 400 invention patents, second only to Thomas Edison.

FEBRUARY 13, 1748
THE LADY LOVIBOND
Kent, England

Goodwin Sands lie several miles off the coast of Kent. Legend tells us that the sandbanks were once part of the mythical island of Lomera, but they are most known for the damage they have caused to British shipping. The shifting sands have sunk many a vessel and devoured their crews. In 1748, *The Lady Lovibond*, a three-masted schooner under the command of Captain Simon Peel, cut through the cold seas not far from the sands. On board were Captain Peel and his new wife, Annette. It has always been thought by seafaring men that bringing a woman on board a ship was bad luck.

The first mate was a man named Rivers, a romantic rival of the Captain. Seeing the Captain and Annette together drove him mad. In a fit of rage, he murdered the helmsman and steered *The Lady Lovibond* into the deadly sands, sinking the ship and killing all on board. But this was not the last time *The Lady Lovibond* sailed the seas. Fifty years later, in 1798, on the anniversary of its sinking, several ships in the same area spied the schooner. Every fifty years after its tragic demise it has been spotted by reputable sources, the last time in 1948. However, with great media scrutiny, it failed to appear in 1998. Perhaps it is finally at rest.

FEBRUARY 14, 1929
THE ST. VALENTINE'S
DAY MASSACRE
Chicago, Illinois

On Valentine's Day in 1929, a police car pulled up in front of the S.M.C. Cartage Company. The brick building was a garage and warehouse for Bugs Moran's bootlegged liquor. Inside the building were six members of Moran's mob, a mechanic, and a dog. Five men, three in police uniforms, exited the squad car and entered the building. Thinking it was a raid, the gangsters didn't resist and lined up against a brick wall of the building. But instead of being arrested, they were brutally gunned down in a hail of machine gun fire. When it was all over, only the dog survived. As it turns out, they weren't cops at all, but rather hit men hired by the notorious Al Capone. The bloody massacre shook Chicago and ultimately ended in Capone's downfall. The ghost of one of the men killed, Bugs Moran's brother-in-law, James Clark, began to haunt Capone almost immediately after the massacre. In 1931, Capone hired a medium to exercise the spirit, but that failed. Until his death on January 25, 1947, Capone could not escape the torment of Clark's ghost.

The building was eventually torn down and a park was built in its place. But there have been reports of phantom gangsters dropping in at the adjacent nursing home. And dogs have been known to bark and growl as they walk by the park. Is the park haunted? Some believe not. Yet it's hard to deny the numerous reports of visitors to the area. The echoes of machine guns and men gasping for their last breath still affirm the horrors of that fateful Valentine's Day in 1929.

TERRIFYING TIDBIT

In 1967 the S.M.C. Cartage Company was demolished. Canadian busi-nessman George Patey purchased the bullet-scarred bricks, while oth-ers were reported stolen. The bricks were sold as memorabilia. It is rumored that the bricks are cursed, bringing ill health, financial ruin, and even death to those who purchased them.

FEBRUARY 15, 1814
OCEAN-BORN MARY
Henniker, New Hampshire

Ocean-Born Mary is one of the most famous ghost stories in New Hampshire. It is so legendary that it is hard to separate the facts from the fiction. What we do know is that Mary was born at sea. Her mother, Elizabeth Fulton, and her husband were immigrating to America from Ireland when pirates off the New England coast intercepted and boarded the ship. When the pirate captain heard the cry of a baby, his gruff demeanor softened, and he told all on board their lives would be spared if they named the baby after his own mother, Mary. Elizabeth agreed, and the legend of Ocean-Born Mary was born. The pirate cap-tain also gave Mary a gift, a bolt of light green brocade silk fabric to be used for her wedding gown. Then the pirates released the ship.

The father died shortly thereafter, and Mary and her mother moved to Henniker, New Hampshire. In 1742, Mary, now a beautiful tall redheaded woman, married James Wallace, and she wore a dress of green silk. After living a full life with James and their children, Mary passed away in 1814, at the ripe old age of ninety-four.

In 1917, a man by the name of Louis Roy purchased the famous Ocean-Born Mary House. However, contrary to the legend, she had never lived in it. Roy, trying to turn a profit, charged a fee to dig in the backyard for alleged buried treasure. Renowned paranormal investigators, Hans Holzer and Ed and Lorraine Warren have all claimed that the house is haunted, but that's not what the current owner says. He has gone out of his way to prove that this was all a hoax. According to him, there is no ghost of Ocean-Born Mary. However there are many credible reports of a tall red-headed apparition seen in the area and even looking out the windows of the Ocean-Born Mary House; it seems the legend may have taken on a life of its own.

FEBRUARY 16, 1945
THE CORROSION HANGAR BAY
Kanagawa, Japan

Used by the Japanese kamikaze pilots, this hangar on the Astsgi Naval Air Base dates back to World War II. When Japan surrendered to the Allies in 1945, many pilots, shouldering the weight of their disgrace, committed suicide (harakari) in the hangar. Today the hangar is haunted. A pair of floating red eyes has been witnessed by some of the base's personnel. The nighttime opening and closing of doors can be heard as well. One evening, a guard saw a Japanese man dressed in a World War II–era uniform walk through the hangar, strutting right past him to the back exit. By all accounts, the ghostly officer was totally oblivious to his surroundings. Some believe that because of their disgrace the kamikaze pilots are bound to the hangar, waiting to avenge themselves. Terrified of what they may encounter, many a serviceman has refused to venture into the hangar after dark.

FEBRUARY 17, 1974
HEADLESS CATHERINE
Franklin, Maine

Motorists driving between the towns of Franklin and Cherryfield often see the ghostly specter of a headless woman. The picturesque mountainous road that winds around Fox Pond then slowly crests the top of the mountain is appropriately named Catherine—as is the phantom young woman that attracts the attention of many a traveler. Legend has it that if you are driving down the short stretch of Route 182 and come across the headless torso of Catherine, you had better pick her up. If you don't, you will meet with a disastrous fate. One story tells of a traveling salesman who drove past the headless ghost. As soon as he had he done so, he looked into his review mirror, and there in his back seat was the phantom woman. He was so distraught, he lost control of the car and swerved into a tree. He died on impact. But who is this ghost and why is she haunting that particular stretch of road? The story goes that Catherine and her boyfriend, driving back from their prom, lost control of the car and hit a tree. Catherine, beheaded, died immediately; her boyfriend's body, on the other hand, was never found. Is Catherine wandering aimlessly looking for her boyfriend? Perhaps. Then again, does it matter why Catherine haunts the area near Fox Pond? Just remember that if you find yourself driving through the beautiful valleys and picturesque mountains of Maine and happen to spy the specter of Catherine, pick her up. Lest you lose your head.

FEBRUARY 18, 1374
THE TOOLMAKER OF
TOMASSKA STREET
Prague, Czech Republic

While traveling down Tomasska street in Prague, you may run into the skeleton of the toolmaker. Back in medieval times there once was a toolmaker who hired a young apprentice. The apprentice was a handsome man who took a fancy to the toolmaker's wife. Without the toolmaker's knowledge, the two began a torrid affair. Afraid that the husband would find out, they decided to murder him. One night while he slept, his wife drove a nail into the toolmaker's skull, killing him. They quickly buried him, and a year later, the murderous pair married. Then the toolmaker's ghost began appearing in his workshop, but nobody thought much of it until they dug up his coffin, as tradition dictated, for reuse of the grave. Lifting the lid, the undertaker found his skeleton with a rusty nail in it. He reported his discovery to authorities, who arrested the apprentice and his wife. They were tried, convicted, and executed. The toolmaker's remains were reburied with the nail still in. Today his skeleton wanders the streets looking for a brave soul to pull out the nail so that he can rest in peace.

TERRIFYING TIDBIT

In many cultures, bodies were only buried for a short period of time. To save space in cemeteries, they were dug up so the plot could be used again. The bones were placed in a vault or catacomb called a bone house. Even more disturbing is that some of the coffin lids revealed scratch marks, denoting that the bodies were buried alive.

FEBRUARY 19, 2000
JACOB FUNERAL HOME
Kokomo, Indiana

In 2000 a local man purchased the old Jacob Funeral Home. It was the only black-owned and -operated funeral home in central Indiana. Dating back to the early 1900s, it had a strange past, and what the new owner found when he began remodeling was even stranger. In the damp basement behind some rubble was a small storeroom. In it were moldy stacks of cardboard boxes labeled "Personal Belongings." The rotting cartons contained the personal items of the deceased that were supposed to be buried with them, but "somehow" got misplaced. They contained a variety of items from wedding bands to children's stuffed toys, and always a photograph of the person who died.

As the remodeling progressed, a series of strange events afflicted the building. Lights and water faucets would turn on and off by themselves. Whispers could be heard echoing in the halls. And the sound of a "high-pitched drilling noise" emanated from the basement, where the boxes had been found. But the creepiest experience of all was the black shadows lurking in the corners, darting back and forth through the building. A minister was called in for a blessing, but things only deteriorated. Psychics refused to enter the building, and heavy and sullen moods began to affect its inhabitants. Finally, the owner decided to sell the items found in the basement on eBay with hopes that the ghosts would go with them. That might be fine for him, but what about the purchaser?

FEBRUARY 20, 1922
ISLE OF THE DEAD
Venice, Italy

Five miles off the coast of Venice is Poveglia, a rather small island with a deadly history. During the Roman era, the island was used much like a leper colony. When the bubonic plague came to Europe in the Dark Ages, with almost a third of Venice's population dead or dying, victims were sent to the island for quarantine. Men, women, and children all met their untimely death on the island, and thousands were thrown in an open plague pit or burned in bonfires. The island was abandoned until Napoleonic times, when it was fortified and used as a supply station.

TERRIFYING TIDBIT
The sound of church bells ringing was said to drive away demons. And when epidemics and diseases plagued cities, the air was thought to be cleared of the illness by the ringing of bells.

In 1922, a mental institute was built on the island, a formidable looking building with a tall bell tower. The inmates began to see and hear the tormented lost souls of the island. Terrified, they reported their complaints to the doctors, which were casually dismissed as symptoms of their condition. One particularly cruel doctor was assigned to the hospital at this time. He began experimenting on the patients, performing lobotomies and other crude procedures, killing and injuring many. He too began to see the ghosts. His own sanity slipping away, one night he went to the top of the bell tower and fell to his death.

The hospital was eventually abandoned and the bell removed.

Today few Venetians dare to step foot on the island. The bones of the dead wash up on the beach, and the soil is so impregnated with the remains of humans that many fear to breathe the dust. The bell from the empty tower continues to toll, but for whom does it toll?

FEBRUARY 21, 1704
THE EUNICE WILLIAMS
COVERED BRIDGE
Greenfield, Massachusetts

The village of Deerfield, Massachusetts was savagely attacked by a band of Mohawk Indians in February 1704. Reverend John Williams and his family were among the 100 captives who were herded together like cattle. The Indians drove their prisoners toward their camp in Canada, striking down any who couldn't keep the brutal pace. The reverend's wife, Eunice, having just given birth to another child, realized she was too weak to survive the ordeal. Coming to terms with her fate, she handed off the newborn baby to her husband, praying at least some of her family would survive the attack. As the captives crossed the river in Greenfield, Eunice, too weak to continue, fell. One of the warriors struck poor Eunice with a tomahawk, killing her instantly. Her family was forced to watch in horror as Eunice's blood flowed into the river. Unable to go to her aid, they and the remaining captives continued onward. Finally, after enduring two years at the Mohawk camps, they were released. The grieving Reverend Williams returned home with all but one of his children.

His eldest daughter, also named Eunice, growing so accustomed to the Indian ways, refused to leave. To her father's horror, she married one of the tribesmen.

Today, Eunice's ghost still haunts the bank of the river in Greenfield. It's also been said that if one stands in the covered bridge and calls out the name of Eunice Williams, she will appear. Many believe her soul remains because of the brutal way in which she died. Others believe her spirit is at unrest, eternally waiting for her namesake, the child that betrayed her, to return.

FEBRUARY 22, 1884
BOOT HILL GRAVEYARD
Tombstone, Arizona

The old "Tombstone Cemetery" was nicknamed "Boot Hill Graveyard," because the majority of its 250 inhabitants, buried beneath mounds of cactus and strangling growths of crucifixion thorns, died with their boots on.

Not all graves tell a tale; however, those that do speak to Tombstone's violent past. Boot Hill, used primarily during 1878–1884, became the final resting place of dozens of prospectors, outlaws, and prostitutes alike. Others that are laid to rest at Boot Hill include five men hanged for the "Bisbee Massacre," the men who took their last breath at the famous gunfight known as the "O.K. Corral," and the poor soul that was hung by mistake.

Since its restoration in the 1940s, Boot Hill has grown in popularity and become a favorite among tourists. Some believe cemeteries to be serene and quiet. After all, burial plots are our final *resting* place, right? Not so for Boot Hill. Considering the numerous reports of strange lights and odd noises said to emanate from within, it's definitely the exception to the rule. In fact, there have been many tourists who, after taking sightseeing pictures, are later surprised to discover they've captured more than their eyes could see. From the ghostly images appearing in the photographs, it seems, the poor souls that have been laid to *rest* are doing anything but!

FEBRUARY 23, 1836
THE SIX MONKS AT THE ALAMO
San Antonio, Texas

The spirits of restless souls still wander the grounds of the Mission San Antonio de Valero, better known as the Alamo. Are these spirits a residual haunting from the famous battle that raged for thirteen days? Or do these ghostly apparitions communicate with the living? If you could reach back in time and ask Colonel Sanchez, you would have your answer. As Sanchez and his detail approached the Alamo to destroy the mission as General Santa Ana had ordered, they were greeted by six screeching monks waving flaming swords above their heads, yelling, "Do not touch the Alamo!" Stunned, Sanchez and his men made a hasty retreat. He returned to the camp and reported to the general what had happened. Not believing his story, Santa Ana accused him of cowardice and decided to take matters into his own hands. He personally returned with additional troops and a cannon. As the gunners were preparing to fire upon the mission, once again the six ghostly monks with their flaming swords appeared. The general was thrown from his horse, and his men fled in fear. Evidently he became a believer because the Alamo and its hosts of ghostly inhabitants still remain today.

FEBRUARY 24, 1555
SMITHILLS HALL
Bolton, England

The roots of Smithills Hall can be traced back to the reign of King John in the early 1200s. During the rule of "Bloody Mary" Tudor, the hall was in the hands of magistrate Sir Roger Barton. Mary was attempting to reintroduce Catholicism in England and worked feverously to quash the Protestant faith. In 1555, an Anglican minister, Reverend George Marsh, was brought before Barton for questioning. He was taken to the "Green Room" where his interrogation began. Frustrated at the proceeding, Marsh fled from the room and ran down the stairs. When he reached the bottom, he stopped and stamped his foot on the fieldstone floor, declaring, "If I am true to my faith, God shall leave his mark." He was taken back to the room and ordered to stand trial for heresy. Convicted, he was sentenced to death and burned alive.

But that couldn't stop Marsh's ghost from returning to Smithills Hall. The spectral image of the minister has been seen on the staircase and in the Green Room, haunting the manor that sealed his fate. Today, if you look at the stone in the floor where he stomped his foot, you can clearly see a rough imprint of it, an enduring reminder of his persecution. Once the owner of the manor removed the stone and placed it outside. Late that night a storm of poltergeist activity rattled the mansion until it was returned. And every year on the twenty-fourth, it is said that the imprint turns red and sticky, a reminder of Marsh's plight.

TERRIFYING TIDBIT

Near the village of Beetham, between two boulders, you will find a tiny set of stairs carved by elves. If you make a wish before descending to the bottom, and can do so without touching the sides, your wish will come true.

FEBRUARY 25, 1912
LA BOHEME BED AND BREAKFAST
Edmonton, Alberta, Canada

According to an article in the *Edmonton Sun*, many believe the La Boheme Bed and Breakfast is haunted. And given its grisly past, why shouldn't it be?

The building was built in 1912 and was once a luxury apartment building. At some time in its history the owner of the building allegedly murdered his wife and dragged her corpse down three flights of stairs into the basement. There he chopped her into pieces and burned them in the building's huge furnace. Mike Comeau, co-owner of the bed and breakfast, pointed out to the reporter that the original coal-fired furnace is still there, although it has been converted to gas. He went on to say that one of his female employees once went into the dimly lit cellar to do the laundry. While working near the furnace, something touched her. She came running up the stairs screaming and never went into the basement again.

Another time, a regular customer named Larry Finnson was staying in Room 7, the most haunted room in the building. He was awakened in the wee hours of the morning, when his bed lifted off the floor. Larry, who once thought of himself as a skeptic, declared, "There's a ghost here!"

Many say that late at night, when the building is still, you can hear thuds of the murdered wife's head bouncing off the stairs as she is being dragged to the basement. That would give even the most ardent skeptic a headache.

FEBRUARY 26, 1965
THE HOLLYWOOD WAX MUSEUM
Hollywood, California

Visitors to the Haunted Hollywood Wax Museum may get more than they bargain for. Thousands of tourists each year walk the narrow hallways admiring more than 350 realistic wax statuettes of celebrities and movie stars. Among the most popular exhibits at the museum is the horror chamber, chock full of ghouls galore—an eerie addition to be certain.

Yet it's not only the wax statues causing a stir. Visitors to the museum have witnessed ghostly apparitions moving among the wax replicas. Strange anomalies have appeared in countless photos, especially when taken at night. It's been reported that one man from the *National Enquirer*, intent on proving or disproving the validity of the haunting, requested to be locked in for the night by museum officials. When they opened the doors the next day, they found the cowering man was white as a ghost (no pun intended). With barely a word, he made a hasty retreat, never to be seen again.

FEBRUARY 27, 2008
KUALA KANGSAR PERAK
Malaysia

A Chinese woman by the name of Kuala Kangsar Perak, first name Lee, claims that continued torture at the hands of a woman's ghostly presence is the cause of her losing forty-four pounds in a two-week period. Her husband, Liang, concerned for his wife's welfare, sought medical attention. Various tests were run, including a brain scan. Still, doctors were at a loss. In their opinion Lee was not physically or mentally ill, and they could find no explanation for her condition.

It all began after the purchase of their new home. The family requested the service of a medium (*jitong*) for a religious blessing. While the jitong was there, she reported that she felt the presence of the spirit in the house. Perhaps it was the former owner who had passed away ten years previously and whose name was also Lee?

Soon after, Lee began seeing a shadow in her living room and bedroom. At night, her temperament changed, as if the spirit inhabited her body, trying to live again, only to vanish with the rising of the sun. During the two-week period, and only during the night, Lee would often talk to herself, become agitated, and provoke family members at every turn.

Not willing to give up, Liang requested the services of an exorcist. During the exorcism, Lee threw a bowl and became so agitated it took six bystanders to hold her down. Unfortunately, the exorcism failed. Unless another solution can be found, it appears that Lee and her tormentor may share her body until her demise.

FEBRUARY 28, 2007
SKIDAWAY ISLAND
Savannah, Georgia

Within the gated community known as the Landings on Skidaway Island sits a lone gazebo. Those brave enough to visit it between the hours of 10:30 P.M. and midnight soon receive the fright of their life, as columns of fog rise up from the murky waters and take human form. Then a battle unfolds before their eyes and transparent soldiers fight for freedom. All the while, the woods come alive with ghostly specters lurking behind the trunks of trees and in the shadows, apparently waiting for their unsuspecting foe.

But if you find yourself in the midst of this holographic horror and wish to exit stage left, think again. It has been reported that often cars refuse to start. Their batteries, much like the ghostly apparitions hovering about, have been drained of life.

MARCH 1, 1867
MUSHROOM TUNNEL
Picton, Australia

Behind the pastoral hamlet of Picton, Australia, the Redbank Range Railway Tunnel burrows through the hillside. Built in 1867, it is more commonly known as the Mushroom Tunnel. Originally used for trains, it closed to traffic in 1919. After that, it saw many different uses until it was converted into a mushroom-growing farm, hence the name Mushroom Tunnel.

In 1916, a local by the name of Emily Bollard lived in a small cottage near one side of the tunnel; on the other side was a farm owned by her brother. When she visited her brother's farm, she would often cut through the tunnel rather than climb the hill. One lazy Sunday afternoon, Emily set off to visit her brother. Half way through the tunnel she heard a train approaching—she had forgotten to check the railroad timetable. A deadly mistake. Emily frantically tried to escape, but to no avail. The train struck and killed her, and her broken bloodied corpse, caught on the cowcatcher, was carried all the way to Picton.

Almost immediately afterward, the townspeople began to see Emily's ghost in and around the tunnel. Strange lights, like that of an approaching train, have also been spotted. Many have felt the temperature drop and a sudden breeze like that of a train passing by. The tunnel is now abandoned except for local ghost tours. And if you are lucky enough to go on one, you too may run into the spirit of Emily Bollard, still trying to escape the spectral train.

MARCH 2, 2007
GHOSTS OF MADRID
Madrid, New Mexico

Madrid, New Mexico, an old mining town, breathes new life—or death, shall we say—into paranormal sightings. It all began 1,500 years ago when the Native American people mined the area for turquoise. When the Spaniards arrived they captured the Native Americans and forced them to mine for silver.

In addition to the turquoise and silver, the mines were rich in various minerals. For hundreds of years gold seekers and coal miners dug up the land.

The town was finally given its name in 1869, and eleven years later the Santa Fe railroad would arrive. However, in 1954 when the coal was depleted, Madrid became a ghost town. Literally.

Today Madrid has been rejuvenated, but many visitors to the town report seeing ghostly apparitions of times past. One of the most haunted buildings is the Mine Shaft Tavern, a saloon that can be found along the old turquoise trail. Reportedly, cries are often heard emanating through the six-inch-thick adobe walls. The saloon doors swing to and fro of their own accord. Glasses thrown by invisible hands are smashed to the floor. Most terrifying of all are the reports of employees who say they have looked into a mirror and, rather than seeing their own image, face a phantom reflection.

TERRIFYING TIDBIT

The popular *Wild Hogs* movie was filmed in the old ghost town of Madrid, New Mexico. It seems that this happening place is an attraction to both the living and the dead.

MARCH 3, 1888
STAGE FRIGHT
Melbourne, Australia

The Princess Theatre first opened in 1854 as the Astley Amphitheatre. Several years later it was renovated and reopened as the Princess

Theatre. This impressive structure, which is listed on the Queensland Historic Register, hosted such notable shows as Gilbert and Sullivan's *Mikado* and *The Phantom of the Opera*. In 1888, The Princess Theatre staged Charles Gounod's opera, *Faust*. The great baritone Federici (aka Frederick Baker) was performing the role of Dr. Faust. During the final act, Federici and the singer who was performing Mephistopheles were dramatically lowered through a trap door into the basement, representing their descent into Hell. During the descent, the great Federici suffered a fatal heart attack and died. After the opera, the cast took to the stage for their final bow, and when the curtain calls were over, they assembled in the back of the stage. There they were informed of Federici's death during the performance. They stood in shock. Several members of the cast spoke up and swore that they had seen him during the final bows. Since that day, many patrons have witnessed the spectral image of Federici in the theater. It became so commonplace that for years the theater management left a seat vacant in his honor. In the 1970s, while filming a documentary at the theater, the camera crew captured a translucent figure on stage. Perhaps Federici, who never got the opportunity to take his last bow in life, is doing so from the grave.

MARCH 4, 1829
THE HERMITAGE
Hermitage, Tennessee

The Hermitage was built in 1821 by Andrew Jackson, the hero of the Battle of New Orleans. It became home to him and his wife Rachael until she died in 1828. A year later, on March 4, 1829, Jackson became the seventh president of the United States and the Hermitage soon became known as the "Southern White House." When his presidency ended, still mourning Rachael's loss, Jackson retired to the Hermitage, where he died on June 8, 1845. Andrew Jackson Jr., the general's adopted son, then inherited the Hermitage, but unfortunately, as he was nearly destitute, Jackson was forced to sell the 1000-acre plantation. Soon after, in 1856, the house, along with remaining property, was sold to the state of Tennessee. However, the state lacked the proper funding to maintain it, and it began to fall into disrepair. In 1889, the state of Tennessee charted the Ladies' Hermitage Association (LHA) to care for the property. Immediately they began making repairs to the crumbling house and opened it up to the public as a museum.

It didn't take them long to discover that Jackson's spirit had never left. The two members of the LHA who were sent to occupy the house as caretakers didn't sleep very well that night. They said they had been kept up all night by General Jackson galloping his horse up and down the stairs. Others, too, reported seeing Jackson on the premises, and Rachael has also been seen, walking in the garden near her tomb. The sightings of Andrew Jackson have diminished over the years, making one think that the general and his loving wife are finally at rest at the home they both loved.

MARCH 5, 1741
THE COUNTRY TAVERN
Nashua, New Hampshire

Elizabeth Ford was a slender woman, five feet seven inches tall, with white hair. Well, at least that's how her ghost is described, who always wears a long white flowing dress. Elizabeth is the resident ghost of the Country Tavern. Back in 1741, when Nashua was known as Dunstable, the Tavern was her home.

Barely twenty-two years of age, she married an English sea captain who spent many long days and nights out on the open sea. One day, after a ten-month absence, he returned home to find that his wife had a baby (do the math here). In a fit of rage he murdered them both, throwing Elizabeth down the well and burying the baby beneath a tree.

In the 1980s Elizabeth's farmhouse became a restaurant, but Elizabeth has never left. It appears she has decided to stay, adding her own personal touch to the place. Unseen hands move salt and peppershakers, silverware, and plates. Glasses and cups are tossed off the shelves, while doors open and close without human intervention. Women diners have the sensation of invisible fingers playing with their hair, and Elizabeth's spirit, described as "opaque not transparent," has made an appearance or two. It seems her favorite haunt is an upstairs window in the part of the restaurant that was once the barn. She has been seen there, gazing out over the property, perhaps remembering another time, waiting for her captain to return from the sea, or maybe she is looking out over her baby's grave.

TERRIFYING TIDBIT

Apportation is the manipulation of objects that are moved from one place to another, seemingly appearing out of thin air.

MARCH 6, 2009
FOB SALERNO
Afghanistan

Two paratroopers from the Second Battalion of the 504th Parachute Infantry Regiment were manning guard tower six at FOB (Forward Operating Base) Salerno. They passed the night away talking and joking about the ghost story going around camp. According to the story, two marines had been manning the tower when one of them saw a little girl in the road with her goat. Startled that she would be out so late at night by herself, they took off their night-vision goggles to try to get a better look, but she was gone. When they put their goggles back on, she was standing right there in the tower with them. Horrified, they left their post and refused to return to the tower. As the two paratroopers continued to poke fun at the story, they began to hear giggling over the radio. It was the voice of a little girl. They contacted the adjacent tower to ask if they had heard anything. They said they hadn't. Chalking it up to imagination, they finished their post.

The next night, while the two paratroopers were on the same duty, they began to experience an icy coldness envelope them. Hearing movement, they looked around, but they were alone. Just then, a voice crackled over the radio. It was the adjacent tower informing them that there was a three-foot-high figure at the base of their tower. The paratroopers went out on the balcony and scanned the area below. Yet they could see no one. The radio crackled again, "It looks like she's waving." Again they looked, to no avail. Spooked, but unable to leave their post, they counted the minutes until their shift ended. The two frightened soldiers made a pact. They promised to never to poke fun at the marines' story, ever again.

MARCH 7, 1867
PHANTOM MONK
Charleston, Tennessee

During the flooding of the Hiwassee River in 1867, a local doctor would make an immoral choice that would haunt this town forever. A train conductor, unaware that the tracks had been washed away by the floodwaters, tragically ran his train into the ravine. Rescue workers labored tirelessly retrieving all but one of the train's passengers. Unfortunately without a hospital nearby, most of the injured were taken to homes, where they died. But what of the sole passenger that remained missing? As it was later revealed, a local doctor had found the passenger, a Catholic monk from Baltimore, and brought him to his office. The monk was already dead, but it seems the doctor had plans of his own for him. He stripped the flesh off of the monk's body and bleached the bones. Once dry, the skeleton provided the doctor with the display piece he had always wanted for his office.

Years later, when all was revealed, the doctor admitted to being haunted by the monk, who apparently wasn't very happy with how his remains had been treated.

In 1932, when the doctor's office was demolished, construction workers found the monk's cloak along with his rosary beads wedged inside a wall of the building. And although the building no longer stands, locals have witnessed the ghostly apparition of the embittered monk walking the tracks, looking for his bones.

MARCH 8, 1713
THE BARNSTABLE HOUSE
Cape Cod, Massachusetts

This three-story Colonial home built in the 1700s is believed by many to be one of the top two haunted houses found on Cape Cod. Truth be told, it has seen its share of tragedy. The story goes that a sea captain, his wife, and his young daughter Lucy inhabited the Barnstable house. The basement of the house was positioned atop a well, with a running stream beneath it.

One day, while her father was away at sea, little Lucy managed to drown in the well.

Overcome with grief, Lucy's mother withdrew to a third-floor bedroom, where she was later found dead from starvation.

Lodgers have told stories of the "captain" assisting children down the steep stairs. Coinciding with the appearance of the ghostly captain, the windows will mysteriously lock and unlock. One witness to the paranormal goings on, a lawyer, watched in stunned silence as a newspaper moved of its own accord from one side of a table to another. With reports of paranormal activity, the New England Society of Paranormal Investigators (NESPI) was offered the opportunity to substantiate the claims. What did they find? Among the most notable phenomena was an EVP of an agitated woman saying, "There are switches!" And, later in the investigation, the team sat at a conference table, politely asking the spirits to communicate with them. A team member, Mike Astin, asked for the spirit of the captain to speak, or to give them a sign. No sooner was the question asked than a fifteen-pound weathervane overturned, startling the group. It seems this band of ghost hunters got their answer.

MARCH 9, 2009
SPIRIT SAVES DAUGHTER
West Virginia

According to a story traveling the Internet, a woman living in West Virginia reports that her apartment, once a funeral home, is haunted. Although uncomfortable with the embalming table and several caskets stowed in the basement, she managed to ignore the strange sounds that emanated throughout the walls at all hours of the day. It wasn't until she heard a persistent man's voice call out her name that she finally grew alarmed.

One day while lying down for a nap she heard her named called out. Snapping to attention, she got up and looked around. Unable to see the source of the voice, she lay back down. Once again the voice called out to her. Feeling uneasy about the determination she heard in the unseen man's voice, she hurried to check on her infant daughter sleeping in the other room. To her astonishment, her child had managed to pull the covers up over her head. Her daughter was struggling, gasping for breath. The voice she'd heard in her sleep had saved her daughter's life.

Further investigation into the history of the funeral home provided a possible explanation. It was said that many years earlier a man had committed suicide by shooting himself in the head in the basement of the building. Perhaps having taken his own life, he was determined to spare another's. Did this man act as the child's mysterious guardian angel? This woman believes he did.

MARCH 10, 1850
GOODY BASSETT
AND PHELPS MANOR
Stratford, Connecticut

Rumors of paranormal experiences abounded at the Phelps mansion in Stratford, Connecticut. In March 1850, a Presbyterian minister by the name of Dr. Eliakem Phelps was so enamored with the supernatural that he inadvertently conjured up the evil spirit of Goody Bassett during a séance. Unbeknownst to Phelps, the mansion was built on the same land on which Bassett had been hanged for witchcraft in May 1651. Mr. Phelps, along with his wife and children, returned from services to find their house in shambles. The doors were wide open, books and personal items were strewn about the home, and atop the bed, sheets and clothing had been arranged as to depict the posture of a corpse.

Out of sheer terror, Phelps roamed his house that night keeping vigil over his family. However, during his rounds, as he made his way back through his kitchen, he spotted dark figures hovering around the room. Turning on the light, he was shocked to find his family's clothing had been stuffed with rags and formed into lifeless bodies. And it had all been done while he had been making the rounds.

The strange phenomena continued each night. The children were physically thrown across the room by unseen hands and beaten by a phantom attacker. Sawdust and dust showed strange scrawlings demanding that the Phelps family leave. No longer able to withstand the torment, the Phelps family did in fact move out. The abandoned home became a shelter for the homeless and drug addicted until it was converted into a hospital in 1947.

But soon after, the haunting began again. The staff and patients heard strange knocking sounds, and doors opened and closed of their own accord. By 1971 the old Phelps mansion was once again abandoned, and it has since been torn down. Did the destruction of the building finally put Goody Bassett to rest? One can only hope.

MARCH 11, 1953
THE HAUNTED HOCKEY HALL OF FAME
Montreal, Canada

In 1953, a nineteen-year-old bank teller by the name of Dorothea Mae Elliot committed suicide. Her coworkers informed the police that Dorothea arrived at work early, pleasantly greeted everyone, and then headed into the second floor restroom with a revolver. They found her with a gunshot wound to her head, and she died soon after.

However, this wouldn't be the last Dorothea was heard of. After the incident there were reports of unexplainable phenomena: flickering lights, windows and doors opening of their own accord, and the feeling of an invisible hand placed on one's shoulder.

The bank eventually closed some thirty-seven years later. Dorothea would be seen again, however, this time by a Toronto musician, Joanna Jordan. In 1993 this historic building hosted an event in the Great Hall. During Joanna's performance, she glanced up and gasped. Above her, peering down from the ceiling was the ghostly apparition of a young woman with long, flowing black hair.

A few years later when the building became the Hockey Hall of Fame, Dorothea would show herself again, this time to a little boy. While visiting the Hall, a young boy screamed and became agitated pointing at something no one else could see. As reported by the *Toronto Star*, the Hall's coordinator Jane Rodney said, "He claimed a woman with long black hair was going in and out of the walls." It appears Dorothea haunts the building, regardless of its function.

MARCH 12, 1832
THE HISTORIC
RICHMOND BRIDGE
Tasmania, Australia

The Richmond Bridge, spanning the Coal River, was built in 1825 to connect Richmond to Hobart. It is the oldest stone arch bridge in Australia. Originally known as Bigge's Bridge, it was built by convict labor, as were many things in Tasmania. In 1832, an official inquest was conducted into the death of a man named George Grover. George was a convict and flagellator (a person who whips others as a form of discipline). He was especially cruel and received great enjoyment in whipping his fellow convicts during the construction of the bridge. On that day in 1832, according to the results of the inquest, he was drunk and either fell or was pushed off the bridge to his death. Most believed he was pushed by some of the convicts he had whipped so cruelly during the bridge's construction.

Ever since that day, his ghost has been seen pacing back and forth on the bridge. When approached, he simply fades away. Another ghost associated with the bridge is a large dog, nicknamed "Grover's Dog." Pedestrians have reported that a dog appears next to them as they walk across the bridge late at night. As they reach the other side, it vanishes. Although George's ghost strikes fear in many, the phantom canine is a welcomed sight.

MARCH 13, 2008
YORK STREET JAIL
Springfield, Massachusetts

According to CBS 3 News, demolition of the old York Street jail, built in 1886, was completed in the spring of 2008. Although it hadn't been home to prisoners for the past sixteen years, a picture taken by local historian Jim Boone tells a different tale. Boone had documented the various stages of the building's demolition, and he witnessed something odd. While he was standing in the rotunda, snapping photos, a fog appeared in front of the lens. It was there one minute, then gone the next. At first he suspected his camera was faulty. But later, when Boone loaded the digital images on his computer, every picture was clear except for one. Rather than fog, however, the image took on a ghostly shape. Coincidently, Boone states, the exact location where he took his picture was the spot where, in 1898, Massachusetts's last legal hanging took place. It appears the executed man is still hanging around.

MARCH 14, 1984
THE GHOSTLY NEIGHBOR
Watertown, Massachusetts

Bety Comerford knew there was something not quite right with her new Watertown apartment. Staying late to paint before the official move-in date, she couldn't shake the feeling that someone was watching her. Yet she was always alone in the room. She wondered if she was imagining things. Then one evening, she received her answer. As she was finishing up painting the last wall in the bedroom, she turned to put the brush down and the skin on her arms suddenly prickled. Slowly raising her gaze, she saw him.

He stood in the doorway, silently watching her; young, blond, and handsome, dressed in tan corduroy pants and a brown jacket with elbow patches. They looked at each other for a long moment, and then he faded. As if his appearance had broken the ice between them, she began seeing him more and more. Each time, Bety was overwhelmed by his sadness.

Finally it was move-in day. After she and her husband were settled, the upstairs couple invited them up for coffee. Plagued by the images of the ghostly visitor, Bety felt compelled to find out more. She brought up the ghostly sightings she'd had with her new neighbors. Awestruck, the woman broke into tears and ran out of the room. Not realizing the impact of her question, and at a loss for words, Bety apologized. The woman's husband explained. "Ten years ago we rented your apartment to a young photographer. He was going through some tough times. We didn't realize how tough. That is, until my wife found him hanging from our back porch."

MARCH 15, 1999
HELLO KITTY
Hong Kong, China

In 1999, three young gangsters kidnapped twenty-three-year-old Fan Man-yee from her home. Ah Map, as she is also known as, was taken to an apartment in the shopping district. She had owed their boss Leung Wai-lun $4,000, and although she had already paid him back $14,000, he wanted more. He beat and tortured her and kept her as a prostitute in order to pay back her debt. For a month, the three men and one of their girlfriends, high on drugs and just for kicks, subjugated Ah Map to every form of grisly torture conceivable. Eventually when her body could tolerate no more, she died on the bathroom floor, next to Melody, the gangster's girlfriend.

Panicking and needing to be rid of the body, they cut it up in the bathtub, boiled the flesh off the torso, and fed the arms and legs to stray dogs.

Soon after, Melody began having nightmares. Ah Map plagued her dreams. Unable to withstand the torment, Melody escaped the apartment and confessed all to the police. Although they did not believe her, they investigated. What they found in the third-floor apartment shocked even the most seasoned policemen. Not much remained of Ah Map except her skull, which had been stashed inside of a large Hello Kitty doll. Thanks to Ah Map's ghost, the men were convicted. The apartment has since been boarded up, but every now and then her shadowy image is captured on closed-circuit cameras as she wanders the neighborhood, searching for her dissected corpse.

TERRIFYING TIDBIT

A traditional Chinese Ghost Festival includes ritualistic offerings and the burning of hell money in order to please the spirits and deities. The festival is a way to connect the living to the dead, earth to heaven, and the body to the soul.

MARCH 16, 2009
THE BUS PASSENGER
China

According to the *Chinese Daily*, when Chen Lai Fu boarded the bus Sunday night, not all the passengers were among the living. Sitting in one of the seats at the rear of the bus, he couldn't help but notice the young boy running around. The boy looked about nine years old, wore a gray jacket and yellow pants, and talked to himself as he played. However none of the other passengers took any notice of him. Moments later, the boy went to the front of the bus and spoke to the driver. Apparently unable to see him, he too ignored the young lad. Finally, when the boy came to the back of the bus and sat next to Chen, like other spirits he'd encountered, he realized the boy was a ghost. The astral child, counting the passengers with his finger, said, "Wow, so many people." He then turned to Chen and tried to strike up a conversation with him, but Chen ignored him as well. Several minutes later, when Chen reached his destination, he exited the bus. As it pulled away, he turned, staring at the boy through the bus window.

When the reporter asked why Chen could see the boy, he replied, "I developed the ability to see spirits after I fell ill with a high fever when I was a child." Is Chen telling the truth? Just ask him, and he will show you the photo of the little boy he captured on his cell phone. It seems seeing is believing.

TERRIFYING TIDBIT

According to Tony Cornell at the Society for Psychical Research, cell phones are to blame for a decline in ghost sightings. It's his belief that the electronic noise produced by phone calls and text messages is drowning out their unusual electrical activity.

MARCH 17, 1078
THE OLD FERRY BOAT INN
Holywell, Cambridgeshire, England

During the time of Edward the Confessor, a young maiden named Juliet Tewsley was jilted by her lover, a woodcutter named Thomas Zoul. Inconsolable, she hanged herself on the banks of the Ouse. Thomas found her, cut her down, and buried her where she had died, placing a stone slab on her grave. Years went by and the Old Ferry Boat Inn was built on the site.

Since then, her spectral image has been seen in the inn and on the banks of the river. In its floor you can see the stone slab of Juliet's grave. But beware, do not set foot on the slab, for it is said to bring bad luck. If by chance you do stumble upon it, buying drinks for the house is the only way the curse will be lifted. Every March 17, the inn throws a huge party in Juliet's honor. Ironically, although she was spurned in life, she is celebrated in death. One has to wonder if the curse was a ploy by a penniless patron.

MARCH 18, 1996
THE OZONE DISCO CLUB
Quezon City, Philippines

The heavy beat of music reverberated off the walls of the Ozone Disco Club in downtown Quezon City. It was just about midnight when a small fire broke out in the club's disc jockey booth. The DJ attempted to extinguish the fire, but it quickly spread. Most of the young patrons thought it was part of the show. They were dead wrong. The fire grew ever so quickly. Screams filled the air, as did the acrid smoke of the flames. The once jubilant crowd panicked. They rushed toward the only exit as terror set in, but there was another problem: the doors opened inward. The crush of the crowd against the heavy doors turned fatal for those trapped inside the burning inferno. One hundred sixty people died that night and another ninety-two were injured. It was the worst fire in the country's history.

Today the building is abandoned, a silent testimony to the tragedy that occurred that night. Or maybe not so silent. When the sun goes down, the heavy beat of music seeps into adjacent buildings. Muffled voices and wisps of screams fill the air. And if one dares to look into the decaying hulk of the Ozone Disco Club, it is said you can still see ghostly figures dancing in the moonlight, just as they did on that night back in 1996.

MARCH 19, 2009
THE SKULL POINT BATS
Manchester, Jamaica

A long time ago on the island of Jamaica lived a slave by the name of James Knight. Embracing the Christian faith, he preached to his fellow slaves. When the master of the Lyndhurst estate heard of his exploits, he became angered and ordered Knight beheaded. His henchmen, seizing the slave without remorse, chopped off his head. As a warning to other slaves, Knight's head was taken to town where it was impaled on a pole for all to see, which is how the name Skull Point came about. As for James Knight, his spirit lives on.

His ghostly apparition has been seen roaming among the ancient gravestones and the abandoned church at Skull Point. Locals speak of frightful cries emanating from the church and other unworldly noises penetrating the night air.

Hearing the rumors and looking for a good story, a local reporter, Robert Lalah of the *Jamaica Gleaner*, decided to investigate for himself. According to his article, he went to the church on a sunny day. He might have been brave, but he wasn't stupid. As he made his way through the weather-worn tombstones, he heard a terrifying screech coming from the gutted church. Gathering courage, he slowly made his approach. Just as he crept through the doorless opening and over the aging rubble something zipped by his head. It was a bat. Looking to the ceiling he saw many of the large creatures, darting back and forth in the shadows. He grabbed his camera and snapped away. After a few more minutes, he turned and left the church. Satisfied with his finding, he returned to the office. But he was dumbstruck when he began thumbing through the developed photographs. The pictures were only of empty rafters. Where were the bats? It appears the mysterious haunting of Skull Point Church remains just that. A mystery.

MARCH 20, 1393
CHARLES BRIDGE
Prague, Czech Republic

The historic Charles Bridge was originally known as the Stone Bridge. Spanning the Vltava River, it connected Old Town with Lesser Town (Mala Strana) and Prague Castle. The cornerstone was laid by King Charles IV on July 9, 1357, and the structure was completed at the beginning of the fifteenth century. Nearly all the citizens of Prague are aware of the ghosts of the Charles Bridge.

During the Middle Ages ten noblemen were beheaded. Their severed heads were displayed on pikes atop the bridge for all to see. Today as you pass over the bridge at the stroke of midnight, you can hear their mournful songs terrifying those who dare to cross.

To add to the terror, there are over thirty gothic statues lining the bridge. One of the most chilling is that of St. John. In 1393 a Cistercian priest, St. John of Nepomuk, was summoned to the castle of King Wenceslas IV. He had heard the confession of Queen Johanna, and the king wanted the details. Saint John refused. The king had him tortured and thrown from the bridge. For 300 years, the ghost of Saint

John was seen wandering the bridge and the banks of the river. In the seventeenth century, a statue of the saint was constructed and placed on the bridge, capturing his vagrant soul. The ghost was never seen again. It has been said that if you have a secret and touch the statue of Saint John, it will be safe forever. One can only imagine the breadth of the secrets he keeps.

MARCH 21, 1897
BOBBY MACKEY'S MUSIC WORLD
Wilder, Kentucky

Bobby Mackey's Music World is a popular location not only for the living but the dead as well. When Bobby and Janet Mackey purchased the building in 1978, they never in their wildest dreams realized the horrific trail of death and destruction that was associated with their new purchase.

Back in the mid-1880s, the site was home to a slaughterhouse. The well in the basement was used to dispose of the blood and animal parts. Eventually the building was abandoned and became used for more sinister purposes. In 1896, during the trial concerning the murder of a young woman, Pearl Bryan, secret rituals that had taken place at the old slaughterhouse were revealed. Pearl, having become pregnant, was decapitated by her lover. And although her body was identified by the shoes she wore, her head was never found. One of the two men responsible for the atrocity had removed Pearl's blond hair, which was later found in his dresser. But it is believed the head was used in a satanic ritual at the old slaughterhouse and then tossed into the well. The two men responsible were hanged in 1897.

But that's not the whole gruesome tale associated with the land. In its history there have been numerous murders and a suicide. One previous owner, a gangster, after discovering his daughter, Joanna, was pregnant from a singer in a band, had the singer killed. The distraught young woman then tried to poison her father. After she failed to take her father's life, she managed to take her own. Her body was found in the basement a few feet from the well.

In 1978 when Mackey opened up the dance club, one of his employees began to see a spirit who told the man her name: Joanna. At first Bobby, along with the rest of the town, assumed the employee was crazy. However, that all changed when his wife was accosted in the basement. The entity pushed her down the stairs and yelled at her to get out. Coincidently, Janet, like Joanna, was pregnant at the time. Since then, more than thirty visitors to the club have reported strange goings-on. Some have witnessed the ghostly apparition of a headless woman dressed in turn-of-the-century clothes. Others have smelled the sweet aroma of Joanna's rose-scented perfume. The jukebox, although unplugged, continues to play. And one gentleman in 1994 even tried to sue Mackey for the ghost that attacked him in the men's bathroom. Not surprisingly, the case was dismissed. Yet, despite the dismissal, Bob Mackey's reputation still attracts paranormal enthusiasts from around the world.

MARCH 22, 1882
AMTRAK HAUNTING
Tucson, Arizona

A current Amtrak station nestled in the town of Tucson, Arizona, was once the scene of a western shoot-out back in 1882, when Wyatt

Earp shot Frank Stillwell dead. Stillwell, along with Ike Clanton, hid and waited at the depot. Their plans? To ambush the Earp clan while they accompanied Morgan Earp (the younger brother) on his way back to California for burial. Instead, Stillwell was the one to meet with his end, as Wyatt shot him point-blank beneath his ribs. Bystanders heard shots fired. Several hours later Stillwell's body was found riddled with bullets.

Today, Frank Stillwell is one of the more prominent ghosts thought to inhabit the railway station. Along with the sound of gunfire captured on EVP (electronic voice phenomenon) devices by various ghost-hunting teams, Stillwell's apparition has been seen wandering near the depot's platform.

Security personal have witnessed many strange occurrences, including the ethereal screams of a woman in distress and the translucent image of a tattered man. A waiter has also reported wine bottles that rise of their own accord, only to shatter as they fall onto the tile floors. So why is this depot in Arizona so ghost inhabited? Is it Frank Stillwell reeking havoc for being bested in his plan of murder, or are there other ghostly visitors in search of a free ride?

MARCH 23, 1828
THE OCTAGON HOUSE
Washington, D.C.

The Octagon is an odd-shaped house with an even odder lineup of ghostly inhabitants. The six-sided building is situated a mere block away from the White House. It was built in 1801 for Colonel John Tayloe III of Virginia. The strongest paranormal activity takes place in the central part of the building, where you will find an ornate oval staircase. Tragedy struck for the Tayloe family during the War of 1812 when one of Tayloe's daughters returned from a secret tryst with a British soldier and upon her return came face to face with her furious father. The two had a heated discussion. Tayloe's daughter lost her balance and careened over the railing, plunging to her death.

It is said that her ghost often returns to re-enact her demise. A flicker of light is seen rising up the length of the staircase, as if someone is carrying a candle. One can then hear a scream followed by a loud thud echoing up from the bottom. Perhaps the memories were too painful, because shortly after the accident the Tayloe family packed up and moved back to their Virginia plantation.

In 1814 British troops set fire to the White House and surrounding buildings, forcing President James Madison and his wife Dolly to find alternative living arrangements. Tayloe graciously offered his home.

When the repairs were completed on the White House, the Tayloe's returned to the Octagon. But once again Tayloe, standing on the oval staircase, caught a different daughter sneaking back in after meeting a forbidden beau. This time, the colonel shoved her in a bout of anger, and she too, like her sister, met her fate at the bottom of the staircase. Guilt ridden, Tayloe died in March of 1828.

It is widely believed that history and haunting go hand in hand. It seems the Octagon is terrible proof of this.

TERRIFYING TIDBIT

During the burning of Washington, D.C., a freak thunderstorm arose, dousing many of the flames of the burning buildings. The tornadoes and lightening killed more than half of the invading army.

MARCH 24, 1878
HMS *EURYDICE*
Isle of Wight, England

The twenty-six gun HMS *Eurydice* was launched in 1843. At the time, it was considered one of the finest ships in the navy. But with the advent of ironclads in the 1860s, it was deemed obsolete and converted into a training vessel. On November 13, 1877, under the command of Captain Hare, the *Eurydice* sailed for the West Indies. Three months later, it completed its training tour and headed home, arriving in the English Channel in March 1878.

TERRIFYING TIDBIT

Since its sinking there have been numerous reports of a spectral three-mast ship, sailing with its gun ports open off the coast of the Isle of Wight, and disappearing when approached. In fact, according to one submarine's log, evasive action was taken to avoid hitting the ghost ship.

According to a BBC report, something quite unusual occurred on the same afternoon of the ship's return. The Bishop of Ripon, Sir John Cowell, and Sir John MacNiell were dining in Windsor. Suddenly, MacNiell stood up and cried out, "Good Heavens! Why don't they close the portholes and reef the sails?" Stunned, Cowell asked him what he meant. MacNiell replied that he didn't know, but went on to say that he had a vision. He saw a ship under full sail cruising up the English Channel with her gun ports open being thrashed by an enormous squall.

MacNiell's vision came true. For at the very moment, the HMS *Eurydice* floundered, capsized, and sank to the bottom of the channel.

All but two of her 330-man crew perished. An inquiry was held. It was found that it capsized because the gun ports were open and it had too much sail. Just as MacNiell had exclaimed.

MARCH 25, 1645
DUDLEYTOWN
Cornwall, Connecticut

Although now closed to the public, with all of its strange occurrences, Dudleytown, an old abandoned settlement in the northwest corner of Connecticut, is believed to be one of the most haunted locations in the United States. Thomas Griffis founded the town in 1645. Rumor has it that the Dudley brothers, after whom the town was named, were cursed, and they brought the curse with them when they settled into the town.

Strange lights have been seen cascading throughout the wooded area and its surrounding forest. Visitors to Dudleytown have reported feeling an evil presence and encountering dark shadows that seem to rise out of the lost and forgotten foundations to chase away anyone foolish enough to enter the former settlement. Is the ghostly force trying to protect or cause harm? The answer to this question may never be resolved.

MARCH 26, 2009
GREY'S ANATOMY
Hollywood, California

As reported by FoxNews.com, the set of the popular TV show *Grey's Anatomy* is believed to be haunted. Controversies and misfortunes among colleagues are not unusual in any workplace, but they seemed so excessive with the show's cast that psychic to the stars Nikki was called in. She believed the set was being plagued by a hostile specter and described him as heavyset and balding—the ghost of a previous facilities manager or maintenance worker. It's this entity that was thought to be behind the rash of bad luck that had afflicted the cast members of the popular medical drama. In what seemed to be a relatively short span of time, T. R. Knight was involved in a three-car accident, Aasha Davis's sister went missing, and an ex-cast member was scheduled to be evicted from his apartment for nonpayment of rent. Nikki foretold of catastrophic events unless the set was cleansed by use of Feng Shui, crystals, and other clearing methods. If not, the unfortunate events would continue. For the sake of cast and ex-cast members, let's hope Nikki's warnings were heeded.

MARCH 27, 1943
ARCHERFIELD AIRPORT
Brisbane, Australia

During World War II, Archerfield Airport was a major military base for Australia, the United States, and the Netherlands. The airport has had several fatal accidents over the years but none more devastating than the one that occurred in March of 1943.

It was just about 5 A.M. when a Royal Australian Air Force transport took off from Archerfield on a flight to Sydney. On board were twenty-three U.S. and Australian servicemen. Less than a minute into the flight, just as the (C-47) Dakota was about to make its ascent, it rolled, plummeted to the ground, exploded, and burst into flames, killing all on board. It was the worst aviation accident recorded at Archerfield.

Since that fatal day, the airport and surrounding area has been plagued by a series of unusual events: phantom lights, unusual sounds, and a spectral airman.

Early morning travelers along Beatty Road have spotted a man dressed in a flight uniform with cap and goggles, sometimes carrying a parachute under his arm. He has also been seen walking about the aircraft at the field itself. In efforts to find out who he is, witnesses have been asked to look at pictures of men from that era, especially the crew who died in the Dakota accident. No positive identity of the spectral visitor has yet been established.

He never seems to be in distress, always smiling and waving at all those he has met. In fact one paranormal investigator is quoted as saying about the ghost, "He may not be Casper, but he sure is friendly."

MARCH 28, 1584
IVAN THE TERRIBLE
Moscow, Russia

Ivan Chetvyorty Vasilyevich, better known as Ivan the Terrible, ruled over Moscow from August 25, 1530, to March 28, 1584, becoming the first tsar of a powerful nation. Ivan met his fateful end while playing a game of chess with Belsky and Godunov, his advisors. Modern belief is that Ivan was poisoned. During the 1960s his tomb was opened and his remains examined. The lab results indicated Ivan's remains were high in mercury. But who could have killed him? Rumor has it that three days prior to Ivan's death, he'd attempted to rape Godunov's sister. His efforts were thwarted, however, when Godunov and Belsky followed the sound of her screaming. It's believed that the two, realizing they were now marked for death, took matters into their own hands.

But was Ivan the Terrible as horrific as portrayed? It is written that he experienced bouts of rage. In fact, he once beat his pregnant daughter-in-law for her lack of modesty, causing her to miscarry. When Ivan Jr. found out what his father had done, an argument ensued, resulting in Ivan the Terrible cracking his son over the head with a pointed staff, killing him. Immediately remorseful, from that day forward, he was never the same. It seems he even lost his enjoyment of persecuting his enemies.

Over the years, Ivan's phantom image presented itself to many of the succeeding tsars and has been seen wandering the bell tower of the Kremlin. The appearance of Ivan's malevolent spirit strikes fear into all who see him, especially since his appearance, more often than not, portends disaster.

MARCH 29, 2002
THE SEVENTH GATE TO HELL
Stull, Kansas

A 1974 article in a Kansas newspaper reported that the Seventh Gate to Hell is located in Stull, Kansas. Above the local graveyard rises Emmanuel Hill, on which sit the ruins of the United Methodist Church. It is this location that is known as the Seventh Gate—a doorway between the two worlds. According to the article, the Devil himself makes an appearance twice a year in the tiny town of Stull. The legend says that he once mated with a local witch and spawned a child, who died shortly thereafter. Twice a year, at midnight, he visits his child and mate, summoning all those who have died violent deaths to dance with him.

There are a plethora of strange stories about Stull. For instance, the pope's plane detoured around Stull to prevent the pontiff from flying over unholy ground. Rain would never fall inside the ruined church, although it was roofless. And strange winds rise up from nowhere. On March 29, 2002, Good Friday, a bulldozer knocked down the last walls of the church, sealing the Seventh Gate of Hell—or at least they hope they did.

MARCH 30, 1826
THE DUEL
St John's, Newfoundland, Canada

Captain Mark Rudkin was a member of the British Army and Ensign John Philpot of the Royal Veteran Companies. Both were stationed in Newfoundland and found they competed for the affection of the same woman, the daughter of a prominent St. John's businessman. One night, during a card game, Philpot and Rudkin had a disagreement over the game. As tempers rose and anger grew, Philpot threw water in Rudkin's face. The captain tried to diffuse the situation and settle it in a gentlemanly manner, but Philpot only pressed him harder. Finally, with his honor at stake, Rudkin challenged him do a duel.

The next day, a mile outside of town, the two men met at a place called Brine's Tavern. Each holding a pistol, they squared off, waiting for the signal. Shortly after noon, the signal was given and Philpot fired, grazing Rudkin's collar. The captain then fired harmlessly into the air, hoping to end the disagreement. But Philpot, refusing to end it, ordered a second round. Tragically, Philpot was shot and killed. Rudkin was tried for his murder and found guilty. However, the judge was not willing to accept the verdict and requested a second vote. This time, Rudkin was found innocent of any wrongdoing and was set free. However, unlike Captain Rudkin, Ensign Philpot doesn't seem to be free; many citizens of St. John's have seen him wandering about the town and countryside. Still as stubborn in death as he was in life, it appears, Philpot is yearning for a rematch.

MARCH 31, 1993
BRANDON LEE
Seattle, Washington

Brandon Lee, the son of the late, famous martial artist, Bruce Lee, was a celebrity in his own right whose promising career was cut short at the age of twenty-eight. It all began during the filming of *The Crow*, which was based on the death of Eric Draven. In the movie, Eric returns from the dead, seeking revenge upon the criminals who took both his and his fiancée's lives.

It's been rumored that during the filming of the movie, a string of bad luck and accidents plagued the crew. With the production company running behind schedule, a few changes had been made. One of the changes, for authenticity, was to place dummy rounds in real cartridges. With cameras rolling, Brandon entered the scene where the script dictated the actor who played "Fun Boy" was to shoot him. The second the gun fired, Brandon's body jerked backward. Falling against the door, he collapsed. Upon realizing he was actually shot and was bleeding from the abdomen, an ambulance was called. The doctors fought to save Brandon's life, but he died of his wound. The shooting was ruled an accident. Brandon's body was laid to rest beside his father, Bruce Lee, in Lakeview Cemetery, in Seattle, Washington.

But is he really at rest? Numerous people have reported the sighting of a young man clad all in black wandering near the grave. When approached, he vanishes. His ghostly apparition has also been spotted at the underground Seattle bus station. The vision is so clear that some people are unaware that they are looking at a ghost—until he mysteriously disappears. Perhaps Brandon is returning to fulfill his role, unaware the movie was completed.

APRIL 1, 1748
THE WITCH OF ST JOHN'S
Burslem, England

Margaret Leigh, also known as Molly Lee, was born in 1680. She was ostracized even from birth. It is said she refused her mother's milk and would only suckle on farm animals. According to Reverend Spencer, she was ugly as sin—so much so, in fact, that he decreed Molly a witch. Margaret eventually found a home in the woods, where she befriended a blackbird and kept a cow, making her living by selling milk.

The Reverend continued his campaign against her. Then one day, at the local tavern, a blackbird appeared, and immediately the beer soured and the patrons, including the Reverend, became ill. The angry townspeople went looking for Molly but found her dead.

After her burial, Reverend Spencer went to Molly's cottage and peered into the window. There, before his eyes, was the ghost of Molly sitting in a chair. The good Reverend wasn't alone in seeing Molly; the rest of the village soon saw her too, walking the streets and howling.

The people of the town, along with the clergy, devised a plan to rid themselves of Molly's ghost. Capturing her blackbird, they lured Molly's spirit to the church, where they trapped it in a pig trough. Then, at midnight, they dug up Molly's grave and moved her body. Instead of an east-west Christian burial, they buried her north-south along with her blackbird. So ended the sightings of Molly Leigh— unless, of course, you dance around her tomb three times singing, "Molly Leigh, Molly Leigh, you can't catch me."

TERRIFYING TIDBIT

Clover is a plant used as a protection against witchcraft and fairy enchantments. The "lucky" few to find a four-leaf clover, it was believed, were given the ability to recognize evil.

APRIL 2, 1851
EXECUTION ROCKS LIGHT HOUSE
Long Island Sound, New York

In 1851, William Craft became the first keeper of the towering lighthouse that was built on the stone ledge known as Execution Rocks. It received its name when the revolutionary spirit was sweeping the colonies. Condemned American prisoners were allegedly taken to the ledge at low tide and chained. Their executioners looked on, waiting for the rising tide, as the terrified prisoners awaited their fate among the skulls and bones of those who went before them. The ghosts of the executed prisoners exacted their revenge when one of the British ships, pursuing George Washington, crashed into the ledge killing all on board.

Another grisly story associated with the lighthouse involves serial killer, Carl Panzram. In the early 1920s he stole a revolver from future president William Howard Taft and went on a crime spree, murdering twenty-one men and boys and dumping many of their bodies a scant 110 yards off Execution Rocks. He was finally caught and hanged on September 5, 1930. His last words were "Hurry it up, you Hossier bastard! I could kill ten men while you're fooling around!"

Although the lighthouse has borne witness to strange noises, unexplained voices, and mysterious fires, most of the ghostly sightings take place at the rocks. Boaters and even Coast Guardsmen have all seen the specters of terrified men stalking the rocks. Whether they are the victims of Panzram or the condemned prisoners of the British, the tortured souls apparently are to forever remain, haunting the cold stone of Execution Rock.

APRIL 3, 2008
THE HAMPTOM LILLIBRIDGE HOUSE
Savannah, Georgia

As reported in the Associated Contents online news, The Hamptom Lillibridge house, built in 1796, is the most terrifyingly haunted house in all of Savannah. After a sailor hanged himself in a third-floor bedroom, a series of tragic events and ghostly happenings plagued the building. In 1963, soon after antique dealer Jim Williams purchased the building, another tragedy occurred. A group of laborers had been hired to move two architecturally similar buildings onto one parcel of land. One of the workers was crushed to death beneath the structure when the smaller of the two houses collapsed.

When the houses were put into place, the workers resumed their duties and the restorations began. However, above the clamor of construction equipment could be heard the sound of disembodied voices and the stomping of feet running up and down stairs. But there were no stairs to run on. Scared witless, many of the thirty workers refused to continue their task.

Soon after, Williams was made aware of the odd find the workers had made beneath his home. They had stumbled upon an empty crypt that dated back to the colonial days. Seeing it empty, they had sealed it back up and buried it again before informing Williams.

Was the crypt the source of the events that plagued the Lillibridge house? We will never know. However, the cries and the mocking laughter Jim Williams heard convinced him to contact an Episcopal bishop. An exorcism on the house was performed on December 7, 1963. Unfortunately for Jim, it was unsuccessful. To this day, the haunting of the Lillibridge house continues.

APRIL 4, 2009
THE HAUNTING IN CONNECTICUT
Southington, Connecticut

The truth about the popular movie, *The Haunting in Connecticut*, was revealed in an interview with People.com. For two years, Carmen Reed, the mother of the boy who had been plagued by a malevolent force, stated the children in the home had been slapped, groped, and terrorized. According to the interview, in order to be closer to the clinic where her son underwent cancer treatments, the family moved into a former funeral home. The torment began the first night they arrived. It started with her son seeing a man with black hair that hung down to his hips. The apparition appeared to him daily. Sometimes the entity would just say his name. Other times, he'd make threats. The doctors, after being informed of the boy's visions, declared him a schizophrenic. Soon after, her son's disposition seemed to change. He began playing cruel tricks on his family. Not sure what to do, the Reed's sent their son to live with nearby relatives. Interestingly the voices and the visions stopped. But now with the boy gone, the entity set his sights on one of Carmen's nieces. One night, her eighteen-year-old niece said, "Aunt Carmen, it's coming, can you feel it?" Terrified, she clung to Carmen. Pulling her away, Reed glanced down and saw the imprint of an invisible hand crawl up her niece's shirt. That's when she realized that the visions and voices that had plagued her son were supernatural. Immediately she reached out for help. Famed demonologist John Zaffis, along with three priests, performed a three-hour exorcism. Zaffis was later quoted as saying, "Compared to that house, the other cases I had been involved with were like dealing with Casper the Friendly Ghost." He continued, "All I wanted to do was get my car keys and get the hell out of that house." Although the exorcism was a success, the Reed family no longer lives there. The torment they'd endured at the hands of the evil that once lurked within their former Southington home will never be forgotten.

APRIL 5, 1765
THE MASON CHRONOMETER
Delaware

Charles Mason and Jeremiah Dixon were astronomers and surveyors. In 1763, they were hired to survey the border between two of the colonies, Pennsylvania and Maryland. They were staying in Delaware while they worked on what became known as The Mason-Dixon Line. Mason also "tinkered." He had high hopes that the new project he was working on would bring him riches. It was a chronometer, an early version of a watch. He went into town one day on an errand and left the chronometer in his tent. While he was gone, a fat little boy came into his tent and ate everything he could find, including the chronometer. When Mason returned and discovered what had happened, he tried to get the chronometer from the boy, but failed. Realizing the situation was useless, he drank to the fat boy telling him he could "keep the chronometer with him until the end of time."

The fat little boy grew up to be a clockmaker. And when he died, he was buried at London Tract Church in Landenberg. Today, his grave is weathered and worn. But if you put your ear to the stone, they say, you can hear Mason's chronometer still ticking.

APRIL 6, 1626
THE GHOST CHICKEN
Highgate, London

According to the BBC, Sir Francis Bacon was responsible for the world's first frozen chicken. One particular frigid day in April, Bacon and his friend Dr. Witherborne, a physician to James I, made a life-altering discovery. While enjoying a carriage ride through Pond Square in Highgate, the men were discussing the possible use of snow to preserve food. As the snow stuck to the wagon wheels, Bacon pointed out to Witherborne that the grass beneath looked new and fresh. Witherborne, not sharing his friend's vision, scoffed at him. Sir Francis, angered by the doctor's disbelief, ordered the carriage halted. Running into a home at the bottom of Highgate Hill, he purchased a hen. He killed and cleaned the bird and removed its feathers, stuffed the cavity with snow, placed the carcass in a bag, and covered it with more snow.

Unfortunately for Bacon, the bird would have its revenge. A few days later, as a result of his freezing the chicken, Bacon contracted acute pneumonia and died on April 9, 1626.

Not long after, the ghost of the chicken began to appear. Many frequenting Pond Square would hear the screeching and clacking of a chicken. Yet none was in sight. At first, the locals thought everyone had been imagining things. They even blamed it on an emotional reaction to Sir Francis's death. But the sightings continued. The featherless fowl was seen on several occasions, shivering and running in circles before vanishing through a brick wall. Over the years there have been countless sightings. In December 1943, a British airman passing through town one night heard the sound of a carriage, followed by a loud screech. When he looked up, although he saw no carriage, there before him was the bird, shivering and running about. As he approached it, it disappeared before his eyes. It's these types of haunting that beg for answers. For instance, do chickens have a soul? And if they do, then this poultry-geist, adds a whole new dimension to *soul* food.

TERRIFYING TIDBIT

In 1907 Dr. MacDougall performed an experiment on the dying. The
measured loss of mass on humans compared to dogs, was a staggering
twenty-one grams to none. To MacDougall this was concrete proof: animals do not have a soul. Somehow I think the chicken would disagree.

APRIL 7, 1775
THE CONCORD COLONIAL INN
Concord, Massachusetts

Erected on a Native American burial ground by John Thoreau,
Henry David Thoreau's father, the Concord Colonial Inn is com-
prised of three houses connected together. Henry David Thoreau
lived there from 1835 until 1837. Today, many of the staff and visitors report strange occurrences. Books have flown off of the shelves
and full-bodied apparitions have been sighted. But the most activity
surrounds room 24, where a woman with dark hair wearing colonial
dress haunts the room. In fact, staff at the Concord Colonial are so
terrified by her ghostly apparition that many have refused to enter the
room. One guest, after being booked into room 24, was so horrified
by the ghost's appearance that she ran downstairs in the middle of the
night. Unfortunately, the inn was completely booked and the desk
clerk was unable to change her room. The guest, refusing to return to
room 24, spent the night sleeping on the sofa in the foyer. The next
morning, both the guest and the maid sent to retrieve her belongings were astonished. Her suitcase had mysteriously repacked itself.
Another visitor of haunted room 24 was awakened in the middle of

the night. Reportedly, she lay in sheer terror as a shadowy mass hovered above the bed. How did her husband respond to her complaints? He said, "Don't worry, honey, the ghost came with the price of the room."

APRIL 8, 2005
THE REALTOR
Tulsa, Oklahoma

Michelle, a realtor, was inspecting a vacant ranch for a client. Her initial impression was positive. It looked in decent condition. She entered the home and, as usual, began doing a clockwise inspection of the property. Upon reaching the kitchen she stopped short. Every drawer and cabinet door was ajar. She counted at least fifty. After a moment's hesitation, she chalked it up to an overzealous realtor wanting to see every last detail and continued with her inspection.

Michelle then peered out a window, spied the backyard with a built-in pool, and decided instantly that that was where she was headed next. Walking out of the kitchen toward the back of the house, she passed a lit basement with its door wide open. Deciding she would save the basement for last, she continued on. Suddenly, the door to the basement violently slammed shut. Startled, she quickly turned around to see who was there, but found she was alone.

Determined to see the backyard, she turned on her heels and headed for the door at the end of the hall. That's when she felt it. The odd electrical sensation that tore through her body made her hair stand to attention. Finally getting the hint that she wasn't welcome, she said, "Fine, I'll leave," and briskly walked out the front door.

After Michelle relayed her experience, the client declined a further look. The house was on the market for two years, and as far as Michelle knows, it never sold.

APRIL 9, 1949
THE WITCH OF THE WOOKEY CAVES
Wookey Hole, England

The Wookey Caves is an extensive cave system located near the village of Wookey Hole in Somerset England. Neanderthals, Celts, Romans, and a ghost or two have inhabited it over the past 50,000 years. It is now a renowned tourist attraction, with ghosts and all, enticing nearly 25,000 people a year. When exploring its caverns, visitors have reported seeing the ghost of a deceased cave explorer in 1949 and the spirit of a nameless little boy who wanders the tunnels and passageways. However, the most famous denizen of the caves is the witch.

Back in the 1700s an old woman lived in the cave with some goats. The villagers blamed the recluse for all the ills that beset the village. Heeding their complaints, the Abbot of Glastonbury sent Father Bernard to exorcize the witch. As the story goes, the priest blessed the water in the cave and then began sprinkling it about. The witch of the Wookey Caves challenged the priest. Standing his ground, he asked her to repent. His request was spurned, and a battle of wills ensued. Finally, Father Bernard doused her with holy water. The wicked witch screeched, her body stiffened, and she slowly turned to stone. Is the story of the Wookey Caves a legend? Maybe yes. Maybe no. In 1912, seasoned cave explorer, Herbert Balch, discovered the skeletal remains of several goats—and an old woman.

TERRIFYING TIDBIT

On July 28, 2009, after about a month of auditions, Carole Bohanan was hired for about $80,000 a year to be the new witch of Wookey Caves. It seems that despite Father Bernard's best efforts, the witch is back.

APRIL 10, 1324
THE SKELETONS OF PRAGUE
Prague, Czech Republic

As you make your way through the charming medieval streets of Prague, you might find yourself face to face, or rather face to skull, with Prague's "Begging Skeleton." In life he was a student at the university who stood six foot six. His stature drew the attention of a professor, who wanted a tall frame for his collection of skeletons. The student, who was much younger than the professor, sold his skeleton to him for thirty dollars, figuring he would easily outlive the much older professor. Collecting his money, he went out for a night of drinking, squandering all thirty dollars. Quite inebriated, he got into a fight and was killed. His skeleton ended up in the professor's collection. Now he wanders the streets looking for a handout so he can buy his skeleton back.

APRIL 11, 1735
THE DOLPHIN HOTEL
Littlehampton, England

Several spirits reportedly haunt the Dolphin, an old coaching inn built in 1735. Two of the most active ghosts are Tom, an older man who once looked after the many barrels of wine, and Molly, a chambermaid who once lived in the old hotel. It seems poor Molly, distraught after being jilted by her lover, entered the old stable block and took her own life.

One credible report of Molly's ghost came from an American serviceman in the mid-1990s. While relaxing at the Dolphin, he was suddenly stunned to see the ghostly apparition of a beautiful young woman walk across the floor in front of him. Further investigation indicated that Molly's apparition had indeed appeared above the old stable block where she had met her tragic end. And since the floor had been raised several feet, it explained the man's odd report: he said that Molly appeared to be wading through water, her ghostly apparition only visible from the waist up.

APRIL 12, 1800
THE GREEN LADY
Burlington, Connecticut

The Burlington Center Cemetery, better known as the Green Lady Cemetery, is one of the oldest graveyards in Burlington. But how did it get its name? Legend has it that a young woman by the name of

Elisabeth Palmiter died tragically at the hands of her husband. Evidently it's not what he did to her, but what he didn't do.

One day, Elisabeth, who lived next door to the cemetery, wandered into the woods in search of her husband, Benjamin. She got stuck in the swamp. When her husband happened across her, he just stood there, lantern in hand, and waited for his wife to disappear beneath the muck, never to breathe again. But Elisabeth, angered by her husband's inaction, returned from the dead and haunted him until he went insane.

Through the years there have been numerous reports of the ghostly apparition of a woman surrounded by green mist wandering throughout the cemetery. One visitor of the graveyard took a picture of the tombstones. Upon reviewing her photo, she noticed a stationary green mist above one of the stones. To her surprise, it was the grave of Elisabeth. Is the legend of the Green Lady fact or fiction? Maybe you should visit Burlington, Connecticut, and find out for yourself.

APRIL 13, 1699
THE POTSFORD GIBBET
Letheringham, Suffolk, England

Back in the 1600s many men were hanged for their crimes, but perhaps more grisly is that their bodies were left to rot in the sun on a device called the gibbet. A gibbet is a gallows with a projecting arm at the top, from which the bodies of criminals were hanged in chains and then left suspended for all to view. In a place called Potsford Wood stands the Potsford Gibbet, an eerie reminder of its horrid past. The last victim was a man named Jonah Snell, hanged there in 1699 for the murder of a miller and his son.

TERRIFYING TIDBIT

In England, gallows were built at crossroads. This was done in the hope of confusing the ghosts of the hanged, in case they decided to return and revisit those who took their lives.

Today, those who venture into the wood have noticed strange twinkling lights darting about the trees. Dark shadows roam around the weathered gibbet accompanied by hideous moans. But even in broad daylight many have been terrorized by a cloaked figure with a skull for a head. The specter of Jonah Snell, perhaps?

APRIL 14, 1912
TITANIC EXHIBIT
Atlanta, Georgia

On April 14, 1912, while cruising through dark, icy waters, the *Titanic* struck an iceberg. Within a few short hours, it sank, disappearing into the black watery depths and leaving more than 1,500 people struggling for their lives in the icy waters of the North Atlantic.

Eighty-two years later, on June 7, 1994, the United States District Court awarded RMS Titanic Inc. salvaging rights. It wasn't until fourteen years after, in 2008, that the salvage company began their worldwide tour titled the "Titanic Aquatic," which featured over 190 artifacts.

It is rumored that a Georgia aquarium, soon after displaying the antiquities, began experiencing a series of unexplainable events. One volunteer, Margarit, felt an invisible hand move through her hair while she was working. She was quoted as saying, "I think it's the lost souls from the *Titanic*."

A spokeswoman for the aquarium stated that she'd received multiple reports of odd goings-on from various volunteers. Soon after, a paranormal investigative team was called in. It seems that during the investigation, members of their team spotted several shadowy figures roaming the aquarium's hallways. The ghostly specter of an elderly woman was seen in the vicinity of the *Titanic* exhibit.

Coincidently, other sites housing the *Titanic* artifacts have reported experiencing similar unexplainable phenomena, lending credence to the notion that the artifacts from the *Titanic* have some of its lost souls still attached.

TERRIFYING TIDBIT

The energy of those who have passed on can remain attached to an item. That would explain why so many cultures treasure their relics.

APRIL 15, 1865
LINCOLN
Washington, D.C.

Well-known actor John Wilkes Booth assassinated President Abraham Lincoln on April 15, 1865, in the Ford Theatre. Booth, carrying a .44 Derringer, jumped Box 7 where Lincoln sat with his wife. Counting on the sound of laughter muffling his shot, he fired at point-blank range.

It is said that President Lincoln foretold his own death when he related a dream to his bodyguard. Of this one cannot be certain; however, tales of President Lincoln being the most active of spirits in the White House abound.

For instance, Eleanor Roosevelt reported feeling the presence of Honest Abe while working in Lincoln's bedroom. During the Roosevelt administration, a clerk reported seeing Lincoln sitting atop his bed removing his boots. Queen Wilhelmina of the Netherlands had a vision of Abraham Lincoln one night during an overnight stay at the White House. Upon hearing a knock at the door, she got up to open it, only to come face to face with the ghost of our dear departed president.

Yet these are not the only sightings. On several occasions, Calvin Coolidge's wife reported seeing President Lincoln staring out the windows of the Oval Office, hands behind his back, appearing to be in deep contemplation. One can only imagine the reason behind the numerous sightings of Lincoln and what he would say if he could speak to those who have seen him.

APRIL 16, 1851
MINOT'S LEDGE LIGHTHOUSE
Scituate, Massachusetts

About a mile off the coast of Massachusetts, between the towns of Scituate and Cohasset, lurks a dangerous reef known as the Cohasset Rocks. In 1847, the government ordered a lighthouse be built there.

After much controversy as to the design, cost-conscious bureaucrats chose the less expensive, metal-frame structure, a decision that would come back to haunt them. The new tower went into service on

New Years Day in 1850. Almost immediately, the lighthouse keeper, Isaac Dunham, began to complain about the stability of the tower. Ten months later, he, along with his two assistants, resigned. The next lighthouse keeper was a man named John Bennett.

On April 14, Bennett went ashore on lighthouse business, leaving the tower in the hands of his assistants, Joseph Wilson and Joseph Antoine. While ashore, a vicious nor'easter raged, preventing Bennett from returning to the lighthouse. The relentless storm pounded the coast, and around 10 P.M., the light went out. The lighthouse had been swept away. Both Wilson and Antoine had perished.

In its place, a new granite structure was built. Since then, several keepers have reported odd occurrences—the sound of ethereal whispers, the feeling of being touched by an unseen hand, and even a shadowy figure spotted in the lantern room. Strange taps have been heard on the pipes (a system of communication used by Wilson and Antoine). And glass soiled by seagulls has been mysteriously cleaned. Fishermen have glimpsed a man screaming at them in Portuguese, "Stay Away! Stay Away!" Coincidentally, Antoine was Portuguese. It seems that although Wilson and Antoine perished on that night in April, they continue to carry out their duties as if they are unaware they are dead.

APRIL 17, 1865
MARY SURRATT
Washington, D.C.

John Wilkes Booth, the man responsible for Lincoln's assassination, was known to frequent a tavern operated by John Lloyd, but owned by Mary Surratt. In April of 1865, Mary Surratt along with Lewis Powell (who had attempted to kill Secretary of State William Seward) and Louis Weichmann, who dropped off a package at the Inn that was later picked up by Booth, were all arrested as conspirators in Lincoln's assassination. Lloyd was pressured into testifying against Mary. But what other proof did the police have on Surratt? The incriminating evidence against Mary was that her boardinghouse, located a few blocks from Ford Theatre, was a convenient haven for Booth while in town. And, to make matters worse, both of Mary's sons were involved in the Confederacy.

Weichmann also testified against Surratt. Later he claimed that he was pressured by government officials to do so.

Many believed that President Andrew Johnson would pardon Mary. After all, up until that point in history, no female prisoner had ever been hanged. Unfortunately for Mary, the pardon never came. On July 7, 1865, Mary, along with three others, was hanged at Fort McNair. One of the men who died along with Mary, Lewis Powell, proclaimed her innocence with his dying breath. But his words fell on deaf ears. That day marked the first woman to ever be hanged in the United States.

Ever since, people have witnessed the ghostly apparition of a woman with her hands and feet bound roaming about the site of her execution, her face barely visible beneath a black hood. And many a soldier's child, when asked who their invisible friend is, happily report, "the Lady in Black."

TERRIFYING TIDBIT

In some customs, people preparing their loved ones for burial would bind the feet. It was believed this act prevented the spirit from returning.

APRIL 18, 1910
McPike Mansion
Alton, Illinois

No one knows why the aging mansion built by Henry McPike who died in 1910 is haunted. Although the mansion has not been occupied since the 1950s, there have been numerous visitors who have roamed its halls in search of paranormal phenomena. They have not been disappointed. Professional photographers have captured the image of an unexplained ball of light. Some believe it to be Sarah, a servant that once lived in the home. And others have felt Sarah's ghostly embrace.

A video recorded in 1999 by a professor from California has yet to be debunked. In fact, analysts have found it so unexplainable that it has been viewed on national television many times.

Upon entering the basement the professor and companions were suddenly enveloped with a white mist that appeared out of nowhere. The mist swirled around them for a few seconds, moved away, and then returned just as quickly. As if it were beckoning the group, it continued its cosmic dance, while the curious yet stunned onlookers followed close behind. Then it stopped abruptly. Their encounter with the ghostly apparition lasted only a moment.

However, when the group was asked to describe what they'd felt while encircled by the mist, they said it felt like an electric charge. And that's not all; during their encounter, the eyewitnesses described the swirling mist as having moved with a purpose, indicating an intelligence. Yet, its presence remains a mystery.

TERRIFYING TIDBIT

A paranormal investigation is an event to either prove or disprove the existence of paranormal phenomena.

APRIL 19, 1602
BRIDGE OF SIGHS
Venice, Italy

Built in 1602, this limestone bridge located in St. Mark's Square in the heart of Venice is haunted. The bridge, which crosses the Rio di Palazzo, connects the old prison to the interrogation rooms in the Doge's Palace. After being tried and sentenced in the Palace, the doomed caught their last glimpse of Venice through the narrow windows in the old stone covered bridge. In the nineteenth century, Lord Byron named the bridge for the groans and sighs often heard from the condemned prisoners as they were led away to their cells.

Over the centuries, visitors to the palace and prison have heard heart-wrenching groans and torturous cries emanating from the walls of the stone covered bridge.

But that's not all. Obviously sound travels, because visitors to Hotel Scandinavia, found right next door, have often reported hearing similar eerie moans echoing within its walls. Oddly enough, the hotel has not experienced any other type of paranormal goings-on. So, many believe the unexplainable sounds originate not from the hotel itself but from its neighbor, the Bridge of Sighs.

APRIL 20, 1827
CASA DE ESTUDILLO
San Diego, California

Constructed in 1827, Casa de Estudillo, the adobe house located in San Diego State Historic Park, is haunted. Through the years it has had many uses, including a church. In fact, it is in the old chapel that the translucent image of a monk dressed in a brown robe has been seen. On several occasions staff and visitors alike have stared in awe as they watched the ghostly specter glide past them, vanishing through a doorway to what was once a priest's bedroom. Museum staff members have witnessed the faint sound of praying and a book flipping pages of its own accord. Unseen hands have slammed the heavy wooden doors shut. The morphing of ghostly, human faces has been witnessed in the antique mirrors. Shadows are seen darting room to room. Flashes of red and yellow lights appearing out of nowhere in the dining room have shocked more than one visitor to this museum. And the ghost of a sad woman dressed in Victorian garb is often seen wandering about. The strange occurrences at Casa de Estudillo have attracted the attention of the paranormal community. Among those to investigate the haunting was the team from the television show *Ghost Hunters*.

It's been said that during their investigation, they captured a few of the ghostly faces on film. The images were so clear that the staff, familiar with the historic residents and with the antique photos of the museum, were able to identify the spirits. In their calculation there are at least nine ghostly inhabitants. However, visitors to the museum believe there to be more. Many more.

APRIL 21, 1910
MARK TWAIN'S MUSEUM
Hartford, Connecticut

The famous novelist Mark Twain, also known as Samuel Langhorne Clemens, is most noted for books such as *The Adventures of Tom Sawyer*, but what most people fail to realize is that he was also a paranormal enthusiast. He spoke of prophetic dreams and channeling the dead and was known to attend séances.

In 1874 Twain moved from Missouri to Hartford, Connecticut, where he lived for the next seventeen years until he moved to Europe. The home in which he and his family lived in Hartford passed hands many times until finally it was purchased in 1929 by a group of local preservationists. In 1963, it was named a national landmark.

The level of paranormal activity experienced in the Twain home has garnered the attention of many notable paranormal investigators. Staff and visitors alike have reported seeing a transparent image of a young woman in a white dress cascading down the stairway. The ghostly apparition is believed by many to be that of Susy Clemens, Mark Twain's daughter who died at age twenty-four in their Hartford home after contracting meningitis. The sounds of laughing children along with the pitter-patter of little feet are often heard running up and down the length of the front staircase.

Once, a paranormal phenomenon was even credited for attracting the attention of the fire department. Late one evening the fire department responded to a smoke detector being set off at the Twain House and Museum. However, when they arrived, they found nothing, expect for the pungent odor of cigar smoke lingering in the air.

Samuel Langhorne Clemens, of course, was known to enjoy a good cigar.

APRIL 22, 2005
GHOST BROTHER INTERVENES
Jackson, Mississippi

A brother, long deceased from a car accident, is credited with saving the life of his sister. As retold, a young woman's tire blew out while driving in the high-speed lane. Her out-of-control car skidded off the road, down a ditch, and through bushes and trees on a path of destruction.

Through the horrifying ordeal, she suddenly heard her brother's voice loud and clear, "Undo your seatbelt, now!" She obeyed. The moment she unclipped the belt, her body, like a rag doll in flight, soared into the backseat. Just then, the car flipped over and came to a halt in a garden. Hearing her pleas for help, the owner of the home pulled the woman's bruised and battered body through the rear window to safety.

Emergency teams arrived, and after taking one look at the wreckage, they were at a loss as to how the young lady had survived her ordeal.

She related to all that her brother had saved her life.

Although there may be some people who are skeptical of her claims, the simple fact remains that the driver's side of the car was crushed and smashed to pieces. Had the young woman not unclipped her seatbelt when she did, she would not be alive to tell the tale.

APRIL 23, 1729
THE FATAL JUDGMENT
Cape Town, South Africa

The impressive star-shaped Fort de Goede Hoop (Castle of Good Hope) was completed in 1679. This massive fortification was the seat of the military and civilian government. Today the castle is the oldest colonial structure in South Africa and is known for a ghost sighting or two.

Several people have reported seeing the gleaming apparition of a tall man walking between two of the bastions in the castle. Disembodied footsteps and cursing have also been heard in the same area. This specter is believed to be the ghost of Pieter Gysbert van Noodt, a former Dutch colonial governor. According to legend, van Noodt was as cold as the Cape Town winter winds and hated by the soldiers stationed there.

In 1729 seven soldiers were caught trying to desert. The ruling council sentenced them to beating and deportation; however, Van Noodt overturned their verdict and sentenced them to death by hanging. As his sentence was being carried out, one of the men cursed him for what he had done. After the men were hanged, an officer went to the governor's chamber to inform him that his sentence had been carried out. He found van Noodt in his chair, dead, his face frozen in terror. It seems judgment came as swiftly for the governor as it did for the men he had condemned. In death, the souls of the deserters seem to have finally escaped the cruelty of van Noodt. The governor, on the other hand, seems damned to roam the grounds of the fort for eternity.

APRIL 24, 1907
LADY ELLIOT ISLAND
Australia

This small Great Barrier Reef island was discovered in 1816 by Captain Thomas Stuart and was named after his ship, *Lady Elliot*. A wood and iron lighthouse was built in 1873.

If one ventures to the island today, not far from the lighthouse is a tiny well-kept cemetery. One of the graves belongs to Irish-born Susannah McKee. Thomas McKee and his family left Ireland promising Susannah a better life. But his job as lighthouse keeper on Lady Elliot Island was far from what he promised. The island was barren and inhospitable. As the years passed, Susannah's constant yearning for a better life, coupled with the desire to escape the isolation became too much for her to bear. Finally in April of 1907, she donned her best dress and plummeted into the sea. The next day, her husband found her body and buried her in the small cemetery. Rumors spread that Tom had pushed her to her death, but nothing could be proved.

Several years later, another lighthouse keeper, Arthur Brumpton, spied the ghost of a woman in old-fashioned dress walking between the lighthouse and the cottage. Brumpton and his daughter saw her several times during their stay on the island but didn't know who she was. In 1940, while Brumpton and his daughter were returning to Brisbane on a ship, the captain of the vessel decided to show them some old photographs of past inhabitants of the island. To their shock, they recognized Susannah as the spectral image they'd often witnessed wandering about the island. To this day, Susannah McKee's ghost can still be seen in the cottages, the lighthouse, and gliding across the island. Ironically, it seems that even in death she still can't escape the loneliness and desolation of Lady Elliot Island.

APRIL 25, 1578
DRAGSHOLM SLOT
Sealand, Demark

Bishop Roskilde built Dragsholm Castle in the twelfth century. The castle became the residence of kings and of several noble families. At least three spirits haunt the colossal fortress.

The saddest tale is that of the Lady in White, the daughter of a nobleman who at a young age fell in love with a common man who worked in the castle. One day, her father, discovering their relationship, became furious and ordered her to be imprisoned in the castle. Today the apparition of a woman in a white dress can be seen roaming the corridors in search of her lover.

Another spirit making a notable impression on the castle is the Earl of Bothwell. In the 1500s he was captured and imprisoned in the castle's dungeon, where he remained for ten years, escaping only in death. His mummified remains were displayed as a relic in a nearby church. Each evening his ghost returns and he is seen riding his gallant steed through the courtyard.

The last of the three is the gray lady. She was a maiden in the castle who suffered from a terrible toothache. The master cured her. Eternally grateful, she returns to watch over the castle.

TERRIFYING TIDBIT

In the 1930s during renovations of the castle, workers knocked down a wall and discovered the skeletal remains of a woman in a white dress. Could this be the Lady in White?

APRIL 26, 2006
BARNLEY PUB
Barnsley, South Yorkshire

Roger Froggatt, the owner of the Yorkshire Pub, encountered the fright of his life one fateful night. The pub's heat-seeking alarm was set off at 1:30 A.M. Froggatt, thinking his establishment had been broken into, went to investigate. Upon entering the empty pub, he immediately noticed that all the televisions had been turned on. He then went to check out the bathroom, where he could clearly hear the toilets flushing. That's when he came face-to-face with the ghostly apparition of a gray-haired woman dressed in white. Stunned, he stood there for a moment and watched in horror as the figure before him turned to stare, her face missing from cheekbone to jaw. Terrified, Froggatt ran out of the bathroom. His fear was so intense he had difficulty speaking, but he managed to call the police. When the police arrived, they too experienced paranormal oddities. There was no sign of a break-in, yet the alarm had been triggered, and when they entered the restroom, the electronic toilets once again began to flush by themselves.

Previously, Froggatt had experienced barrels in the basement had been inexplicably moved and the gas jets turned on. At first he thought it was nothing more than his overactive imagination. Not anymore. Roger has decided to call in the help of a priest to exorcise the evil spirit that he now is convinced haunts the establishment.

APRIL 27, 1976
THE HAUNTED HOUSE OF ROSALYNN CARTER
Plains, Georgia

In 1976, during an interview with the *National Enquirer*, Rosalynn Carter shared her family's haunted house stories.

Between 1954 and 1959, the Carters rented an old Southern house in Plains, Georgia. Although she was not a true believer of ghosts, she recalled several instances of strange goings-on in the house. In fact, her experiences with the house started long before moving in. As a child growing up in town, she would do her best to avoid the house at all cost. But on the occasions when she did pass the empty house, she would often see flashing lights emanating from the attic.

Former residents of the home spoke of sleepless nights when blankets were torn from their bodies as they lay in bed. A white dog had been seen on the front porch on several occasions, yet when approached, it would vanish. Another resident reported that one night his body was lifted out of his bed and placed on the floor, only to be placed back in bed again.

Legend has it that the activity began after the building had been taken over by Union soldiers. The tortured souls of the soldiers killed during the skirmish are believed to still reside within its walls.

She was so distraught by the rumors of haunting, Rosalynn decided to turn the "haunted bedroom" into a sitting area when the Carters moved in. During the years they rented, Rosalynn also reported that her son inadvertently uncovered a hidden room beneath the fireplace with nothing but a lone chair in it. Mrs. Carter believed that the Union soldiers hid in this room, and perhaps this contributed to the rumors of the haunting.

But did she have a ghostly encounter herself? Although she never saw a ghost, she does admit to hearing eerie sounds each night that echoed in an empty attic. Sounds that sent chills up her spine.

APRIL 28, 1945
HOTEL BURCHIANTI
Florence, Italy

The Hotel Burchianti is more difficult to find than its ghosts. Tucked away in the Old World Florence streets, this quaint hotel has been home to some of Italy's "most famous" residents, such as opera singers, poets, and politicians, including Italian dictator Benito Mussolini. Many visitors to Burchianti have witnessed several spirits. A little girl who likes to skip down the hallways, an old woman who knits in a chair, a spectral doorman, and a maid who continues her duties with care and attention to detail can all be seen within the walls of the hotel. But it is the Fresco Room that has garnered the most attention. Guests who have spent the night there have had the uneasy feeling of being watched. Some have experienced the sensation of a phantom entity as it crawls in bed with them. Others have seen a man, whom they believe to be Benito Mussolini, enveloped in a pink haze. Perhaps most chilling are the occasions when guests have been awakened by an icy breath upon their face. Although the Burchianti Hotel only has eleven rooms, these chilling experiences have earned it a spot on the list of The World's Most Haunted Hotels.

APRIL 29, 1865
LINCOLN SPECIAL
East Coast, United States

Abraham Lincoln has long been associated with the paranormal. It is a well-known fact that he attended séances and foresaw his own death, and his ghost has been witnessed in several locations, including the White House. After his death on April 15, 1865, it was decided to transport the president's body to his final resting place, Springfield, Illinois. A powerful steam locomotive, dubbed the "Lincoln Special," was designated for this journey. On board were both Lincoln's body and the coffin of his son Willie, who was disinterred for reburial with his father; as well as 300 mourners; an honor guard; and, to keep the body fresh looking, since Lincoln was not embalmed, a mortician. The train departed Washington chugging along up the east coast. Finally it arrived in Springfield on May 4, nineteen days after his death.

Through the years there have been eyewitness accounts of the spectral Lincoln Special. From these reports it appears to be taking the same route as it did back in 1865. People near the tracks have reported hearing an old-fashioned steam whistle and seeing dense gray clouds of billowing smoke, which are followed by a change in the atmosphere. Nearby crossing gates close as if a train is passing by, but there is none. And for those fortunate enough to spy the train, it is a scene they will never forget. A blue light emanates from the engine, which is followed by a flat car with a band of skeleton musicians in Union uniforms, playing music that no one can hear. The next car contains Lincoln's black-draped coffin and an honor guard of skeletons in both Union and Confederate uniforms. As the train passes, there is a rush of warm air, no matter how cold the night is. Eyewitness accounts have slowly diminished through the years, making one believe that Lincoln's phantom funeral train may be slowly fading away.

APRIL 30, 1945
ADOLF HITLER
Berghof, Germany

On April 30, 1945, as the Third Reich crumbled around him, Hitler and his wife of one day, Eva Braun, retired to their bedroom in the fuehrer's underground bunker and committed suicide. Their bodies were burned, and seven days later, Germany surrendered and the war was over. But apparently it wasn't the end for the fuehrer. From the end of the war to the present, Hitler's ghost has been seen in the area around the Berghof, Hitler's home in the Bavarian Alps.

The Berghof was heavily damaged at the end of the war. Countless visitors have claimed to see Hitler strutting about the ruins, barking out orders, and wildly waving his arms in the air. Other times, he has been seen sitting in a chair, his head in his hands, despair on his face. When he was alive he would look out the picture window of the Berghof and say, "It is here where Germany will find me for a thousand years." It appears he may be right.

TERRIFYING TIDBIT

Brian Singer, the director of the 2008 movie *Valkyrie*, told the *National Enquirer* that he was convinced Hitler's ghost was haunting the set. Among the unexplainable events that happened during the filming was a runaway tank that nearly hit actor Tom Cruise.

MAY 1, 1791
CROW ROCK
Crabapple, Pennsylvania

One Sunday, the four young Crow sisters were walking through the woods on the way to visit a neighbor. It was a warm peaceful day when they reached a ford in the creek that ran through their property. As the sisters were crossing the ford, three men—two Indians and a savage white man named Spicer—came running out from behind a large boulder. The men had been hiding, lying in wait. Frozen in fear, the sisters were easy prey. They were brutally attacked with tomahawks, but the sisters fought back. In the commotion, one sister escaped. By the time the rescue party came back, it was too late. The sisters had been scalped. Two were dead and one lay dying in the hot sun. She later perished at home. All three were buried in the family plot.

Today, some say that if you go to that boulder by the ford on a hot summer's night, you can still hear the terrifying screams of the sisters. And every now and then, you can even see their wandering spirits searching for their scalps by the rock that bears their name, Crow's Rock.

MAY 2, 1946
ALCATRAZ
San Francisco, California

Indigenous people believed Alcatraz island to be inhabited by evil spirits. From the 1850s to 1933, the island was used as a military prison for deserters and depraved soldiers. In 1934, The Rock, as it is sometimes known, became a federal penitentiary. It was home to some of the country's most notorious murderers, including Chicago gang lord Al Capone and the "Birdman of Alcatraz," Robert Stroud. Alcatraz was reputed to be the toughest prison system and where the most hardened criminals were locked away. Although some prisoners came close to escaping, they never succeeded. Inmates who were unable to endure the cramped quarters, torture, deprivation, and physical abuse eventually died at the Rock. Some died of natural causes, some at the hands of guards or other prisoners. During the prison's heyday, six cells on D block made up "the Hole." They were used to house the more troublesome inmates. However, one of the six cells, the most isolated, was called, "the Oriental." The story is that in the 1940s, one prisoner, after being stripped of his clothes, was tossed into its dark chamber. Throughout the night the man howled and screamed claiming a creature with red eyes was attacking him. Laughing it off, the guards ignored his cries. The next morning when they opened the door, they found the man dead, his throat laced with unexplainable claw marks. Later, the guards lined up the prisoners to take a head count. To their astonishment, they noted one extra inmate. As soon as they recognized him as the man who had mysteriously died in the Oriental, the ghost vanished.

Everything from inexplicable cold breezes to the loud sound of unearthly clanging has been reported from prison guards and their families who inhabited the island. Many believe that those who had been imprisoned on the island still remain. Evidently, even in death, Alcatraz is inescapable.

MAY 3, 1810
ST. SIMONS LIGHTHOUSE
St. Simons Island, Georgia

During the construction of St. Simons Lighthouse many workers bitten by mosquitoes died from disease, an omen of things to come. In 1880, while Frederick Osborne was keeper, an argument broke out between him and his assistant, John Stephens. Apparently the trouble began when Osborne spoke "inappropriately" to Stephens's wife. A violent fight occurred between the two, and Osborne was shot and died from his wounds. Stephens was arrested for his murder, but he was acquitted and continued tending to his duties. However, he was not alone. It appears that Osborne, even in death, continued his duties as well.

Through the years following the murder, many of the keepers, as well as their wives, claimed to hear the sound of heavy footsteps on the tower's staircase and to feel Osborne's presence. In fact, one account published in a newspaper in 1908 retells how a keeper's wife, having problems with the light mechanism while her husband was away, called out to the spirit of Osborne. There was a "clink and a rattle," then she saw the ghost of Osborne working on the mechanism. Shocked, she fainted. When she awoke, she found that the mechanism had been repaired. As the years passed, fewer sightings of Osborne have been reported, making one think that good keepers don't die, they just fade away.

MAY 4, 1471
THE CHARGING HORSEMAN
Prestbury, England

In 1471, a messenger during the War of the Roses charged down a path headed for the camp of Edward IV. He soon met his end as a Lancastrian arrow sailed through the air, plunging deep into his chest. His mission had abruptly been put to an end.

Today, the glowing image of this messenger can still be seen galloping through various locations in Prestbury, specifically along the Burgage, which is reportedly one of the most haunted roads in Prestbury.

During construction on the roadway, workers found the skeletal remains of a man with the head of an arrow buried deep within his rib cage. It seems that this poor messenger is forced to relive his failed mission for eternity.

MAY 5, 1937
BANTA INN
Tracy, California

In Tracy, a bar called the Banta Inn was originally a saloon built by reputed outlaw Frank Gallegos. In later years it served as a bordello, before finally meeting its end in a fire in 1937. As a cost savings, all the unburned timber was recycled and used to rebuild what would later become the Banta Inn. It is said that among the ghosts to frequent the bar are two people who lost their lives in the fire. Objects have been seen levitating as well as shadow people dashing to and fro. But the most popular ghost to visit Banta is Gallegos's son-in-law, Tony Gurkan. Gurkan and his wife, Jenny, took ownership of the bar in the early 1960s. While alive, Tony had the habit of leaving the cash drawer open with neatly stacked coins visible for all to see. He was also known to sit by himself at the corner of the bar. In 1968, Tony suffered a heart attack and died. In the years since, those who have bar tendered have recalled tossing coins in the cash drawer and closing it, only to find the drawer open and the coins stacked into neat little piles. And from all appearances, death hasn't stopped Tony from enjoying a good hand of cards. He's often been seen, sitting by himself, in the corner of the room, playing poker. And that's not all. Apparently when we cross over to the other side, humor remains. Staff of the Banta have heard the jukebox playing *Spirits in the Material World*, by the Police. And it wasn't even plugged in!

TERRIFYING TIDBIT

Severe psychokinetic phenomena are moving or levitating objects. It is often associated with some of the following: doors slamming, objects sliding across a table, pictures sailing off the walls, and furniture moving of its own accord.

MAY 6, 2006
DEAD AGAINST TOLL ROADS
Richmond, Virginia

It seems that not only the living are adverse to toll roads, but the dead as well. Pocahontas Parkway is alive with paranormal activity. At least it was. According to the *Richmond Times-Dispatch* motorists, toll operators, and road crews were plagued by ghosts. One truck driver was forced to scare away the torch wielding Algonquian ghosts with the horn of his big rig. His opinion: the Native Americans were protesting the road being built over what once was their village. One evening, during a night of highway construction, a worker spotted what he thought was a man in a Native American costume riding a horse across the highway. At first he just assumed it was an eccentric out on a joy ride, but he changed his mind when he approached the man to ask him to leave. Before he could say a word, the ghostly specter vanished. Toll workers on the late-night shift have reported the bone-chilling sounds of "whooping" and screams emanating from the woods. Even a spokesman for the local state police commented that the eerie high-pitched screams were made by more than a dozen voices.

Interestingly enough, it appears that the Algonquin protestors caved in, or, should we say, they gave up the ghost. Because they've barely been seen or heard from since.

MAY 7, 1663
THEATRE ROYAL
London, England

The notoriously haunted Theatre Royal was built in 1663. In its day it was the leading theatre in all of London. But what of the ghosts that reside there? The host of characters include: Dan Leno, whose clog dancing is still heard coming from the empty dressing rooms; the remorseful Charles Macklin, who in 1735 took out an eye of a fellow actor with his cane; Joe Grimaldi, the deceased clown who is believed to assist actors in finding their correct spot on the stage, ridding them of their jitters; and last, but not least, "The Man in Gray", an eighteenth-century nobleman dressed in a gray cape, three-cornered hat, and powdered wig, who makes his presence known during various rehearsals. Word has it that this last ghostly visitor is not only sought after, but also highly celebrated, especially since his past appearances correlated with such theatrical successes as *Oklahoma*, *Carousel*, *South Pacific*, and *The King and I*. So where did the mysterious ghost of the Man in Gray originate from? In 1848, the skeletal remains of a man with a knife wedged between his ribs, was found behind a wall at the Royal.

MAY 8, 1815
THE WOODBURN MANSION
Dover, Delaware

Built in the 1790s by Charles Hillyard III, the Woodburn mansion once served as a stop on the Underground Railroad; today it is the governor's mansion. The first reported ghostly sightings in the house were in 1815. The Bates family, who resided there at the time, had a houseguest by the name of Lorenzo Dow. On his way down to join the family for dinner, he passed an elderly gentleman on the stairs. When he joined his hosts at the dinner table, he asked if the old man was going to join them. Bates informed Dow that there was no one else home. But through Dow's description, he quickly learned the man described was none other than his own deceased father. Another owner of the mansion claimed to have a run in with the elder Bates as well. One night he came down to the dining room and discovered a man drinking his wine. It was the ghost of Bates. Several other spirits are known to frequent the mansion: the spirit of a little girl who has a habit of tugging on unsuspecting people's clothes and vying for attention, a colonial soldier, and a Southern slave raider. Little is known about the soldier, but it has been said that the slave raider accidentally hanged himself in the old poplar tree. At night you can hear his moans of agony. The many ghosts of the governor's mansion are reflected in its history. Who knows, those who are living in it now may haunt the house in the future.

MAY 9, 1131
TINTERN ABBEY
Tintern, Monmouthshire, Wales

Walter de Clare, Lord of Chepstow on the banks of the River Wye, founded Tintern Abbey. It was a Cistercian order and thrived for 400 years. In 1349 bubonic plague swept through the area killing many monks and perhaps explaining the disappearance of the neighboring village of Penterry.

Today the abbey and Saint Mary's Church lie in ruins, deserted except for the ghosts. Nocturnal visitors have reported hearing the somber sound of chanting and witnessing the processions of torch-bearing spectral monks. The most terrifying story associated with the abbey speaks of a group of men who went into the abbey's orchard in search of antiquities. After a day's labor, they had dug up two skeletons. That night in the church, they celebrated, drinking heavily and taunting the spirits of the monks. The skies grew dark. A heavy wind came up. Lightning flashed about the area. Soon an eerie mist began to swirl around them. Out of the mist came a knight. Other figures emerged: hooded men and the white-robed monks of the monastery. The ghostly knight raised his arm, pointing toward the doorway of the abbey. The men, scattering in fear, left what they'd brought behind. It is said that they did not stop running until they reached the next village. Since that day, few dare to dig on the abbey's grounds fearing that they too might raise the wrath of Lord Strongbow, the Earl of Pembroke, and protectorate of Tintern Abbey.

TERRIFYING TIDBIT

Sin eaters refer to persons, who through eating food and drink, take on the sins of the deceased, thereby absolving their soul and allowing them to rest in peace.

MAY 10, 94 B.C.
HISTORY'S FIRST GHOST HUNTER
Athens, Greece

It has been said that one of the oldest recorded ghost sightings in history comes from a Roman magistrate named Pliny the Younger. What he described in his writings is what we would assume today to be a typical haunted house. Pliny writes that a philosopher by the name of Athenodoros Cananites (74 B.C.–A.D. 7), having heard of the haunted house, decided to investigate the situation for himself. You might say that Athenodoros was a paranormal investigator way ahead of his time. He rented the haunted location then waited for the ghostly apparition to make its move. We don't know how long the stoic philosopher had to wait, but what we do know, as recorded in Pliny's record, was that Athenodoros found what he was looking for. Apparently the disheveled spirit of an old man bound in chains appeared before him. Without whispering a word, the spirit beckoned Athenodoros to follow him. The spirit of the old man led him out of the home and into the garden before vanishing into thin air. Not one to ignore a message, the philosopher marked the spot, then brought men in the next day to dig.

Once again Athenodoros was rewarded for his efforts when the skeleton of a man bound in chains was discovered. What happened next? Well, the way Pliny described it in his writings, when they respectfully removed the chains and properly buried it, the haunting of the home came to an end.

TERRIFYING TIDBIT

According to Greek legend the soul of a deceased person roams the earth for forty days and forty nights.

MAY 11, 1833
THE WALLET MAN
Morristown, New Jersey

Antoine Le Blanc, an immigrant sailor from the West Indies, was hired by the Sayer family to help out on the farm. Little did they know how deadly that decision would turn out to be. Le Blanc, tiring of his duties, convinced an unsuspecting Samual Sayer and his wife to enter the barn, where he then beat them to death with a shovel and buried them in a dung heap. Next, he entered the home where he located Phoebe, the maid, and bludgeoned her with an axe as she slept.

While attempting to flee the state he was captured and brought to trial. Found guilty of his hideous crimes, he was sentenced to death by hanging. After his death, his body was given to a Princeton scientist and a local doctor for dissecting. Later, his skin was tanned in Morristown, and soon after, souvenir wallets and purses, book jackets, and lampshades were made and signed by the local sheriff to prove authenticity.

Since the gruesome murders, the Sayer family's farm, now believed to be haunted, has changed hands several times. Twice when it was a restaurant, waitresses and visitors alike have sworn that the spirit of Phoebe still remains. A delicate, yet blood-soaked hand has been seen reaching from a painting on the wall. Customers have been repeatedly touched on the shoulder by an invisible hand. Objects have been seen moving of their own accord, and the coldest spot in the building is . . . where else, Phoebe's room. Exorcisms have been done on the property, but the activity still remains.

While Phoebe haunts the old Sayer farm in search of justice, the "Wallet Man" has been seen roaming around the old courthouse, perhaps looking to collect his skin.

MAY 12, 2009
PFISTER HOTEL
Milwaukee, Wisconsin

Reports of a Milwaukee haunted hotel abound. Word has it that the previous owner of the luxurious, 116-year-old hotel, Charles Pfister, is still interested in keeping tabs on the goings-on in his establishment. Many visitors who have seen the ghostly specter have reported him to be a well-dressed, older gentleman with a welcoming smile. But how do they know it's Mr. Pfister himself? When shown his portrait, his image matches what they'd seen.

Well-known baseball players staying at the hotel have been so unnerved with the strange occurrences that they have slept with a bat for protection. One player turned off his iPod only to have it continue to play. The Marlins visiting Milwaukee for a series against the Brewers were so disturbed by the rumors that they decided to bunk up together as a preventative to paranormal activity.

A "visitor" presumably fitting the description of Mr. Charles Pfister is still being reported from guests and staff. Apparently Pfister is returning to ensure all is well with his earthly clientele, taking customer satisfaction to new heights.

MAY 13, 1878
HOSPITAL HORRORS
Danvers, Massachusetts

Danvers State Hospital, built in 1878, later became home to the mentally ill, the drug addicted, and the criminally insane. It's believed that many of these unfortunate souls were torn from their rooms, placed under restraint, and forced to undergo various experimental treatments. In the 1950s the experimental phase included electroshock therapy, hydrotherapy, and lobotomy. The latter technique did little but leave the patient in a vegetative state. Not only did this facility treat the mentally ill, but Danvers was also a tuberculosis site, where multitudes of deaths were recorded.

Under these conditions, it's no surprise to hear why Danvers State Hospital was thought to be among the most haunted of locations. For years it sat vacant and was a paranormal playground for those who dared to enter its premises. Over the years there have been reports of ill feelings, hands emanating from the inner walls, spooky apparitions, and shadows cascading down the hallways.

The torturous cries and sobs of the desperate have plagued many a visitor.

With construction complete, new condominiums now stand on the land that once echoed the horrors of the poor tortured souls of the Danvers State Hospital. One has to wonder if the new tenants are able to get a good night sleep.

MAY 14, 1810
FARNSWORTH HOUSE
Gettysburg, Pennsylvania

The Farnsworth House, built in 1810, was the homestead of the Sweney family during the Battle of Gettysburg. While the battle raged, Confederate sharpshooters occupied the house. The hundred bullet holes in the south side of the building bear testimony to the ferocity of the battle. Elon John Farnsworth, the newly appointed brigadier general, after whom the house was named, led the ill-fated charge against the Confederate right flank. Sixty-five of Farnsworth's men died that fateful day.

The O'Day family purchased the Farnsworth House in 1972 and today it is a restaurant. Staff and visitors to the Farnsworth have heard the shuffle of booted feet pacing above them on the empty attic floor, along with the occasional sound of a mouth harp reverberating off its rafters. And while many have witnessed ghostly Confederate soldiers pacing the confines of the attic, others have seen the ghosts of Union soldiers in the basement, which makes sense, since the basement had been converted into a makeshift hospital for the Union army. But the most often seen ghost is Mary, a woman believed to have been visiting her brother when the battle broke out. Rather than leave, she remained to tend to the wounded. Her ghostly apparition, dressed in a white satin dress stained in blood, has shocked many visitors. Other spirits have been seen wandering about the dining room. So, if you get a chance to visit Gettysburg, Pennsylvania, and are looking for something to quench your thirst, make sure to stop in at the Farnsworth for a "spirit" or two.

MAY 15, 2009
PARANORMAL PAWS
St. Augustine, Florida

As reported on hubpages.com, a café chef in St. Augustine, Florida, working the second shift, befriended a large Himalayan cat one night when he walked home from work. The cat accompanied him for several weeks during his walk home. Concerned for its well–being, he checked the collar, which clearly read, "Mr. Jeeves."

One day while paying his rent, he asked his landlord and his wife about the cat. Suddenly, at mere mention of Mr. Jeeves, the elderly couple became extremely upset and refused to continue the conversation.

Later he was informed by another tenant that she too had seen Mr. Jeeves. According to the woman, seventeen years earlier, the landlord and his wife had an eleven-year-old daughter by the name of Helen who had been killed while crossing the busy front street. She had not been alone. Her cat, Mr. Jeeves, died beside her.

It began to make sense. It explained why the cat never allowed the chef to pick him up. One evening after finding out that Mr. Jeeves was a ghost cat, the chef attempted to take his picture. However, although he could see the cat with his eyes, when he developed the film, Mr. Jeeves was nowhere to be seen! Perhaps this spectral cat would give even the biggest skeptic pause, or, should we say, "paws."

MAY 16, 1916
THE WUNSCHE BROS.
HOTEL AND SALOON
Spring, Texas

The Wunsche Bros. Hotel and Saloon was built in 1916. This historic landmark in Spring is a well-known restaurant that was once used to accommodate railroad employees and travelers. It's even rumored that the infamous Bonnie and Clyde once used the saloon as a stopping place after robbing one of the town's banks. Today, many believe the crotchety ghost of Charlie Wunsche haunts the building. You see, poor Charlie wasn't always a cantankerous old man. The story is told that in his youth he fell deeply in love with a woman who never loved him back, and he spent the rest of his life pining after his lost love. Staff at the saloon hesitate to speak of Charlie. Ever since they remodeled the place, it seems the old man has been on a tear. On several occasions, it seems he's even locked employees out of the building.

Not long after Charlie passed away, an artist who was sleeping in his old room was abruptly awakened during the night. There before him was an elderly man, who just stood there staring at him. Taking a pad of paper and charcoal, he drew a sketch. The man in the drawing was immediately identified; it was Charlie Wunsche. Sadly, it seems that poor Charlie's broken heart has sealed his fate—and the fates of those who will have to live with his ghostly presence.

MAY 17, 1970
BERNARDSVILLE PUBLIC LIBRARY
Bernardsville, New Jersey

The Bernardsville Public Library was dedicated in May 1970. The red brick building once was the Vealtown Tavern, which was constructed during the Revolutionary War. It is believed to be haunted by the ghost of Phyllis Parker, the innkeeper's daughter. In 1777, soon after Phyllis's marriage to Dr. Byram, Byram was hanged as a British spy. His remains were sent back to the tavern in a casket. Unaware of its contents, Phyllis opened it and found the glassy-eyed stare of her beloved. Unable to bear the horror, she went insane. Her weeping can still be heard in the oldest part of the library, the reading room, where it is said that poor Phyllis opened the casket.

In 1974, after beginning renovations, her ghostly apparition began appearing to employees. In an attempt to contact Phyllis a séance was held in 1987, the results of which can be replayed during a visit to the library. And it appears that the ghost of Phyllis has remained all these years, because in 1989, a young child reported seeing a woman in a long, flowing white dress, in the reading room. In fact, the library staff has seen Phyllis Parker so often that they even issued her a library card.

MAY 18, 1613
THE HAUNTED CROSSROADS
Pluckley, England

Just outside of the old village of Pluckley there lies a crossroads that is called Fright Corner—and rightfully so, because this was the ambush point for a murderous highwayman by the name of Robert du Bois. Next to the crossroads stood a hollow oak tree. Du Bois would hide inside the old oak until his unsuspecting quarry passed, then he would jump out of the tree and rob them of their money and possessions. As his infamy grew, it became common knowledge that the tree held a nasty surprise. One day, a traveler venturing up the road decided not to take any chances. He knew the story of Robert du Bois, so he drew his sword and ran it through the tree. Du Bois was hiding in it. Do you get the point? Robert did, and he died that day. Today the tree is gone, but the ghostly apparition of Robert still haunts the crossroads, looking for his next victim.

TERRIFYING TIDBIT

According to the 1998 edition of the *Guinness Book of Records*, Pluckley was officially recognized as the most haunted village in England, with officially twelve ghosts.

MAY 19, 1536
TOWER OF LONDON
London, England

Anne Boleyn had been the wife of Henry VIII slightly more than three years. Henry, in love with another woman, grew tired of Anne, especially since she lacked the ability to provide him with a male heir to his throne. Soon, a rather unconventional solution to his current dilemma presented itself. Unable to find a way to divorce Anne, he claimed he had begun to hear tales of her infidelities. Not only would she be branded as an adulteress, but also she would be charged with high treason, a crime punishable by death. Although lacking any supporting evidence, her alleged extramarital affairs became suspected as a conspiracy to murder the king.

All of her supposed lovers endured brutal endings: burning, decapitations, disembowelment, castrations, and so forth. As for Anne, she lost her title of queen not long before she lost her head. On May 19, 1536, Anne was led to a scaffold where she was beheaded. But this would not be the last anyone would see of poor Anne Boleyn.

In 1864 a guard nearly court-martialed for falling asleep at his post was spared by his tale. Apparently that night, he'd encountered a headless figure approaching him. Horrified, he charged the apparition with his bayonet, but he passed right through her and fainted.

Another tale comes from the captain of the guard who, upon witnessing a light emanating from a locked, empty chapel, decided to take a closer look. After climbing a ladder to get a bird's-eye view, he peered down into the White Tower. There before him was a procession of people in ancient garb. One slender, elegant woman, whom he quickly recognized by her portraits hanging on the Tower's walls, led the procession. It was Anne Boleyn. The poor soul, to this day, it seems, not only carries her torturous memories, but her head as well.

MAY 20, 1927
THE *DELTA KING*
Sacramento, California

The *Delta King* is a completely renovated 1920s riverboat that is permanently docked in Old Sacramento, California. From 1927 until 1940 the *Delta King* was alive with activity, offering its patrons everything from fine dining to live entertainment. And during its rich history, it was even used as a navy barracks. However, now it is an active restaurant and hotel where patrons and employees alike have reported strange goings-on. There have been several reports of hearing the pitter patter of little feet as a young girl walks down the hallway singing "Ring Around the Rosie." In fact, after seeing the bare footprints of a small child appear out of nowhere, one horrified employee quit on the spot. And one guest even requested that the hotel staff ask the little girl to stop playing in the hallway, as she was disrupting his sleep. Apparently, he was unaware that the little girl was not among the living.

Another spirit frequenting the riverboat has been nicknamed the captain, as his ghostly apparition appears wearing a dark cap and pants and a crisp white shirt. Employees have caught sight of the captain in their peripheral vision as he quickly moves to and fro about the ship. Since the captain has become a regular part of the crew, it seems that no one has the heart to tell him that his "presence" is no longer needed.

MAY 21, 1935
HULL HOUSE
Chicago, Illinois

Hull House was built by real estate magnate Charles Hull in 1856. In 1889, Jane Addams and Ellen Starr Gates founded the first United States Welfare Center in the previously abandoned building. The center provided a variety of services to the poor.

In 1913, as the legend goes, a Catholic woman married an Athe-
ist. They were about to have their first child when the woman hung
a picture of the Virgin Mary over their bed. Her husband became
furious, removed the picture, and said that he would rather have
Satan in his home then sleep under that. A short while later, his
young wife gave birth to what could only be described as a demon
child. It had scales for skin, pointed ears, horns, hooves, and even
a tail. The Devil Baby could walk and talk and was reported even
to smoke cigars. With a sinister laugh, it threatened the father.
Frightened beyond belief, the father took the Devil Child to Hull
House, begging for Jane Addams to take care of it. She agreed, and
attempted to have it baptized. The creature escaped the clutches of
the priest and scurried away over the pews. The members of Hull
House captured it and imprisoned the creature in the attic until it
passed away.

The Chicago newspapers got hold of the story and soon Hull
House was besieged with visitors looking for a glimpse of the Devil
Child. Jane always denied its existence and took the secret to her
grave when she died in May of 1935. The story eventually became
the inspiration for the book and movie *Rosemary's Baby*. And even
today, people still report seeing a demonic-looking being peering at
them from the attic window, craving its freedom, even in death.

TERRIFYING TIDBIT

During colonial times it was believed that water had the ability to trap
souls. Towns that had creeks run through them would have two cemeteries, one on either side, for fear that carrying the deceased over the
water would trap his soul.

MAY 22, 1123
ST. BART'S HOSPITAL
London, England

Rahere was a jester in the court of King Henry I. One night he had a dream about St. Bartholomew that inspired him to become an Augustinian monk. Eventually, he founded Bartholomew-the-Great, the second-oldest church in London, and nearby St. Bartholomew's Hospital, affectionately known as St. Bart's. Rahere died in 1143 and was entombed in the church. His ghost has often been seen in the church he founded.

TERRIFYING TIDBIT

A vortex can sometimes be captured on film. Spirits requiring a lot of energy to manifest, will often use this high-energy signature, as a precursor to manifesting their presence.

But the hospital has a ghost of its own, "Nurse Pinkie." Whenever doctors or nurses would administer drugs, they would hear a whisper in their ear, "Check it! Check it!" Patients would refuse medicine, saying a nurse in a pink uniform already gave them it. She was also credited with awakening medical personnel who fell asleep on the job. It is believed that Nurse Pinkie, having misread a label, accidentally killed a patient by administering a mistaken overdose. She subsequently committed suicide. The ghost of Nurse Pinkie, in her attempt to make amends, is monitoring the staff of St. Bart's Hospital, from the other side.

MAY 23, 1253
HOUSKA CASTLE
Blatce, Czech Republic

The roots of Houska Castle can be traced back to 1253. The Gothic-style fortress has been described as the most evil castle in the world. According to local legend, the castle was built over a deep cavern known as the Gate to Hell. Black-winged creatures and horrific beasts, half-man and half-human, dwelled in the pit. During the castle's construction, prisoners were given a reprieve if they volunteered to be lowered into the pit and report back. The first volunteer that disappeared into the pit was pulled out screaming. His brown hair had turned snow white.

TERRIFYING TIDBIT

Portals are thought to be a dimensional doorway, from this world, to the next.

Built directly over the pit to keep the evil in, the walls of the chapel are covered with strange paintings of demons and dragons being slain.

During World War II, the Nazis used the castle for experiments on dimensional portals. Today visitors to Houska feel the presence of evil. Eerie sounds, screams, growling, and voices in strange languages emanate from within the chapel. And an endless line of humans chained together with big black hellhounds nipping at their heels is often seen. The plethora of demonic presences makes one wonder if the evil that lurks below Houska Castle has ever been contained.

MAY 24, 2007
GADSDEN HIGH SCHOOL
Anthony, New Mexico

Students attending a high school in Anthony, New Mexico, tell tales of tragedy and murder. The story goes that during a school dance, two male teens lured a young woman by the name of Ana into the basement, where she was brutally raped and murdered. Other stories speak to the possibility of Ana's suicide. Regardless, sometime in the history of Gadsden High School, the young woman met her end.

Or did she? Students have seen the luminescent spirit of a young woman peering out a window at the north side of the building as if longing to join them. Others have reported seeing a white ghostly mist float down the hallways from one side of the building to the other. Supposedly by viewing a picture of the basketball team in an old yearbook one can see her ghostly image. Although poor Ana is gone, it seems she is still longing to complete her education.

MAY 25, 1904
THE WITCH'S GRAVE
Yazoo City, Mississippi

On the banks of the Yazoo River lived an old ugly woman. Labeled a witch, she was rumored to lure fishermen into her house in the woods and kill them. In the fall of 1884, a local boy by the name of Joe Bob Duggett was passing by her house when he heard horrible screams. Sneaking over to the window, he peeked inside. To his shock, two men lay dead on the floor as the old witch chanted over them. Duggett ran for help. Upon returning with the sheriff, they broke in, but no one was there. Making their way to the attic, they slowly opened the door. The two stared in horror at the skeletal remains of two men hanging from the rafters. Fish bones littered the floor as dozens of mangy cats prowled the room. Hearing the witch outside, they chased after her into the swamp. But by the time they caught up, it was too late. She had fallen into a patch of quicksand. Sinking deep into the sand, she cursed in a cackling voice, "I shall return from the grave and burn down the town on May 25, 1904." With one last breath, she disappeared beneath the muck. The next day they removed her body and buried her in Glenwood Cemetery, placing heavy chains atop her grave to keep her there.

Years came and went. Few remembered the curse of the witch, until the morning of May 25, 1904, that is. What started as a small fire, driven by unearthly winds, soon engulfed the town in a raging inferno that destroyed it completely. Remembering the curse, a delegation of elders inspected the witch's grave. To their astonishment, the chains had been broken. Twenty years later, just as promised, the town burned. If you think this is just a legend, then take a journey to Glenwood Cemetery and witness the broken chains for yourself. Just be careful not to become the next victim of the Yazoo witch.

MAY 26, 2008
GHOST PHOTOGRAPH VERIFIED
East Lothian, Scotland

A photograph taken by a gentleman by the name of Christopher Aitchison has caused quite a stir in the paranormal community.

The picture was of a mid-fourteenth-century fortress, the Tantallon Castle in Scotland. And although Christopher does not remember physically seeing a person staring out the barred window of the castle, there is clearly someone to be seen. The figure captured on film is so clear that one can make out the fifteenth-century garb of the ethereal being.

It has been said emphatically that Tantallon Castle does not use mannequins or have tour guides that wear costumes. So, how does one know that the photo was not tampered with? Ghost skeptic and psychologist Professor Wiseman from the University of Hertfordshire, launched an investigation into the authenticity of the photograph. Wiseman sent the photo to three independent experts. The results astounded the professor: all three proclaimed the photo to be legitimate, not edited or manipulated in any way. This left the skeptic at a loss for words.

MAY 27, 1933
THE HEARTLAND GHOST
Atchison, Kansas

According to Legends of America website, the popular haunting of Sallie, the "Heartland Ghost," has been the subject of several paranormal television shows. But the Heartland Ghost story is more than just an entertaining tale, especially for the family that lived in the home when the phenomena first began. In 1993, immediately after a young couple rented the home, a ghost began playing pranks. Picture frames were turned upside down, gas jets were turned on, and toys were strewn about the nursery.

Before long, the pranks turned menacing. No longer able to endure it, the couple sought the assistance of a psychic. Soon they learned that there were two entities in the home: a young child by the name of Sallie and the more sinister spirit of a woman who had allegedly set her sights on the husband. The psychic informed the couple that the ghost woman wanted the husband for herself and through all of her ghostly acts had tried to form a wedge between husband and wife. When that didn't work, she began attacking the husband. The psychic also informed the couple about Sallie. It seems that sometime in the history of the home, a doctor, practicing strange methods, had attempted to operate on a girl for appendicitis. However, the child had panicked when she'd seen the tools, and rather than wait until she was under anesthesia, the doctor held her down and began to operate.

During the production of the television show *Sightings*, researchers working on the story of the Heartland Ghost uncovered uncanny historical data corroborating what the psychic had relayed. At the beginning of the nineteenth century, a doctor whose unorthodox medical practices were under scrutiny had in fact lived in the home. And oddly enough, to the shock of all present, welts and red scratches dripping blood developed on the husband's body before everyone's eyes.

Finally, unable to put up with the torment, the family moved. And ever since they left, it appears the haunting has come to an end. Or has it? Perhaps there has yet to be another man the evil entity is ready to fight over.

MAY 28, 1922
THE MOSS BEACH DISTILLERY
San Mateo County, California

This former speakeasy was built in 1922 by Frank Torres. Legend has it that in its heyday over seventy years ago, a young woman had an affair with a pianist in the building, now home to the Moss Beach Distillery. Even though this woman was married and had a young child, her love was so strong for this musician that she frequently visited the bar. It's been said that once her enraged husband discovered the illicit affair, he murdered her in cold blood. Today, rumors of a haunting abound at the distillery. Her spectral image, wearing a tattered blue dress, has been seen on so many occasions that she's earned the nickname "The Blue Lady." Some believe her name to be Elizabeth Claire Donavan. And Cayte, as she likes to be called, has not only appeared to many, but has been known to move glasses. Lamps swing of their own accord, books fly off the shelves, and visitors to the Distillery have felt Cayte's presence at the very moment the odd occurrences are taking place. Perhaps she remains at the distillery trying to recapture the romantic memories of her forbidden love. If you're ever among the visitors to partake in the "spirits" of the Distillery, you too may be lucky enough to meet Cayte in person.

MAY 29, 1546
CARDINAL BEATON
St. Andrews, Scotland

Cardinal Beaton was the ruthless Archbishop of St. Andrews, a key figure in Bloody Mary's Persecution of the Protestants. In March

1546, he had Protestant George Wishart arrested. In a speedy trial he was convicted and sentenced to death. Wishart was dragged from the castle and burned alive as Beaton looked on. But Wishart had many sympathizers who plotted their revenge. In the early hours of May 29, they entered St. Andrews Castle and roused Beaton from his bed. Despite the cardinal's pleas, they stabbed him to death, stripped off his clothes, and hung his body over the castle wall for all in the town to see. Few prayers were recited for Beaton that day.

Although the Castle of St. Andrews lies in ruins today, there are those who have seen the ghostly image of the cardinal peering from the windows, especially the one from which he witnessed Wishart's death. Others say that when the tide is high on the East Sands, and the clock strikes the midnight hour, a black coach with skeleton footmen and a headless coachman materializes before you. Staring from within the coach's window is the ashen face of Cardinal David Beaton. Beside him sits the Devil, returning to the gates of hell.

MAY 30, 1894
HECETA HEAD LIGHTHOUSE
Yachats, Oregon

Constructed in 1894, Heceta Head Lighthouse was named after Spanish explorer Bruno de Heceta. Now it is a bed and breakfast, and it seems it has a permanent guest. Most know her as "Rue," the spirit of an old woman who doesn't appreciate visitors. Sometimes she is called the "Gray Lady" because of the gray mist that makes up her essence. She appears to be a benign spirit, but likes to make her presence known.

She rearranges objects to suit her fancy and even opens and closes cupboard doors while snooping in the cabinets. Some claim to smell her perfume, while others feel her presence. But who is this mysterious ghost?

Most think she is the mother of a baby girl who is buried on the lighthouse property. Others wonder if she may be a keeper's wife. But everyone agrees that "Rue" still believes that this is her house and she'll run it as she pleases.

MAY 31, 1912
St. James Theatre
Wellington, New Zealand

The St. James Theatre was built in 1912. There have been several reports of ghosts in the theatre. The most noted one is the ghost of Yuri, a Russian performer. He died when he fell onto the stage from above, some say under mysterious circumstances. His ghost has been known to switch the lights back on again once the theatre has been locked up for the night. Another specter associated with the theatre is known as the "Wailing Woman" because she has been heard crying and moaning throughout the theatre. After receiving a poor response to her performance on stage, she went into the dressing room and killed herself. Perhaps the most unusual ghost or ghosts haunting the theater is that of a boys' choir. The choir played their last performance at the St. James during the Second World War. They boarded a ship to go on tour and were never seen again. Patrons and workers often hear their music in the seating area. The plethora of spirits may just earn the St. James Theatre the title of the most haunted theatre in New Zealand.

JUNE 1, 1735
FALL HILL
Spotsylvania County, Virginia

The Thornton family plantation, Fall Hill, was built in 1735 and is said to be home to the ghost of a Sioux Indian princess. Katina was captured in the late seventeenth century and was given as a gift to the Virginia governor, who in turn willed her to the Thornton family. Before departing this world in 1777, Katina was the loving caregiver for three generations of Thornton children. Even in death, it appears she took her job very seriously. One time, two boys sleeping in the nursery awakened to find the apparition of a Sioux woman staring over them. Upon realizing she'd been seen, she turned around and vanished through the wall. It wasn't until a few years later, during the remodeling of the nursery, that the door that would have been used by Katina to enter the nursery was discovered to have been in the same wall the boys had seen her disappear through.

Another guest, while resting, saw the door in the nursery open and there before her was not only the Indian princess Katina, but Francis Thornton II, the only male child in the home and her presumed favorite. Once again, she vanished, along with the young boy. Evidently Katina's bond is eternal, as even in death she continues to care for the Thornton children.

JUNE 2, 1863
RUEBEN'S GRAVE
Armstrong County, Pennsylvania

The sound of hooves echoed in the night as a young lad rode his horse into Shott's Cemetery. Stopping at the base of a looming oak tree, he placed a noose around his neck. He tied the other end to a sturdy branch. At the youthful age of seventeen years, spurned by a lover, he could take no more. Hesitating for only a moment, he spurred the horse and hanged himself. As his body swayed in the moonlit night air, a legend was born.

His name was Rueben Briney, and he was buried in that same cemetery. Etched in the cold granite of his gravestone was the following, "As you are now so once was I. As I am now you will be; remember me as you pass by. Prepare to die and follow me." His stone is gone today, toppled and smashed, but according to *www.hauntsandhistory.blogspot.com* it can be seen within the pages of a 1974 Ford City High School yearbook.

So, if you venture to Armstrong County and find yourself near Shott's Cemetery, beware of the ghost of Rueben. Riding a white horse with flaming red eyes, he searches for his lost love. But do not pity him, for all those who gaze upon his image will die a horrible death within a year. Or at least that is what the legend says.

JUNE 3, 1981
VIKING LONGSHIPS
Reykjavik, Iceland

Two American couples on an Icelandic vacation were standing on a beach near the capital city of Reykjavik. A shifting breeze patted their faces as the sun slowly dipped into the cold waters of the ocean. They were mesmerized by the moment, until jolted by the sound of wood slapping the water. Off to the right, their eyes slowly focused upon the silhouettes of not one, but two Viking longships. Frozen as if in a dream, they stood, their mouths agape as they watched the two graceful boats glide past them. On the bow of the lead ship perched a tall man with a long beard. "Kling hoff Ogden," he shouted, as the ships slowly disappeared into the sunset. The couples, excited about what they had just seen, returned to town to talk to their tour guide. A nervous smile slid across his face. Pausing for a moment, he spoke in broken English, "You have just been lucky enough to see the ghost ships of Iceland." He went on to say that every third of June, if you stand on the beach around 8 P.M., spectral longships continue on their eternal journey.

TERRIFYING TIDBIT

On June 23 each year, Viking longboats are supposed to appear off the coast of L'Anse Aux Meadows, Newfoundland—twenty days after they are seen in Iceland.

JUNE 4, 1896
BRIGGS LAWRENCE COUNTY LIBRARY
Ironton, Ohio

This library is a perfect example that a haunting is not always the result of the building but the land on which the building stands. According to Firefox News, the staff have reported keys rattling, doors closing, and a computerized card catalog being toyed with. The staff believe it to be Dr. Lowry, whose house once stood where the library is now. Back in 1896, Dr. Lowry ordered a casket for his petite wife. The doctor special ordered the casket, but once he received it, he returned it, refusing to pay the bill. A short two years later, the undertaker would have his revenge. As it turned out, Lowry died under mysterious circumstances and his body was sent to the unfairly treated undertaker for burial. This was the opportunity the mortician had waited for. He would bury the doctor in the previously ordered casket and bill his estate for money owed. There was one problem however: Lowry was too tall and too fat for the coffin. So the mortician broke Lowry's legs and removed his intestines. Unfortunately for him, suspicions surrounding Lowry's death led the police to investigate. Exhuming the body, the atrocities done to the doctor's remains were discovered. Fortunately for Lowry's heirs who were suspected of murder, the remains were no longer viable for testing.

Today, it's believed the sometimes disruptive spirit that roams the halls of the library is the restless ghost of Dr. Lowry looking for his internal organs. This ghost story goes to show: be careful of the enemies you make while you're alive. Or like Lowry found out, it just might come back to haunt you.

JUNE 5, 1692
LYCEUM RESTAURANT
Salem, Massachusetts

This haunted Salem restaurant was built upon the former site of Bridget Bishop's apple orchard. It's believed that Bridget's restless spirit haunts the building to this day. In 1692, she was accused of witchcraft. Found guilty, Bridget spent the next year in prison, until the fateful day that she was led to the gallows and hanged.

Sadly for Bridget, she would come to be memorialized for being the first witch to have been executed in the Salem witch trials.

Years later, a historic lecture hall was built on the site of the apple orchard; it would host such notables as Hawthorne, Thoreau, Emerson, and the prominent inventor, Alexander Bell. In fact, in 1877, history was made from this location, as Bell demonstrated his invention here and made the first public phone call.

In 1989 George Harrington purchased the building, and the Lyceum Bar & Grill soon opened. Ever since, employees and patrons alike have witnessed scores of unexplainable phenomena. Above the hectic activities of a bustling restaurant, many people have heard a female voice whisper in their ears. Shocked patrons have given George countless photos depicting unexplainable light anomalies. Some employees have seen the ghostly image of a woman staring out a second-floor window, only to have her vanish upon their approach. And there are those that have caught the sweet, succulent scent of apple blossoms wafting in the air. When the staff are questioned about the origin of the floral aroma, they state that it's a gift from Bridget.

JUNE 6, 1879
THE PROSTITUTE THAT LOST HER HEAD
Griffintown, Montreal

According to the *Montreal Gazette*, 129 years ago two prostitutes, Mary Gallagher and Susan Kennedy, drank two bottles of whiskey while they enjoyed each other's company. Inebriated, the women picked up a man named Michael Flanagan and took him back to Susan's home. Later in the evening, when Flanagan lay unconscious, the two women fought. Apparently, Kennedy was jealous of Gallagher. Enraged that Gallagher could so easily pick up a trick, she retrieved an axe and chopped off Mary's head, which was later found in a bucket beside the stove. At first, the unconscious Flanagan and Kennedy were charged with murder. But the police soon realized that since Michael had no blood on him, he was innocent of any wrongdoing. The press went wild with the story. In Victorian times, women were considered to be gentle, not cold-blooded murderers. The downstairs neighbor, who reported that at 12:15 A.M. she heard the loud thud of a body dropping to the floor, further corroborated the tale of horror. She continued to say that for a period of time after hearing the loud bang, she heard the disturbing sound of chopping. Kennedy was tried, convicted, and sentenced to hang; however, her sentence was commuted. Susan Kennedy spent the next sixteen years in prison. But that's not the end to this gruesome story. It appears that the day Mary died, a legend was born. Every seven years, the ghost of Mary Gallagher returns to the streets of Griffintown, seeking revenge and looking for her head.

JUNE 7, 1873
ST. AUGUSTINE LIGHTHOUSE
St. Augustine, Florida

St. Augustine Lighthouse towers 165 feet above sea level and is located on Anastasia Island near America's oldest city. The lighthouse has seen its share of tragedy. The first keeper died of unknown causes, another fell to his death, and a third died of illness. However, the most tragic occurrence was in 1873. The superintendent overseeing the construction at the time was a man named Hezekiah Pittee. He had moved from Maine with his family. To aid with construction, a tram was built from the ocean to the station. The family's five children loved to ride in the tramcar. While riding in the tram one day, the car derailed and the children fell into the water. Nearby workers were able to save a boy and a girl, but three of the girls drowned.

Today it is said that staff and visitors often hear laughter in the tower, and one astral girl appears to be wearing the same blue dress she drowned in.

JUNE 8, 1693
BOSTON COMMON
Boston, Massachusetts

Established in 1634, Boston Common is the oldest public park in the United States. Known for its swan boat rides and Frog Pond skating rink, it has a much darker side. On the west end of the park stood a tall oak tree with a sinister purpose. It was the Massachusetts Bay Colony's dreaded hanging tree. Up until the new gallows were built in 1769, many a poor soul met his or her demise on its wretched limbs.

The tree is no longer there, but the misery and terror it brought to so many of its victims remains. The homeless stay clear of the spot, especially in the evening. And many visitors have felt an uneasiness and heaviness in the night air. There have also been many reports of ghostly apparitions through the years, including that of two fancy-dressed women seen walking together in the Common.

On June 1, 1660, Quaker Mary Dyer was hanged from the old oak because of her religious beliefs. In 1693 Elizabeth Emerson met the same fate for murdering her two children. Although the two women never knew each other in life, perhaps they have bonded together in death, fighting the loneliness of eternity.

TERRIFYING TIDBIT

Female prisoners tried to look their best for their executions, often buying new clothes. If they were too poor, it was not unusual for friends, neighbors, or even the authorities to provide them with a new outfit. I guess you would call them clothes to die for!

JUNE 9, 1912
THE VILLISCA AX MURDERS
Villisca, Iowa

After 1912, life would never again be the same for many of the residents who lived in the peaceful, booming town of Villisca Iowa. The Moore family of six consisted of Sallie, her husband Josiah (or J. B.), and their four children. They, along with two young girls, friends of the Moore children, headed home after the Child's Day program came to an end. It was 9:30 P.M., and it was the last time anyone would ever see them alive.

The next morning, a neighbor and J. B.'s brother discovered their lifeless, blood-covered bodies. All six family members, along with the two young girls who were visiting had been slain. Their heads crushed with an ax.

The news of the massacre quickly spread through the town of 2,500. Before the police knew what was happening, the crime scene was compromised by curiosity seekers as hundreds of people walked through the Moore home, some even taking souvenirs as they left. The police had very little to go on. And although there were several suspects, the murders were never solved.

This home has since passed through many hands. However, in an attempt to preserve history, Darwin and Martha Lynn purchased it in 1994. Through the use of old photographs, they meticulously restored it, replicating the way it looked that fateful night when the Moore family lost their lives. That's when the haunting began. The home has been opened to overnight visitors, many whom have been awakened by the sound of children's laughter when there are no children in sight. Investigators who have stayed at the home have captured many strange sounds, and curious anomalies have showed up on video. Objects move of their own accord. And loud banging can be heard during the night. Sadly, it seems the horror of the family's demise has stained the home forever.

JUNE 10, 1915
JULIAN GOLD RUSH HOTEL
Julian, California

In the late 1800s Albert Robinson, a freed slave from Missouri, moved to the small gold-mining town of Julian. He was hired as a cook for a local ranch, where he met Margaret Tull. They married shortly thereafter and started a restaurant and bakery. A few years later, they constructed the Hotel Robinson. Known for its good cooking and hospitality, the hotel became a hot bed of social activity.

Albert died on June 10, 1915, but because he was black, he wasn't buried in the town's "whites only" cemetery. Although it was protested, he was laid to rest forty-five miles away. His wife ran the hotel until 1921, when she sold it, and it was later renamed the Julian Hotel.

Through the years, the place somehow acquired an evil spirit, which showed itself as a ball of light, breaking windows, scaring employees, and moving objects. An exorcist was called in to quell the spirit. It appeared to be successful because the destruction of the property has subsided. But some believe Albert's ghost still remains. His spectral image has been seen throughout the hotel but especially in his old room. When entering room 10, furniture is often rearranged and the bedding disturbed. Quite often, Albert is seen, pipe and all, in mirrors throughout the building. The faint odor of tobacco also lingers in the air. So, although the hotel has changed hands, it seems Albert is unable to move on, destined to remain in the Robinson for eternity.

JUNE 11, 1201
SILENT POOL
Shere, England

Near the small village of Shere in the county of Surrey lies a tranquil pond—and a not-so-peaceful legend. Back in the eleventh century, during Saxon times, a hardworking woodcutter lived in the forest with his son and daughter. On a warm summer's day, his daughter,

Emma, went to the lake to bathe. Removing all her clothes she walked out into the cool water.

Suddenly she heard the clamor of hooves as a rider approached. Since she could not reach her clothes in time, she waded deeper into the lake, but the stranger on horseback spotted her. He tried to lure her out of the water, but she only waded deeper, shunning his advances. Angered, the stranger rode his horse into the lake chasing after the girl, who began screaming. Her brother, who was in the nearby woods, heard her cries and ran to her rescue. He dived into the lake and tried to pull her to safety. But he was a poor swimmer, and they both disappeared beneath its dark waters. Meanwhile, the stranger rode away.

The woodcutter searched and searched for his children, but to no avail. Finally, several days later, the heartbroken father found the bodies of Emma and her brother. No one knows for sure who the mysterious rider was, but legend tells us that he was none other than the evil Prince John, of Robin Hood fame.

Today if you go to Silent Pool, the deathly stillness haunts you. But if you take the time to listen, you can hear Emma's screams of terror. And on a warm summer's night, as a soft mist covers the pool, maybe you too can see her ghost gliding over the surface of the water.

JUNE 12, 1731
DEVIL STONE INN
Devon, England

The Devil Stone Inn dates back to the fifteenth century. In its rich history, among some of its uses were a poorhouse and a coaching inn. Legend has it that the nearby "Devil Stone," a huge boulder, had fallen from the Devil's pocket on his descent from heaven to hell. And thus, the inn's name was born. But who haunts the inn? According to visitors who frequent the pub, the ghostly specter of an elderly gentleman has been seen in and about the bar. The playful spirit of a young girl enjoying the occasional game of hide and seek is often seen in the upstairs bedrooms. And a grumpy old man has been seen in the upstairs rooms as well. Perhaps his bad mood could be attributed to a repetitive ethereal game of hide and seek. But that's not all. Staff members report that the taps have turned on by themselves during the night, and disembodied footsteps have been heard throughout the hallways. The paranormal activity even induced Richard Felix from the popular television show *Most Haunted* to pay a visit. Through the use of glass divination, séances, and table tipping, Richard, along with several investigators, reached out to the ghosts of the Devil Stone Inn. It appears, from footage of the show, that the spirits didn't disappoint them.

JUNE 13, 1776
THE WOMAN IN SCARLET
Boston Harbor, MA

During the Revolutionary War, William Burton and his wife, Mary, were aboard a British ship blockading Boston Harbor.

A cannonball fired from Long Island Battery struck the ship, splintering the hull. A flying shard, like a dagger, drove into the back of Mary's skull. Poor Mary did not die instantly. Rather, she suffered for days, all the while pleading to her husband to not bury her at sea. On behalf of Mary, a flag of truce was waved, and William was granted permission to come ashore with her body. Before he buried her at East Head, he lovingly sewed her remains into a red blanket and promised to return.

In 1804, fishermen stranded on the island, not far from Mary's marker, started a fire to keep warm. They were at first startled by the eerie moans, then by the ghostly apparition of a woman wearing a scarlet cloak. As she strode by, the blood dripping from a wound to her head was clearly visible. Moments later, she disappeared over the dunes. Mary was also spotted during the War of 1812, when Private William Liddell reported a story nearly identical to the fishermen.

Perhaps Mary is still waiting for her husband's promise of return to be fulfilled.

JUNE 14, 1954
TUG HILL ANNIE PUT TO REST
Plum Island, Massachusetts

In 1954, Anna J. Machowski Tebidor's life came to a gruesome end. Anna and her friend, Jan, after purchasing wine at a local store, were driving back in a 1949 Studebaker truck when Anna made a crucial mistake that would cost her life. Anna, traveling too fast, could not make the sharp curve along Sears Pond Road. The truck flipped, landing on its roof in an adjacent field. A young man who had witnessed the accident hurried to the scene. When he arrived, he found Jan beside the truck. Although alive, his body was bruised and he was going into shock. Anna had not been as lucky as her friend. Her body was still, arms by her side, while her severed head lay six inches away.

But that was not the last anyone would see of poor Anna. Many visitors have reported seeing the spirit of a headless woman wandering around the shoulder of Sears Pond Road. Over the years, the notoriety of Anna's fateful end attracted many a visitor, all with the hope of catching a glimpse of the headless apparition, which had received the nickname "Tug Hill Annie" from the location where she'd perished.

In August 2008, a group of paranormal investigators, having heard the tales of her ghostly presence, decided to go looking for Anna. And although they expected to find no paranormal activity, they were soon convinced that the rumors of Anna's existence were not rumors at all. Although none of their team had been walking around, they all heard gravel crunch as if it was being walked on. Strange mists and light anomalies appeared in their photos. The mists, oddly enough, contained facial features that matched Anna's picture.

Convinced that poor Anna's restless spirit needed to be put to rest, they made a return trip. This time they were joined by several members of the Tebidor family and a medium.

They performed a sunrise ceremony to help Anna to cross over. Since then, Anna's headless ghost has been seen no more. It appears she listened.

JUNE 15, 2008
OLD ELLERBE ROAD SCHOOL
Shreveport, Louisiana

Realhaunts.com reported a story of an evil janitor from the Old Ellerbe Road School in Shreveport, Louisiana, who molested a collection of children. He then gathered them up, locked them in the gym, and set fire to the building, leaving them to burn alive. It is said that the mournful cries of children can still be heard throughout the crumpled remains.

Curious to find out if the tales were true, without permission, a group of teens decided to investigate. On their drive there they shared laughs, making light of the rumors. How could someone be so gullible to fall for such crap?

Once they arrived, they stepped over the fence, disregarding the "do not disturb" sign. By the fading beam of their flashlight, they walked past the graffiti-covered walls and took in the sight of the devastation. There before them, in place of lockers loomed a life-size mural of the grim reaper. Not deterred, they continued on. Slowly, reverently, they walked through overgrown weeds and dirt-filled halls until they reached their final destination, the gym. They could tell by the black, charred bleachers that they had found what they were looking for. That's when it happened. A door slammed shut. The sound of a school bell ringing echoed in the night, followed by the muffled cries of children calling for their mommies.

Terrified, the group ran out of the building and sped away. Whether or not the experience will fade from their memories remains to be seen, but it's said that one thing is for certain: their ride home was a lot more somber.

JUNE 16, 1881
MARIE LAVEAUS
New Orleans, Louisiana

The Saint Louis Cemetery has been the target of countless vandals, and it appears the hoodlums have awakened the ghost of voodoo queen Marie Laveaus. A woman wearing a turban has been seen gliding along the narrow pathways between the old crypts. Her mumbling of voodoo prayers have been heard by many a tourist.

But who is Marie Laveaus? She was a Louisiana Creole who practiced voodoo. A free woman of color, Laveaus had become highly feared and revered for her magical abilities. Her rituals and religious beliefs, among other things, were an eclectic mix of Catholicism and voodoo.

Today Marie is visited by scores of people who come to pay homage to her, bringing voodoo offerings of food, dolls, statues, Mardi Gras beads, and so forth, hoping that the long-ago queen of voodoo will repay them with her blessing. And if they are lucky enough, she may even grant them a wish or two.

Many a tourist has reported seeing the ghostly apparition of Marie Laveaus exiting her tomb while visiting the site. Then again, there are those who believe her soul has revealed itself many times by entering the body of a black cat. Either way, the fact remains that Marie Laveaus will forever be the queen of voodoo.

JUNE 17, 1959
SUPERMAN RETURNS
Los Angeles, California

George Reeves was found dead in his mansion in June 1959. Reeves, a popular actor of his time, had been best known for his role as Superman in the 1950s television show. His friends reported that while they were throwing an impromptu party they awakened George, who, investigating the racket, decided to join the gathering. However, he didn't stay long. Instead, being in a foul mood, he enjoyed only one drink before retreating back to his bed. Not long after, his fiancée, Lenore Lemmon, and two friends heard a gunshot ring out. George's death was ruled a suicide. Although never substantiated, there are some who believe his ex-lover, Toni Mannix, or her husband, Eddie Mannix, had something to do with it.

Today, there have been several reports of supernatural phenomena. Lights flicker; objects move of their own accord; and dogs bark at the doorway to his bedroom, refusing to enter. The rotten-egg smell of gunpowder singes one's nose. And every now and then George Reeves make an appearance near the foot of his bed, wearing his Superman costume. Perhaps this method actor is taking his role to new heights, racing through time and space to thwart his foe. It looks like Superman has returned!

JUNE 18, 2001
RAMOJI FILM CITY
Hyderabad, India

In Ramoji Film City, Hollywood India, most of the hotels are haunted. The city is said to be built on the war grounds of the Nizam sultans. Witnesses have reported that the lights at the studio continually fall and that the operators who man them have been known to be pushed. Some have been seriously injured. And whenever food gets left behind in a room, it's thrown about by an unseen force. The most bizarre incidents are the inexplicable marks that appear on the mirrors. Most are in script resembling Urdu, the language spoken by the sultans. The ghosts appear to be attracted to women, apparently finding some sort of supernatural amusement by tearing their clothes and knocking on the bathroom doors while they are in them.

Attempts to exorcize the spirits have failed. So the women of Ramoji Film City will have to continue enduring the spectral wrath of the Nizam sultans.

JUNE 19, 1864
VILLAGE INN
Dracut, Massachusetts

Formerly known as the Black North Inn, the Village Inn is one of the oldest restaurants in Dracut. Rumors that it was involved in Prohibition were substantiated when a hidden bunker was found on the property. But is it haunted?

If you talk with some of the staff, they will quietly tell you it is. During the evening, disembodied footsteps have been heard, the swinging doors have opened and closed by themselves, and the ghostly image of a woman has appeared in the barn. But Chris, the current owner, who is a bit of a skeptic, told the most compelling story. One night while he was working in the tunnel between the restaurant and the barn, he saw a young boy with suspenders and a straw hat. Knowing the young man didn't belong there and fearing he would get into the liquor, he chased him. Before he could catch him, the boy simply disappeared. He searched everywhere, but could not find him. All the exits in the barn were locked, so there was no escape, yet he vanished. No one can explain his disappearance to this date. Now Chris isn't as skeptical, as he once was.

JUNE 20, 1893
LIZZIE BORDEN HOUSE
Fall River, Massachusetts

This popular bed and breakfast was once the scene of gruesome ax murders. On the morning of August 4, 1892, Lizzie Borden allegedly "found" the bodies of her father, Andrew Jackson Borden, and her stepmother, Abby Durfee Borden, bludgeoned in their home. Seven days later, Lizzie was arrested for the crime. During the investigation, the police located what they believed to be the murder weapon, or part of it. A hatchet, missing a handle, was found in the basement. The theory was that the handle must have been removed because it was soaked in blood. And although the police had been unable to find blood-soaked clothing, Lizzie, a few days after the murder, admitted to burning her dress that had been soiled and torn. Despite the belief of many that Lizzie was responsible for this heinous crime, she was acquitted on June 20, 1893. And it wasn't until 1927 that she succumbed to pneumonia and met her demise.

But do the souls of Lizzie's slaughtered family still roam the halls of the Borden estate? Many who have visited say they do.

Guests at this B&B have witnessed shoes slide across the floor. Others have reported that their sleep was interrupted by the heartbreaking sound of a woman weeping. Electronic devices malfunction and repeatedly turn themselves on. And perhaps if you make a visit to the Lizzie Borden Bed and Breakfast, you could be the next patron to experience being tucked into bed by unseen hands. Hopefully, unlike Abby Borden, you will escape your stay without developing a splitting headache.

TERRIFYING TIDBIT

For a small price, you can bring a little bit of the Lizzie Borden house home. The gift shop sells authentic brick dust, collected from decaying bricks in the haunted basement.

JUNE 21, 1300
THE OSTRICH INN
Colnbrook Berkshire, England

The village of Colnbrook on route from London to Bath was a stage-coach stopover. Many wealthy travelers carrying large sums stopped there before continuing on their way for an appearance at the courts of Windsor Castle. The owner of the inn, a man named Jarman, devised a plan to alleviate them of their burden. He would offer them his best room and provide them with an overabundance of ale until they were sufficiently drunk. After they retired, he would wait until they nodded off and then undo two bolts in the ceiling that caused the bed to tilt downwards, sliding the unsuspecting guest into a boiling vat. Once they were out of the picture, he would steal their horses and belongings. This went on for several years, until one of his potential victims got up in the middle of the night to relieve his bladder of all the ale he'd drunk and thus escaped his fate. Jarman was tried, convicted, and executed. Before he gasped his last breath, he confessed to the jailer that he had killed sixty people. Today, Jarman's victims are said to haunt the inn; unfortunately for them, they learned the true meaning of being "dead drunk."

JUNE 22, 1893
MESSENGER GHOST
Tripoli, Lebanon

The battleship HMS *Victoria* was the flagship of the Mediterranean Fleet under the command of Vice Admiral Sir George Tryon. While completing a complex set of maneuvers off the coast of Lebanon, the ship was accidentally rammed by the battleship HMS *Camperdown*. Heavily damaged, within fifteen minutes of the collision, it capsized and sank. Although most of the crew had abandoned ship, many were dragged below the surface by the giant whirlpool created by the sinking ship.

Meanwhile, in the seaside town of Broadstairs, England, Mrs. Kingston was busy in her upstairs bedroom. Suddenly, a loud bang, the sound of an explosion, frightened her. Her heart raced as a phosphorous orange light appeared in the corner of the room. Unable to react, she stood in awe as the eerie glowing mass began to change, morphing into a human shape. Her son, a sailor, appeared before her. How could that be? After all, he was at sea thousands of miles away.

He smiled, then spoke, "I'm safe now, mother. Don't worry. I'll see you soon."

Then, as quickly as he had appeared, he vanished. Although it disturbed her, Mrs. Kingston slowly pushed the event out of her thoughts, chalking it up to her imagination. Several days later, on July 3, there was a knock on the door. It was a messenger with a telegram from the Admiralty. "We regret to inform you but your son has drowned with his ship, HMS *Victoria* on June twenty-second." The same day he appeared in her room!

JUNE 23, 1882
THE GHOST OF THE LOS TIRADITOS
Benson, Arizona

The story goes that back in the 1800s, when Arizona was still a territory, three Mexican men were wrongly accused of robbing a train. The railroad town of Benson was typical of the wild west, where gunslingers, thievery, and gambling had become common. Ignoring other possible suspicious characters, the town fixated on three Mexican men. They were subsequently hanged on the main street of the town and, due to public disapproval, were not permitted to be buried within the hallowed grounds of the cemetery. Rather, they were buried across a wash, outside the perimeter of the Seventh Street Cemetery, in shallow graves marked by wooden crosses.

Since the hanging, the Mexican community has proclaimed the men's innocence. As a way to pay tribute to Los Tiraditos (the lost castaways) they tend to their graves and place beautiful handmade paper flowers atop them. Candles are often lit, especially during All Saints Day, when the poor souls of these men are remembered.

However, legend has it that if you walk through the cemetery at night, you can still hear the moans of Los Tiraditos pleading for their bodies to be dug up and buried within the walls of the graveyard.

Unfortunately, due to erosion of the ground, their pleas for help will forever go unanswered.

JUNE 24, 1974
ROBERT THE DOLL
Key West, Florida

Robert Gene Otto was born in October 1900. His parents were known to be cruel to their servants. When Robert, now called Gene, was six, one of the servants, who practiced voodoo, made him a doll. Naming the doll Robert, Gene made it his constant companion. When things went wrong for Gene, he blamed it on Robert. Visitors to the house swore they had seen Robert move and heard him giggle. Finally, in an attempt to bring peace to the house, Robert was banished to the attic.

Gene grew up to be a great artist, and when his parents died he moved back into their house with his wife, Anne. He found Robert and once again they became constant companions. Robert was moved to the turret room, where he sat in a chair looking out the window. As children walked by the house, they grew frightened by the doll, which they believed to be moving.

As Gene grew older, he became more reclusive. Eventually Gene died with Robert right by his side. Anne sold the house and left Robert behind, and the daughter of the new owners found the doll. Tortured by Robert's presence, the family gave it away to a museum. The house is now a bed and breakfast with a couple of permanent tenants. Anne they say, haunts the turret room. And the spirit of Robert splits his time between the attic and the doll at the Key West Martello Museum. It has been said that the servant used a voodoo spell to entomb an evil spirit in Robert all those years ago. And those who visit him today just might agree.

TERRIFYING TIDBIT

Tourists who visit Robert at the museum are advised to ask permission of the doll when taking his picture. If you do, it's been said, fortune will come your way, while those who do not will suffer the consequences.

JUNE 25, 2007
KELLS IRISH PUB
Seattle, Washington

According to the *Seattle Times* many of the shops located in and about Pike Place Market are haunted. One of the more active locations is Kells Irish Pub, and when looking into the history of the building, it's easy to understand how the ghosts found their way to this drinking establishment. At one time, E. R. Butterworth and Sons, a mortuary, inhabited the building Kells now occupies. The mortuary's business was thriving so much that in 1923, short on space, it had to be relocated to Capitol Hill. The Irishman who owns the pub, Patrick McAleese, informed the *Times* that his business is located where the embalming room and crematorium once existed. Perhaps this explains the scores of ghostly sightings associated with the pub. Karen McAleese, the owner's sister, first noticed the ghost of a tall man in a suit jacket with long, thin hands as he meandered out of the kitchen, walked to the end of the bar, and disappeared into thin air. Patrick recalled an experience years earlier when his parents had owned Kells. A mirror hanging on the back of the bar crashed to the floor and shattered. His sister added that the mirror had inexplicably shattered into a neat little pile. When the parents ran back into the closed bar to see what had happened, aside from the broken mirror, all they found was a single candle burning. It's ghostly activity like this that has made Kells Irish Restaurant and Pub the happening place for "spirits."

JUNE 26, 1970
USS *HORNET*
San Francisco, California

Decommissioned June 26, 1970, the USS *Hornet* aircraft carrier (CV-12), nicknamed the *Grey Ghost*, rests its weary bow as a museum in the San Francisco Bay.

The *Grey Ghost* has seen its share of tragedy. Beginning with its maiden voyage in 1943, she destroyed more than 1,400 Japanese aircraft. However, over 300 men lost their lives on board, through combat, suicides, and accidents, and it is from among these that the USS *Hornet*'s paranormal activity is believed to emanate.

The onboard catastrophes included explosions, men walking into the propeller blades, and the decapitation of at least three men when the cable to the plane-launching catapult snapped. On more than one occasion, a headless sailor has been spotted roaming the catapult area of the ship. Footsteps and disembodied voices are often heard echoing throughout her empty halls. Toilets flush of their own accord. Tobacco smoke hangs thick in the air. And sightings of phantom officers have been reported. But has there been any proof? In fact there has. One witness to the paranormal anomalies was a young man who photographed an empty chair. Upon review of the photograph, he noticed the transparent figure of a man in an old fashioned uniform sitting in the chair. Apparently the chair wasn't so empty after all.

JUNE 27, 1864
GHOST RIDER
Kennesaw Mountain, Georgia

In 1864 William T. Sherman met Joseph E. Johnson of the Confederates at the battle of Kennesaw Mountain. Four thousand brave soldiers lost their lives that day. Today, the area is known as Kennesaw Mountain National Battlefield Park. While driving through the park, a man and his teenage son encountered the fright of their lives. According to *www.11alive.com*, they were startled by the sudden appearance of a man crossing the road with his horse. But this wasn't just any man. It was a ghost.

The father frantically hit the brakes as the ghostly apparition continued to move toward them. The image of the soldier was so clear that both the driver and his son were able to make out the Union uniform he wore and the saber he carried. Then, while the pair looked on in fright, the soldier and his steed crossed the road and vanished through a fence.

The driver of the vehicle also told his story to a professional ghost hunter, Kevin Fike. It is Fike's belief that the man and his son encountered a residual haunting; emotionally charged locations, such as battlefields, become the prime locations for these types of hauntings.

TERRIFYING TIDBIT

In a residual haunting, the spirit does not interact with the living. It is more like a video clip that is associated with a traumatic event. The event, for whatever reason, is known to replay over and over again.

JUNE 28, 1914
THE AUTOMOBILE THAT STARTED WORLD WAR I
Sarajevo, Bosnia

Graf and Stift made some of the most luxurious automobiles of their time, and one of the most prestigious customers of the company was the Austro-Hungarian court. So it was only natural that Archduke Franz Ferdinand would take his new red Graf & Stift limousine on a state visit to Bosnia.

While driving through the crowded streets of Sarajevo, he was approached by a man named Gavrilo Princip. Gavrilo drew a gun from beneath his coat, firing two shots into the open touring car, killing the Archduke and his pregnant wife Sophie. It was the event that started World War I. It appears the violent demise of the Archduke and his wife left a ghostly imprint on this stately limousine.

After the Archduke's death, the car was purchased by General Potiorek, who developed mental problems and later died in an insane asylum. It was then purchased by an army captain who died in an accident after hitting and killing two peasants in the road. The next owner was the governor of Yugoslavia, who had four accidents in four months, one causing the amputation of his arm. He sold the car to a doctor, who lost his life when the car overturned and crushed him.

The tragedies continued with each successive owner either injured or killed in tragic accidents. In all, thirteen people associated with the car died until it was taken out of service. The apparently haunted Graf & Stift automobile now sits in the War History Museum in Vienna, where it can do no more harm.

JUNE 29, 1869
THE MURDER OF LOUISA FOX
Belmont County, Ohio

Not willing to allow their thirteen-year-old daughter to marry a local coalminer, Thomas Carr, the Fox family withdrew their consent for the two to wed. They told Louisa she was too young and warned her of Carr's reputed taste for violence. Agreeing to her parent's wishes, Louisa broke off the engagement. It seems the Fox family never predicted just how violent Carr could be. On January 21, 1869, while Louisa and her little brother walked home, an enraged Carr crouched behind a fence at the corner of the road that led to the Fox homestead. Just as his ex-fiancée strode past, Thomas sprang from his hiding place. As later reported by Carr, he sent Louisa's brother, Willie, on his way so that the two could talk. Then, after a few moments, Carr retrieved a razor out of his pocket. Kissing her goodbye for the last time, he slashed her throat from ear to ear. Releasing his rage, he stabbed poor Louisa fourteen times, before dumping her in a ditch. Willie, who watched in horror from a distance, raced home to report what had happened.

Carr spent the night in hiding then, after realizing he would be caught for his crime, attempted suicide. He first tried to shoot himself. When that didn't work, he cut his own throat. But death did not find him that easily. Rather, he was arrested, convicted of his barbaric crime, and sentenced to hang. On June 29, 1869, moments before his sentence was to be carried out, Carr confessed to fourteen other murders.

Today, Louisa's ghost is most often seen wandering throughout the valley where a self-proclaimed serial killer cut her life short. Passersby have witnessed the apparition of a young girl weeping. Her tears of sadness and betrayal touch the hearts of all who hear her.

JUNE 30, 1900
MOUNT WASHINGTON
New Hampshire

Alan Ormsbee and William Curtis were hiking up Mount Washington in the summer of 1900. Not an easy task, since the mountain is the highest peak east of the Mississippi. But they were well-equipped, experienced climbers, so they had little to fear, or so they thought. A ferocious snow and sleet storm developed out of nowhere. The wind-driven sleet pelted the men as they made their way up the precipitous peak. But the treacherous ice and snow made their journey impossible. Just two miles from the Summit Hotel, beaten by the elements, they died. Three days later, rescuers discovered their frozen bodies in the snow.

A wooden cross was erected near the spot where Ormsbee had succumbed and a bronze plaque was eventually placed where Curtis had died. A weather observatory was built at the summit. Soon after, the presence of the two climbers was felt. Dark figures have been seen moving about the building, objects move on their own accord, distorted faces have been seen in boarded up windows, and worst of all are the sounds. Crews from the observatory have heard the thud of footsteps, rowdy disembodied voices, and even the melody of ethereal music reverberating off the walls of empty rooms. One night during a raging snowstorm there was a knock at the door. Puzzled, one of the workers went to investigate. No one was there. Yet there on the ground was the heavy brass plaque dedicated to Curtis. When the weather cleared, the plaque was returned to its original location and refastened to the rock. But that was not the end of it. Defying logic, the event has replayed itself several times. There are those that believe these unexplainable events are the results of William Curtis's ghost completing the journey in death that he was unable to complete in life.

JULY 1, 1863
THE PHANTOM SURGERY
Gettysburg, Pennsylvania

If tragedy and blood-soaked land are a root cause of hauntings, then it only seems logical that locations like Gettysburg, Pennsylvania, would abound with paranormal phenomena. On July 1, 1863, the Civil War raged in Gettysburg. It lasted for three hellish days. By the end of the third day, it had left more than 51,000 casualties of wounded, maimed, and dying upon the fields. In the struggle to tend to the wounded, the dead had been left where they had fallen. But soon, the blistering sun would take its toll on the 7,000 dead. In fact, the smell of rotting corpses was so heinous, that the living could not leave the house without the aid of a scented handkerchief.

Many of Gettysburg's structures quickly became makeshift hospitals for the thousands of wounded, who, even under the best of circumstances, were forced to endure prolonged misery, witnessing piles of amputated limbs while they waited their turn for medical assistance.

Countless visitors to Gettysburg have seen the ghostly apparitions of soldiers walking through the mist-shrouded fields. And there is hardly a home or restaurant that doesn't have a ghost tale or two.

Mark Nesbitt, an authority on Gettysburg's hauntings, related one of the many stories he'd heard. One night, while two administrators from Gettysburg College rode an elevator from the fourth floor to the first, they unexpectedly ended up in the basement. When the doors opened, they had the shock of their lives. Before them lay the dead and dying. They stood frozen for a few seconds as they both watched blood-soaked surgeons frantically work on the countless soldiers littering the basement. In a panic, they pushed the button on the elevator, their horror only relieved at the closing of the elevator doors.

JULY 2, 1895
CAPTAIN JOSHUA SLOCUM
Atlantic Ocean

Two days out of Yarmouth, Nova Scotia, the thirty-six-foot sailing sloop *Spray* cut through the cold ocean waters. At the ship's wheel was its captain, Joshua Slocum, the only person aboard. He was attempting to do what no man had ever done before, circumnavigate the globe, alone. The trip had been uneventful until now. Without warning, a violent ocean storm descended upon the *Spray*. The small ship was tossed about like a child's toy in the waves. Towers of water cascaded over its decks. The able captain battled the tempest for three long days until his battered body could take no more. He dragged himself into the cabin, falling onto his bed, awaiting certain death.

Hours passed as the exhausted captain slept. When he opened his eyes, the storm was still raging, but something was different. Monstrous waves pounded the ship, but the *Spray* ran smooth and true, slicing through the heaving waters. Captain Slocum staggered to the door of the cabin, peering at the cockpit. Frozen in terror, he watched as a heavyset man in fifteenth-century garb manned the wheel. As his fear subsided, the captain spoke, demanding to know who he was. After a long moment of eerie silence, the shadowy figure spoke, "I am the helmsman of the *Pinta*." Slocum's eyes widened. How could this be? The *Pinta* was one of the ships under Christopher Columbus's command when he discovered America, in 1492. As the captain was about to speak again, the spectral helmsman dissolved into the misty sea air. An awe-inspiring wave of renewed strength surged through his body. He grabbed the ship's wheel and guided the *Spray* through the turbulent seas. The storm subsided, and Captain Slocum continued his perilous journey. On June 27, 1898, the *Spray* sailed into New Port Harbor. Traveling over 46,000 miles, Captain Slocum became the first man to sail single-handedly around the world.

In November 1909, while on another journey, Captain Slocum and the *Spray* disappeared, never to be seen again. He had cheated death once, but it seems his luck had run out, or was it that he lacked the services of the helmsman from the *Pinta*?

JULY 3, 1971
THE GHOST OF JIM MORRISON
Paris, France

Jim Morrison, the infamous lead singer of the Doors, died under what was considered mysterious circumstances in a Paris bathtub on July 3, 1971. In 1997, rock and roll historian Brett Meisner made a graveside visit to Père Lachaise Cemetery in eastern Paris. Little did he know at the time that a casual picture taken of him would later reveal a ghost standing behind him with his arms stretched out. Was this the spectral image of Jim Morrison? Many people believe so. In fact, Chris Fleming, the paranormal expert of the show *Dead Famous*, when viewing the photo, was quoted as saying it was "the best he'd ever seen."

At first, Brett was enthralled by the scores of people who approached him regarding the photo, stating that they too had been in contact with the late Jim Morrison. But no longer. It appears that ever since the media got hold of the photo, Brett has experienced nothing but bad luck, including a failed marriage, the death of a friend to a drug overdose, and the loss of many prestigious clients. A spiritual advisor and friend has told Brett that the photo of Morrison is cursed and should be disposed of respectfully. In an effort to find closure for himself and provide the ghost of Jim Morrison the peace he so rightfully deserves, Brett has been searching for a reputable foundation to donate his collection of pictures and negatives to. So far, all have declined.

JULY 4, 1809
FORT CONSTITUTION
New Castle, New Hampshire

Originally known as "The Castle," the first seeds of the fort were planted in 1631. In 1692, the fort was expanded and renamed Fort William and Mary by the British. Just prior to the beginning of the Revolutionary War, four hundred colonials raided the fort. They commandeered sixteen cannon and ninety-seven barrels of gunpowder, which were later used in the battle of Bunker Hill in 1775. After the war, the fort continued to be improved upon and eventually became known as Fort Constitution.

On July 4, 1809, while the fort's commander, Captain Walbach, entertained guests inside the officer's house there was a terrible explosion. When the captain and his guests made their way from the heavily damaged building they were greeted by a grotesque scene. Body parts were scattered about the fort as the screams of the wounded pierced their ears. Eight men and boys died in the explosion, and two more died later from their wounds. According to local lighthouse historian Jeremy D'Entremont, one body was actually blown over the fort's wall and landed adjacent to the nearby lighthouse. An official inquiry into the explosion deemed it an accident.

Today the fort is a state park. Photographs taken there often reveal strange light anomalies. Visitors sometimes smell the faint odor of gunpowder and feel a deep sadness near the site of the explosion. During an investigation by medium Maureen Wood of The New England Ghost Project, contact was made with the spirit of a terribly disfigured soldier near the lighthouse. According to Wood, he felt great remorse. She also picked up on the name, Daniel. Oddly enough, one of the men killed in the explosion was a soldier by the name McDaniel. Is he roaming the grounds of the fort forgotten, unable to rest? Plans are now underway to erect a plaque to the men who died in that terrible explosion. Perhaps, after it is erected, Private McDaniel will soon be able to rest, knowing that he and the men that perished that fateful day will not be forgotten.

JULY 5, 1677
THE DEMON HOUNDS
Buckfastleigh, UK

In the county of Devon, not far from the moors, stands the burnt-out shell of the Holy Trinity Church. Among the ancient graves surrounding the church, you will find an odd structure. This large "penthouse tomb" known as the "sepulcher," is the site of the Cabell family plot, or to be more precise, Squire Richard Cabell.

Squire Richard Cabell lived in the 1600s, and by all accounts he was an evil man. He was described as immoral, quick tempered, and an avid hunter. It is rumored that he murdered his wife and even sold his soul to the Devil. Few tears were shed when he died in 1677. His body was entombed in the sepulcher, but it didn't lie in rest. Late that night, a pack of ghost hounds came from across the moors to bay at his grave. These demonic creatures with glowing red eyes howled all night and then disappeared back into the mist of the moors.

Alarmed by the frightening happenings, the villagers placed a heavy slab on the squire's grave and as an added protection constructed a large building with iron bars around it to prevent his ghost from escaping. But their attempt obviously failed. There have been many reports of people seeing Squire Cabell leading the pack of ghostly hounds across the moors. Others report a strange red glow emanating from his tomb. The church has been broken into several times and burned—some believe by Devil worshippers.

Legend tells us that if you go to the Squire's tomb, run around it seven times, and stick your hand through the bars of the building, it will be bitten by a ghost hound, Squire Cabell, or the Devil, himself. But then again, it's only a legend, isn't it?

JULY 6, 1685
SEDGEMOOR BATTLEFIELD
Westonzoyland, Whales

In the early morning hours of July 6, 1685, the forces of the Duke of Monmouth, the illegitimate son of Charles II, met the Royalist troops of King James II on the muddy fields of Sedgemoor. The duke's forces were routed as he fled the battlefield like a cowardly schoolgirl. He was eventually captured and executed, as were most of his followers. One particular soldier, a well-known athlete, was captured by Royalist troops. His lover, who happened to live nearby, pleaded for his life. The soldiers agreed that if he could outrun a galloping horse, he would be spared. He accepted their challenge, and to their astonishment, he succeeded, only to be gunned down in cold blood in front of his lover. She became so distraught that she drowned herself in the River Carey.

The tragedy and carnage of the battle has left a bloody imprint in the swampy ground of Sedgemoor. Locals speak of phantom horsemen, ghostly voices, and even the spectral image of the Duke, reliving his cowardly escape for eternity. But the saddest specter is that of the young maiden, whose ghost has been seen at the site of her lover's tragic death. Those who wander to the site feel the thunder of spectral hooves, the heavy breathing of an invisible runner, and a rush of cold air, painful reminders of Sedgemoor's tragic past.

JULY 7, 1898
THOMAS PLATER
St. Andrews, Scotland

In 1393, at St. Andrews Cathedral, there was a canon named Thomas Plater. One day, he had a heated disagreement with Prior Robert Montrose. In a fit of rage, Thomas stabbed Montrose to death. Plater was tried and convicted for the murder. He was sentenced to life in prison, but he died shortly after his conviction. For years Plater rested peacefully, and then his spectral image began to appear in the cathedral and the surrounding grounds. One day, in 1898, his vision appeared to a Catholic hotel worker. He pleaded with the man to bury his bones in consecrated ground. Upon investigating the specter's request, the hotel worker discovered that Plater's remains had been dug up during an archeological dig. In July 1898, with the full rites of the church, his bones were reburied on the South Side of St. Rule's Chapel. The ghost of Thomas Plater was seen no more; once again, he was resting in peace.

TERRIFYING TIDBIT

A ghost pig with human eyes has been seen near the ruins of St. Andrews. It is said that the spectral swine is full of desperation, sadness, guilt, and shame, and it begs for your understanding and compassion.

JULY 8, 1758
MAJOR DUNCAN CAMPBELL
Fort Ticonderoga, New York

Late one stormy night in 1747, Duncan Campbell was at his ancestral home, the Scottish castle of Inverawe, when a stranger, bloodied and tattered, pounded at his door. In a hurried voice he told Duncan that he had just killed a man in a fight and asked him for asylum. Reluctantly he agreed, swearing an oath on his dagger. A short time later there was another knock on the door. This time it was the fugitive's pursuers. The armed men informed Duncan that a man had just killed his cousin, Donald. Duncan remembered the oath he had just taken and professed that he new nothing. After they went away he retired to his bedroom and fell asleep. He was soon startled from his dreams by an awful moaning. When he opened his eyes, he saw the ghost of his cousin Donald, standing beside his bed. In a deep muffled voice the specter uttered, "Inverawe! Inverawe! Blood has been shed. Shield not the murderer!"

For several nights the ghost visited, each time pleading with Duncan to hand over his murderer. Disturbed by his vision, he confronted the killer. Yet when reminded of his oath, he was forced to back down. Once more the phantom appeared and said, "Farewell, Inverawe! Farewell, till we meet at Ticonderoga!"

Donald's words meant nothing to Duncan, and as time passed, he forgot all about it. Until 1758, that is, when he and his regiment were sent to the colonies to battle the French and their Indian allies at the fort of Carillon, also known as Ticonderoga, a name he hadn't heard in ten years. Convinced of his destiny, he fought like a man possessed. The attack was a failure and he was ordered to retreat. He was elated.

Duncan had survived the battle with only a flesh wound to the arm. And more importantly, he had survived the curse of his cousin Donald. Or had he? The wound festered and gangrene set in. The surgeon amputated his arm and did his best to save him, but the ghost had his way in the end, and Duncan died ten days later.

JULY 9, 1935
THE VOGUE THEATRE
Los Angeles, California

In 1901, catastrophe struck Prospect Elementary School, when the small schoolhouse burned to the ground, killing Miss Elizabeth and her twenty-five students. In 1935, the Vogue Theatre was built in its place. After fifty-seven years, the theatre closed down and the building was abandoned. In 1992, the old Vogue Theatre became home to a parapsychology group, the International Society for Paranormal Research (ISPR). Soon they realized the building was haunted, and the group utilized the location as a research center rather than offices, as originally planned. For four years thousands of visitors, scientists, and psychics alike communicated with the nine spirits that haunted the old theatre, among them six children, Miss Elizabeth, and a projectionist by the name of Fritz, who had worked for the Vogue for forty years. Fritz's career had abruptly ended when back in the 1980s he died of a heart attack in the projectionist's room.

On numerous occasions, the spirits made themselves known to the visitors by moving objects and appearing before them as full-bodied apparitions. But is the old Vogue Theatre building still haunted? The leading parapsychologist of ISPR, Dr. Larry Montz, says no. The group, having completed their research, cleared the property of all ghostly specters.

JULY 10, 2009
GHOST THROWS TEENAGER
OUT OF HOUSE
Hartlepool, England

According to the website In Pure Spirit, a family was so terrorized by a ghost that they rushed to St. Paul's Church in Hartlepool, England, for help. The mother, returning from picking up her five-year-old from school, found her thirteen-year-old son outside the front door of their home in the fetal position. Allegedly, the young man was in the home listening to music when something unseen lifted him up by the leg and dragged him across the floor before throwing him onto the front stoop. The attack lasted for at least five minutes. Based on the heavy breathing he'd felt while being dragged through his living room, the young man believed the entity was male. When the mother found her son, she helped him up. Together they tried the door, but it was locked. After unlocking it, they attempted to enter, but the sound of banging from within had them quickly running for safety.

Their parish priest, Father Richard Masshedar, visited the troubled home the next day to offer up prayers and bless the building. Although the home has been cleansed, the family have decided to relocate as soon as there is a place available. There are some who believe the boy's claims to be nothing more than a scam to procure a larger place to live. Then again, maybe the young man told the truth.

JULY 11, 1023
LOKRUM ISLAND
Croatia

A great fire erupted in the city of Dubrovnik in 1023. As it spread unchecked, the authorities panicked. They made a pact with Saint Benedict; if he would intercede on their behalf and save the city, they would build a monastery in his name. The fire was extinguished immediately. True to their word, the thankful citizens of Dubrovnik erected a church and Benedictine monastery on the nearby isle of Lokrum. In the fourteenth century, a French occupying general ordered the monastery closed and the removal of all of the monks from the island was ordered. Three prominent Dubrovnik families were sent to carry out the order. Before leaving the island the monks gathered together for one last time. With incense burning and solemn hymns, they conducted a secret liturgy. Walking out of the monastery in single file, they marched around the island, each carrying a candle upside down, allowing the wax to drip to the earth, thus cursing the ground. The solemn mystifying procession circled the island three times, as the monks chanted in unison, "Whosoever claims Lokrum for his own personal pleasure shall be damned!" After they completed their ceremony, the Benedictines boarded a boat and left the island, vowing never to return. Thus, the curse of the island was born.

The three aristocrats who were sent to evict the monks met untimely deaths: one jumped from a window, one was killed by his servant, and one drowned on a trip to the island. But this was just the beginning. Kings, queens, noblemen—all those who subsequently possessed the island suffered financial ruin, ill health, and even death. Lovers venturing into the beautiful garden of the monastery were said to have their heads cut off and their hearts sewed to the woman's dress by lecherous demons. Convicts were tossed from the cliffs to their deaths.

Today, Lokrum is a tourist attraction, but few locals venture to the island, especially at night. During storms, the pounding of the waves against the rocky cliffs echoes the sound of coffin lids being closed. And during moonless nights you can still see the flicker of the candles carried by phantom monks as they circle the island, renewing the curse.

July 12, 1807
The Ghost Bride
Cape Elizabeth, Maine

Lydia Carver, the daughter of a popular Freeport banker, was returning home from a trip to Boston on the schooner *Charles*. She and her wedding party had gone to Boston to purchase her wedding dress and trousseau. This joyous occasion soon turned deadly when a fog bank rolled in and the *Charles* was smashed on Watt's Ledge near Cape Elizabeth, Maine. The next morning Lydia's body was discovered washed up on Crescent Beach. Next to her was a trunk containing her never-worn wedding dress. She was buried in a small cemetery just above the beach.

Today a five-star hotel is located next to the cemetery where Lydia is buried. The Inn by the Sea, as it is called today, has many visitors, including one of a spectral nature. Lydia is known to haunt the inn, turning lights on and off, riding the elevator, and making her presence known to pending brides. One of the best-known stories associated with Lydia deals with a woman who was about to get married. The wedding party checked into the inn the night before the wedding. The next morning the bride told her mother that she was exhausted and hadn't slept a wink because her satin gown had danced about the room all night.

So if your wedding plans include a visit to the Inn by the Sea, be sure to leave an extra place setting for the special party crasher, the ghost bride Lydia Carver.

JULY 13, 2004
THE GHOSTLY FACES
Belmez de la Moraleda, Spain

According to the *Guardian's* website, the most famous haunted house in Spain was put up for sale in 2004. Thirty-three years ago, scores of ghostly faces began appearing in the concrete floor of the kitchen. No longer able to stand looking at the them, Maria Gomez hired someone to chip away at the kitchen floor. However, rather than being rid of these spying ghostly specters, dozens of other faces began to appear. As word of this paranormal phenomenon spread throughout Spain, curiosity seekers lined up every weekend for a tour. The haunting had garnered such attention that a state-run, scientific investigation team closed off the kitchen, performing a series of tests. At first, the scientists believed that Gomez had painted the images herself. But after three months of investigation, under the supervision of a notary, the kitchen was reopened and the faces were still there.

To find a root cause of the unusual occurrence, a two-meter trench was dug. And what did the investigators find? A long lost graveyard, believed to contain members of the Gomez family, some of whom had been massacred during Spain's civil war. Strangely, the numerous other skeletal remains, dating back to the 1300s, were all headless.

JULY 14, 2008
THE GAS STATION SPECTER
Petrich, Bulgaria

A Bulgarian gas station seems to have been visited by a ghostly apparition. Film footage from the security camera reveals a startling image, and although no one can explain why the dark form made the visit, it can be easily seen by all. In the film, a black shadow seemingly appears out of thin air. At first the source of the shadow was thought to be the result of a butterfly in front of the lens. Then skeptical viewers of the image insinuated that it had been fabricated. But their opinions soon changed when they saw the shadow, which took form atop the linoleum tiles, morph into what looks like a human shape. It took several steps toward the rear of the station and then floated up to the ceiling, where it dematerialized several seconds later. In fact, the news anchor who was replayed during the showing of the film of the ghostly specter, "Ghost Shot by a Camera in a Petrol Station in Bulgaria," on VidoEmo, appeared to be at a loss for words. The owner decided it would be best to have his station blessed to prevent future hauntings.

TERRIFYING TIDBIT

Bulgarian traditions dictate that the church bless all new buildings. Unfortunately for the gas station, this had never been done.

JULY 15, 2009
MICHAEL JACKSON'S GHOST
APPEARS ON CNN
Santa Barbara, California

Is the king of pop still posing for the camera? Many people believe so. Miko Brando, a close friend of Jackson's, provided Larry King with an intimate tour of Jackson's Neverland ranch in Santa Barbara County, CA. During the show, the CNN camera pans down a long, desolate hallway when, suddenly, a dark shadow glides across an open doorway. The eerie image caught on film triggered a buzz on the Internet, as excited fans believed that the camera might have captured the moonwalking ghost of Michael Jackson. Despite CNN's denial of the alleged evidence, many see this as a sign that Michael has made one more appearance from the grave.

JULY 16, 1865
JUMEL MANSION
New York City, New York

The Morris-Jumel Mansion was once used as Washington's headquarters during the Battle of Brooklyn in 1776. It was later purchased in 1810 by a French wine merchant named Stephen Jumel and his newly-wed wife, Eliza. Eliza was a voluptuous blonde with a checkered past.

Eliza's reputation did not improve much after her marriage. She was often seen cavorting with the likes of Alexander Hamilton, Aaron Burr, and Thomas Jefferson. But what's worse is that, according to rumor, she pushed her husband out of a moving carriage, then stood by and watched as he bled to death. No one can be certain if Eliza's murderous act really happened. However, the fact remains that Stephen Jumel's death made her a very rich woman, a woman who 200 years later is said to still haunt the Morris-Jumel Mansion.

The Jumel House's rich, lengthy history has attracted scores of ghostly visitors. In the 1960s, a group of unruly children glimpsed a blond woman in a violet gown walk out onto a second floor balcony. She shushed them, then turned and vanished into thin air. Eliza? Possibly. However, another sighting took place when one teacher brought her students on a field trip. In her excitement she wandered into an area closed off to tourists. But her excitement soon turned to fear when she caught sight of a Revolutionary soldier as he stepped out of a painting. She fainted dead on the spot. And last but not least, yet another teacher, after coming face-to-face with a ghostly apparition at the mansion, suffered a fatal heart attack. In past years, curators have been known to downplay the hauntings. However, the Jumel Mansion's history speaks for itself. Literally.

JULY 17, 2002
THE JUNKYARD GHOST
Oklahoma City, Oklahoma

A family claims that the ghostly image they viewed on the surveillance camera at Puckett's Auto is in fact thirty-three-year-old mother of twins Tracy Martin. Sadly, on June 30, eighteen days before the video was captured, Tracy, who hadn't been wearing her seatbelt, was involved in a fatal crash. Her vehicle was towed to Puckett's salvage yard. On July 17, 2002, her truck was moved to another location within the yard, and not more than five hours later, a ghostly apparition was spotted.

Kathy, an employee of Puckett's, while monitoring the security camera, noticed the brief apparition of someone darting about the wrecked vehicles. She sent another employee out to check for intruders, but none could be found. When they rewound the videotape and took a closer look, they were astounded at what they saw. The ghostly image, wearing what appeared to be overalls, floated above the ground, moving in a circular motion. It seemed to be searching for something. Intrigued with what they'd seen, the workers reported their curious finding to the local news station. Not long after, Tracy's family stepped forward. It appears that the ghostly presence wandering about the wreckage, possibly looking for her recently moved truck, was none other than Tracy Martin. Although there are those who are skeptical that this video is real, Tracy's family is convinced it was her. Tracy, they said, favored her overalls.

JULY 18, 2004
DALE EARNHARDT SR.'S
GHOST SAVES SON
Sonoma, California

Did the ghost of Dale Earnhardt Sr. save his son's life? Dale Jr. believes so. In an interview with Mike Wallace of the CBS show *60 Minutes*, Dale Earnhardt Jr. revealed the strange circumstances surrounding his fiery wreck and rescue at the Infineon Raceway.

During the first lap of warm-ups for the American Le Mans Series, Dale's yellow Corvette spun out of control and slammed into a concrete wall, bursting into flames. While trying to escape the car he felt a hand underneath his arm, dragging him out of the burning vehicle. Seconds later, he collapsed to the pavement.

As rescue workers carried him away from the fireball that was once his car, he asked about the "guy" who helped him from the car. They informed him that there was no "guy." Dale suffered burns to his legs and neck, but survived.

Wallace asked if Dale thought the "guy" was his father, who had died three years earlier in a fatal racecar accident.

A spooked Dale, replied, "Yeah, I don't know. You tell me. It . . . freaks me out today just talking about it. It gives me chills."

JULY 19, 1463
THE HAUNTED BED
London, England

In the V & A Museum in London sits a rather large bed, measuring 133 inches long and 130 wide. This monstrosity was built by Jonas Fosbrooke for King Edward the IV who used it for his own personal use. It was passed on to his son, Edward V, and then eventually sold. The bed, reputed to be haunted by its maker, was sold several times, passing through several inns in Ware. Once during a festival, when no one could find a room, twelve couples slept in the bed, or at least tried to. The spirit, known as Fosbrooke, harassed the couples all night long, pinching and scratching them in "a most unpleasant manner." The attacks of Fosbrooke became so well known that guests would offer up a toast before they bedded down with his ghost. Today, you can bear witness to the infamous

Fosbrooke ghost by visiting the V & A Museum, where the "Most Haunted Bed in England" resides.

JULY 20, 1878
PORTSMOUTH LIGHTHOUSE
New Castle, New Hampshire

This forty-eight-foot iron-and-brick tower was built in 1878. For over 130 years it has stood guard over Portsmouth Harbor. A long line of keepers oversaw the Portsmouth Lighthouse until it was finally automated in 1960. The keeper who served the longest was Joshua K. Card, who retired in 1909 after 35 years of service. When people would ask Joshua what the letter K on his uniform stood for, he'd tell them "captain." He died in 1911, but it seems that he has never left.

Coast Guard workers at the nearby station have reported hearing footsteps and seeing someone moving in the old keeper's house and near the tower. Others working in the tower have heard disembodied voices and unusual noises. Although most of these incidences have happened at night, one visitor to the lighthouse met the "Kaptain" in broad daylight. She was walking on her way to tour the lighthouse when she noticed a man in a uniform. However, when she reached the lighthouse he was gone. Later, the visitor was able to identify Card from a photo. There have been several investigations with great results. However, the New England Ghost Project has collected the most interesting piece of evidence to date. While recording EVPs in the tower, one of the investigators asked, "Is anybody here?" The reply on the recorder said, "It's the Kaptain."

JULY 21, 2006
HAUNTED HOUSE FOR SALE
Sanford, Florida

According to Central Florida's *Local 6 News*, a historic home believed to be inhabited by the spirit of an elderly woman was listed for sale. The ad told all prospective buyers that the house was, in fact, haunted. Intrigued by the story, *Local 6 News* interviewed the realtor.

While in the home, to the amazement of the reporter, just as the realtor described the ghostly apparition that had appeared before her near the armoire, the cabinet doors suddenly opened and closed of their own accord.

However, it seems that the real estate agent and the reporter are not the only ones to have witnessed these events, as several others have also reported the bizarre ghostly goings-on In fact, the mortgage banker had also witnessed the cabinet doors opening, closing, and slamming of their own accord. And another time, a penny that had been left on the banister when no one else was in the home mysteriously showed up in the tub.

Although the realtor had listed the home in a blind ad indicating that the home came with a ghost, she stated that some people appeared intrigued, while others were deathly afraid.

TERRIFYING TIDBIT

In Massachusetts, if a home is known to be haunted, the seller must inform the prospective buyers only if the seller is asked. However, this law varies from state to state.

JULY 22, 1929
BARON CASTLE
Cairo, Egypt

Visitors to Cairo today cannot miss Baron Castle. The ornate structure looks more like a Hindu temple than a castle. Belgian Baron Edward Louis Joseph Empain came to Egypt on business, but to everyone's surprise, decided to stay. Some say it was because of his love for the sensuous Yvette Boghdadli, while others claim it was for the love of the country.

In 1905 he began construction of the new city of Heliopolis, ten miles outside of Cairo. Just two years later, he began construction of Baron Castle with the help of French architects Alexander Marcel and George-Louis Claude. They designed an extraordinary structure, melding the characteristics of a Hindu temple, a Renaissance cathedral, and a Cambodian temple all into one.

The Baron died in 1929. Upon his death the building began to fall into disrepair. As the years passed, rumors of its haunting grew. It changed hands several times and eventually was abandoned. Satan worshippers and the dregs of society violated the crumbling structure for sinister purposes. To preserve its past, the Egyptian government declared it a national monument. The building is now being restored under guard, but the rumors of haunting still continue. Doors and windows open by themselves, and the occasional ghost makes an appearance.

Some say it is the Baron himself who is seen wandering the halls, unable to find peace until his home has been restored.

JULY 23, 1938
GRIDLEY TUNNEL
Yokosuka Naval Base, Japan

The narrow Gridley Tunnel is one of twenty tunnels on the Yokosuka Naval Base. Through the years, several reports of supernatural activity have surfaced. They all involve people driving through the tunnel on rainy nights. The odd happenings usually take place between midnight and one in the morning, when there is only one car on this secluded patch of road. From out of nowhere the ghostly apparition of a samurai appears.

Some believe that this honor-bound samurai was ambushed and killed while on a mission for his lord. Sworn to complete his mission, he is damned for eternity until it is completed.

If you find yourself driving through the Gridley Tunnel at midnight on a rainy evening, beware of the samurai, or you find yourself swerving off the road in sheer terror.

JULY 24, 1915
OPRAH'S STUDIO
Chicago, Illinois

Is Oprah's HARPO studio in Chicago, Illinois, haunted? According to the *Enquirer*, some of the staff believe so. And although Oprah has chosen to no longer speak about the haunting, at one time she felt strongly enough about the paranormal activity in her studio to devote an entire show to it. But how did this storage building that once housed weapons become haunted? One need only look back to July 24, 1915, the day Chicago suffered one of its most horrific tragedies.

On route to their picnic, Western Electric Company employees along with their families boarded the *Eastland* steamer. The *Eastland*, which had known design flaws, had reached its passenger capacity. The theory is that prior to embarking on their twenty-minute excursion a large number of passengers stood to one side of the steamer to take a photo, which set it off balance. An engineer, trying to correct for the shift, opened a ballast tank. But rather than stabilizing, the *Eastland* steamer capsized. Eight hundred men, woman, and children died. Their bodies were pulled from the water and placed in the Second Battalion Armory's gymnasium, the building now known as HARPO studios.

Many unexplained sounds echo throughout the building. The mournful sobs of tormented souls still collecting their dead can be heard, as well as giggling children running up and down the length of the halls. Is this residual energy? If so, it doesn't explain the "Lady in Gray," that is often seen moving about the building. Is she still looking among the dead for her love, or was she a victim herself? We may never know for sure.

JULY 25, 1920
KIMBALL CASTLE
Gilford, New Hampshire

Kimball Castle, overlooking Lake Winnipesauke, was built in 1895 by railroad baron Benjamin Ames Kimball. He borrowed the design from a castle he saw while on a summer vacation in Germany. Kimball used the castle extensively as a summer home for his family. In 1920 Kimball died, and shortly after, his only son, Henry, passed. His wife had died earlier, so the property was passed on to his son's wife, Charlotte. She lived in the castle until she died in 1960. The property was then willed to the Mary Mitchell Humane Society, along with funds necessary for the upkeep of the castle. However, the Humane Society failed to maintain it, and the castle fell into disrepair. Eventually, the property was sold to the town. Through the years, vandals and the weather have turned this once splendid monument into crumbling ruins. And perhaps because of its sad condition, ghost stories abound. Since Charlotte's death, a caretaker has remained on the property, and his experiences have driven its haunted reputation. On several occasions, the heavy oak door of the castle has closed by itself. Lights have been seen in Mrs. Kimball's old sewing room, even though there is no electricity. And the apparition of a woman has been witnessed in the kitchen and walking about the grounds. As the castle slowly deteriorates, one can only wonder if the ghost of Charlotte will remain or simply fade away with the castle.

JULY 26, 1978
CHEZ BRIANN
St. Johns, Newfoundland, Canada

When one looks at a building, it is sometimes difficult to imagine the types of businesses that have come and gone since the original structure was built. Chez Briann is one of those. Today it is a modern bistro in downtown St. Johns, but several businesses before, it had a darker side. The building was used as a funeral parlor. After the funeral parlor went out of business, it became an inn. This is when its dark secrets were first revealed. Late one night, a tenant was awakened by a specter of a man hovering above her bed. He stared at her with an evil smile, attempting to place coins on her eyes. With the sound of her screams, he vanished into thin air. Another time, the ashen spirit of a woman was seen in the hall. Her naked torso revealed a long jagged scar, like that of an autopsy. Other tenants have reported hearing faint whispers and unexplained weeping. From time to time, the inexplicable sickly sweet aroma of flowers has filled the air. The employees in the bistro have reported paranormal activity of their own, but none so drastic as those experienced in the past.

TERRIFYING TIDBIT

Coins on a dead persons eyes are there to pay the ferryman, Charon, to take the deceased across the river Styx into Hades.

JULY 27, 1689
KILLIECRANKIE PASS
Pitlochry, Scotland

In Perthshire County, along the River Garry, lies the Pass of Killiecrankie. On a warm summer's day in 1689 it was the site of a great battle. Thirty-four hundred troops of William of Orange met a smaller force of 2,500 Jacobite highlanders loyal to the deposed King James VII of Scotland under the command of "Bonnie Dundee." The highlanders held the higher ground, and when the bright summer sun passed behind them, Dundee gave the order to attack. A volley of

musket fire rained down on the government troops, as the screaming highlanders descended upon their quarry like a hungry school
of piranhas. Blinded by the sun, the Royalists panicked, and fled in
terror as Dundee's men sliced their way through them. The ground
ran red with blood as the highlanders inflicted a crushing defeat to the
troops of William of Orange.

Today, some say that on the anniversary of the battle, the Pass of
Killiecrankie glows with a red hue. Many have heard the sound of
musket fire and the screams of the dead echoing from the slopes of the
gorge. And some have even been startled when they are confronted
by the sudden appearance of spectral troops, still engaged in the battle
of the Pass of Killiecrankie.

TERRIFYING TIDBIT

During the battle, a fleeing Royalist by the name of Donald Macbear
was being pursued by a group of highlanders. When he reached the
rocky shore, he jumped eighteen feet across the river to the other side,
escaping his pursuers. Today that area is still known as "Soldiers Leap"
in his honor.

JULY 28, 1900
BORLEY RECTORY
Borley, England

Built in 1863 on the site of an ancient Cistercian monastery, the Borley Rectory is thought to be the most haunted house in England. No
sooner had Reverend Henry Dawson Ellis Bull and his family moved

in than they became besieged by ghostly apparitions. The most notable was a nun who was seen in the garden by the rector's daughters in July of 1900.

After the Bull family left, Reverend Eric Smith and his wife moved in. While cleaning, they found the skull of a young woman wrapped in brown paper. With their discovery, paranormal activity began to escalate, so much so that objects were now being tossed about. So they called in renowned ghost hunter Harry Price. When the activity failed to cease, the Smiths gave up and moved out. Filling the Reverend's position was Reverend Lionel Foyster and his wife, Marianne.

Marianne quickly became the center of the entity's attention. Objects were thrown at her by invisible forces, bells would ring of their own accord, but perhaps even stranger were the messages scribbled on the walls by an unseen hand. "Marianne, Please get help." The violence toward Marianne increased until the family could take no more. They too, moved out.

In 1937, Harry Price rented Borley Rectory and lived there with forty-eight team members. They conducted several experiments including a planchette séance, a ghost writing device. During the séance Price contacted the spirit of Marie Larrie, an ex-nun who was murdered by her husband and buried in the basement. She told them she could never rest until her bones were found and she received a proper Christian burial. The séance ended when another spirit came through who threatened to burn the building down.

Price's lease ended and he and his team moved out after documenting hundreds of incidents of paranormal activity. In 1939 the Borley Rectory burned in a fire, fulfilling the spirit's threat. In 1943, Price returned, finding bones in the cellar and bringing peace to Marie Larrie but not to the Borley Rectory.

JULY 29, 1993
DEVIL'S HOPYARD

East Haddam, Connecticut

One of the most picturesque state parks in Connecticut is none other than Devil's Hopyard. Besides the fact that during the eighteenth century a malt house was located beside the nearby Eight Mile River, why on earth would it be referred to as the Devil's Hopyard? Because Satan himself has been said to visit the sixty-foot cascading Chapman Falls. Legend has it that the violin-playing Prince of Darkness has been spied sitting atop a boulder at the top of the falls, while his minions have been seen lingering beside the pool below. Since the early Puritan days, dark shadows and phantom specters have been witnessed slithering through the woods. And today, visitors to the woods have reported hearing the sound of ethereal, evil laughter. Others have captured the presence of orbs and inexplicable strange mists on film. If you are wondering how such a place of beauty could be inhabited by the Devil, there's only one way to know for sure. If you mysteriously find yourself in the vicinity of East Haddam, Connecticut, visit Devil's Hopyard and find out for yourself.

TERRIFYING TIDBIT

Orbs are thought by many to be the souls of those that have passed. They can be transparent or solid. Sometimes they contain an image within, such as a ring or a face.

JULY 30, 1927
HOTEL BEN LOMOND
Ogden, Utah

Hotel Ben Lomond, formerly the Bigelow Hotel, was built in 1927. Early in its history the building served as a boarding house for prostitutes, madams, and gangsters. The tunnel beneath the hotel was used during Prohibition to smuggle booze, and many believe it's the hotel's checkered past that has conjured up a spirit or two.

Employees avoid the tunnel at all cost, stating they frequently have the uncomfortable feeling of being watched. There are some who have even been pushed by a pair of unseen hands, while others have witnessed torsoless legs strutting past them.

It is said that the ghost of a bride inhabits room 1102. While on her honeymoon, the young bride tragically drowned in the bathtub. Staff have reported that the bathtub mysteriously fills by itself and the front desk often receives phone calls from an empty room. Yet when they answer, the line goes dead.

A little further down the hall is room 1106 with yet another ghost, and another story. During World War II, a woman became a resident of the hotel while her son was away fighting in the war. She waited and waited for his return. He never came back. It is said she died of a broken heart, and her spirit still lingers in the room. Impressions on the bed have been seen, and unusual cold spots appear in the room. These are just two of the ghostly inhabitants of Hotel Ben Lomond. If you wish to meet the rest, perhaps you should book an overnight stay. But be on guard, you don't want to become the next victim to be incorporated into the hotel's haunted reputation.

JULY 31, 1614
THE BLOOD COUNTESS
Cachtice, Slovakia (Hungary)

It was a cold winter's night when Count Thurzo and his party of armed men made their way up the steep cliffs of the massive Castle Csejthe. It was a reluctant mission, yet a necessary one. The count was related to his quarry, the Countess Elizabeth Bathory, a formidable opponent. Her husband was the "Black Hero of Hungary," brave victor over the Turks. Elizabeth was nearly untouchable; she was also related to kings, cardinals, and many nobles. But the rumors had to be investigated.

For the past thirty years villagers had complained to the king about strange happenings at the castle: black magic, sorcery, and worst of all, the disappearance of their young daughters. Yet their complaints were overlooked; after all, the countess was royalty. But when the daughters of lesser nobility started disappearing, she could be ignored no longer. What Count Thurzo and his party found that night was beyond comprehension. Rotting corpses were strewn around the torture chamber. Young girls barely alive were chained to the walls, their once youthful skin now shriveled and pale.

Unable to excuse such atrocities, Count Thurzo arrested the countess and her cohorts.

The trial stunned the royal court. Evidence showed that for the past thirty years the countess and her accomplices had killed over 600 young girls. The girls had been tortured, sexually abused, and drained of their blood.

As punishment for their crimes, several of her cohorts had their fingers ripped off before they were burned alive. Another was beheaded and burned. Elizabeth, on the other hand, being of royalty, was exempt from such punishment. However, she could not escape judgment. It was ordered that she be walled up in the tower of the castle with just a slit in the wall so her jailors could feed her.

She died three years later, alone in the darkness. When they tore down the walls to retrieve her body, they found a document written by the countess. It was a curse calling for ninety-nine cats, familiars of witches, to do her bidding and tear out the hearts of her accusers.

Today, the ruins of Castle Csejthe still exist. Not many venture to it at night, but those who do have reported hearing the horrific screams of tortured souls. Are these the echoes of the victims of the countess, or perhaps the screams of Elizabeth's final agony?

AUGUST 1, 2008
ASHEVILLE HIGH SCHOOL
Asheville, North Carolina

Is Asheville High haunted? The faculty, especially a teacher by the name of Martha Geitner, believes so. During Martha's interview with the local news channel she said, "It's a ghost! Of course it's a ghost! It's the ghost of some former student who is really angry with his teacher and has come to get back at the teacher, and he's just making himself known at this time."

But what has gotten everyone so riled up? On August 1, 2008, at precisely 2:51:03 in the morning, the motion sensor was set off and the video surveillance system captured a dark shadow gliding across the rotunda. At first glance, the shadow was passed off by the executer of public relations as nothing but a bat flying across the room.

But that all changed on playback, when the strange image continued to change shape. Instead of batlike, it looked human. A child perhaps? In one frame, the shadowy figure took a few steps. In another, it floated above the elevator, eerily casting its own shadow.

The reporter requested the service of a local paranormal investigative team, asking their opinion of the video. After viewing the video they had difficulty debunking it. In their opinion, it was definitely not a hoax.

AUGUST 2, 1100
KING WILLIAM II
Minstead, Hampshire, England

On the afternoon of August 2, King William II arrived in New Forrest with seven trusted friends for an afternoon of hunting. Early in the evening, the party split up. Sir Walter Tyrrel and William, or "Rufus" as he was known, went in one direction and the rest of the party in another. Shortly after they separated, the second group came upon the body of the king with an arrow in his chest. Tyrrel explained that it was an accident. Afraid of being accused of regicide, William's companions fled back to their castles, while Tyrrel fled the country. Later, a peasant named Purkis found the king's body and threw it into a wooden cart. As the cart bounced along it left a trail of blood all the way to Winchester. And ever since that day, on the anniversary of his death Rufus's ghostly specter has been spotted from New Forrest, where he was killed, journeying all the way to Winchester. Even in death, the king tracks the blood trail. Unfortunately for this hunter, rather than animal blood, it is his own.

AUGUST 3, 1343
THE LIONESS OF BRITTANY
Clisson, France

In 1330, after the death of her first husband, Jeanne-Louise de Belleville married Count Oliver de Clisson. The count was a wealthy nobleman who had a vast estate including Clisson Castle and a manor house in Nantes. They were extremely happy together, but these were difficult times. On the throne of France was the ruthless Philippe IV. Although Oliver had helped defend Brittany from the English, his loyalty fell under suspicion. He was lured to the Duke of Brittany's castle, where he was arrested on trumped-up charges and taken to Paris to stand trial. Betrayed by his friend Charles de Blois, he was found guilty and beheaded. His head was sent to Nantes and displayed on a pole.

Jeanne de Clisson was devastated and refused to leave the castle. She slowly began to sell the estate until only the castle remained. With the money she acquired, she secretly purchased and armed three ships. They were painted black with red sails. One dark night she left the castle to take command of her black fleet. Thus began a reign of terror on French shipping. With ruthlessness, Jeanne hunted down and destroyed the ships of King Philippe, killing all on board except for one, who was freed to report back to Philippe her treacherous act. Even after Philippe's death, she continued her wave of terror, taking particular enjoyment in personally beheading any French nobleman she captured. After thirteen years, the Lioness of Brittany scuttled her fleet and took refuge in England. Later she returned to France, and it is believed she died in 1359. But even today the gray spectral image of the Lioness of Brittany can be seen walking the halls of Clisson Castle. It seems even revenge couldn't bring rest to her grief-stricken soul.

AUGUST 4, 1577
BLACK SHUCK
Bungay and Blythburgh, Suffolk, England

There have been many reports of hell hounds and demon dogs through the years, but none as chilling as the event that happened on a Sunday morning in 1577. As villagers were attending services in the small town of Bungay, the skies darkened and a violent storm arose. Thunder and lightning shook the church to its foundation, but despite the clamor, service continued. Then a black dog with glowing red eyes and fire on its claws appeared in the church. It thrashed about the church terrorizing the parishioners, killing two and severely burning another. As quickly as it appeared, it was gone.

Meanwhile several miles away from Bungay, in the town of Blythburgh, the same demonic hound burst through the doors of yet another church, tearing through the sanctuary, killing two and collapsing the church steeple. Then, once again, it was gone.

Some people believe it was lightning that terrorized the two churches that day, but there were too many witnesses to dispute it. The villagers of Bungay have immortalized that day with a weathervane depicting a black hound riding a lightning bolt. And a little further down the road in Blythburgh, the "Devil's fingerprints" can be seen as scorch marks on the church's door—a reminder left by the Black Shuck of the day the Devil came to church.

TERRIFYING TIDBIT

The Black Shuck is a large spectral hound of British folklore. This enormous creature has thick black hair and glowing eyes. The deadly beast can be found in cemeteries, crossroads, and abandoned castles. As recorded in history, this beast has been known to kill unsuspecting humans by snapping their necks with its powerful jaws.

AUGUST 5, 1962
HOLLYWOOD'S ROOSEVELT HOTEL
Hollywood, California

If you're planning to visit the Hollywood Roosevelt Hotel, be sure to take a moment to glance at your reflection in the full-length mirror situated on the first level by the elevators. There's a pretty good chance you may catch a glimpse of the glamorous actress who shockingly died on August 5, 1962, at age 36, Marilyn Monroe. Numerous guests have reported that while glancing into the mirror they've seen the actress standing behind them, only to turn and find she is gone. Interestingly enough, most visitors, including the ones who have reported seeing Marilyn, are unaware that the mirror was once hung in the very room that Marilyn Monroe frequented.

Is Marilyn the only ghostly presence seen at the Roosevelt? Certainly not; although there are a number of spirits who frequent the hotel, one more notable visitor is actor Montgomery Clift. His presence has been felt primarily on the ninth floor, where loud noises are often heard coming from his old room: 928. One guest even reported being touched on the shoulder from an invisible presence.

It's been said that during the days Montgomery Clift lived at the Roosevelt he was often seen pacing the halls while studying his lines for the movie, *From Here to Eternity*, a movie whose title suggests that, just maybe, Montgomery Clift and perhaps even Marilyn Monroe are rehearsing their lines forever more at the Hollywood Roosevelt Hotel.

TERRIFYING TIDBIT

In many cultures it is believed that mirrors can capture the soul of an individual.

AUGUST 6, 1801
THE BANSHEE
Dublin, Ireland

Sir Jonah and Lady Barrington were attending a party in Dublin Castle. Among the guests was Lord Rossmore, commander-in-chief of British forces in Ireland. Just before the stroke of midnight and after a pleasant evening, Lord Rossmore left. The Barringtons followed suit shortly thereafter, and returned home to retire for the evening. At 2 A.M. they were awakened by what Sir Jonah described as "a plaintive sound" rising from below his window. Throwing the drapes open, he looked out, seeing neither man nor beast, but the mournful sound continued. Finally, at 2:30 A.M., it ceased. A melodic voice called out, sending shivers down his spine, "Rossmore! Rossmore! Rossmore!" Then silence.

The next morning a messenger arrived. Lord Rossmore was dead. Sir Jonah was stunned. After all, he had seen him the night before and he looked in perfect health. He pressed for details and discovered that Rossmore's servant had heard a mournful sound emanating from Lord Rossmore's bedroom. He threw open the door and hurried in, discovering his master in great distress. Lord Rossmore died shortly later, at 2:30 A.M.

Sir Barrington later documented this encounter, writing, "Lord Rossmore was dying at the same moment I heard his name pronounced." What was the strange cry he had heard? His Irish staff advised him that it was the howl of the banshee. The eerie shriek haunted Sir Jonah all the rest of his life.

TERRIFYING TIDBIT

According to Irish folklore, a banshee (woman of the fairies) is a female spirit whose wailing foretells death in a house.

AUGUST 7, 1631
ANNE WALKER
Durham, England

The ghost of Anne Walker, seeking justice, reached out from the grave to get it. In 1631, a widower by the name of John Walker enlisted his relative Anne to keep house for him. Not long after, John seduced her. When she became pregnant, he devised a plot to be rid of her. John convinced Anne to go away with a pitman from Lancashire, Mark Sharp, who, John told her, would see to her care. She would stay in seclusion and be cared for until the baby was born. Trusting her relative, she packed her belongings and left with Mark.

Soon after, John's neighbor, John Grahame, while working by candlelight in his mill, received the fright of his life. The air shifted, his blood ran cold, and the hairs on his neck prickled to attention. To his horror, the ghostly apparition of a woman stood before him, blood pouring from gashes in her head. She told the terrible tale of her demise, giving her name, the name of Grahame's neighbor, John Walker, and the plot her cousin had devised with Mark Sharp. Sharp had lured her to a secluded ravine near the Old Mill Wood and, using a collier's pick, had ended her life as well as the life of her baby. She also named the location where Grahame would find Sharp's blood-soaked socks and the murder weapon and the coal pit where her body could be found.

Before disappearing, Anne made Grahame promise to alert the authorities. He agreed. But when he went home, fearing people would believe him mad, he put her spirit out of his mind. Refusing to be ignored, Anne appeared once again. This time she vowed to haunt him for eternity unless he informed the law. The next morning, keeping his promise, Grahame alerted the authorities. Anne's remains, the murder weapon, and the bloodied socks and shoes were all found just where she'd said.

In August 1631, John Walker and Mark Sharp were arrested and tried for young Anne's murder. Judge Davenport, who presided over the court, sentenced them the same day. Both men were executed. This haunting proves that even in death a woman scorned is a force to be reckoned with.

AUGUST 8, 1797
THE VEILED LADY
Turin, Italy

In 1797, a rather brash artillery lieutenant by the name of Enrico Biandrà was visiting a coffee house when he noticed a very attractive young lady wearing a thin black veil over her face. He approached her, and they spoke. From her accent, it was obvious that she was of foreign descent. After some pleasant conversation, she asked him to escort her home. They parted in front of the San Lazzaro Cemetery. Over the next few days, she visited him at his apartment. After one such visit, she asked once again to be escorted home. This time on their way home, they passed through the San Lazzaro Cemetery. As they were walking, the veiled lady stopped by a grave. She pointed to the tombstone, smiled at Enrico, and faded into the atmosphere. The grave was that of Russian princess Barbara Beloselski, who had died in 1792 at the age of twenty-eight, five years earlier.

The spectral princess appeared several time through the years, and her description given by her new lovers was always consistent with Biandrà's account. Some thirty years after the Biandrà encounter, her grave was moved to another cemetery, but still the sightings continued. In the 1970s her grave was moved again to make way for apartment buildings and a park. And although she has been seen from time to time, we do not have many details of the encounters. Today, we hear little of the veiled lady, making one think that she has finally found her true love.

AUGUST 9, 1812
The Chase Vault
Oistins, Barbados

The Chase family vault is in the cemetery of the Christ Church Parish on the island of Barbados. Built in 1724 for James Elliot, this twelve-by-six-and-one-half-foot underground tomb was never used by him.

In 1807, records show that one Thomasina Goddard, in a wooden coffin, was interred there. A year later, the vault came into possession of the wealthy and influential Chase family. Thomas Chase, patriarch of the family, was well known for his quick temper and his vicious cruelty.

In February 1808, Thomas's two-year-old daughter, Mary Ann, was interred in the vault. Four years later, his other daughter joined her sister. Unlike Goddard, they were both buried in lead coffins. Barely a month later, in August of 1812, Thomas Chase passed away to the delight of many. When they opened the tomb, both of his daughter's coffins had been moved, but Goddard's was undisturbed. They were righted and the tomb was sealed.

Over the next seven years the vault was opened three more times and each time, the coffins were found in disarray.

Finally, the governor, a man named Lord Comberermere, ordered a complete investigation and personally viewed the vault. Unable to explain the movement of the coffins, he ordered the bodies righted and placed a fine layer of sand on the crypt's floor. The door was then cemented and the official seal was applied.

In April 1820, the governor and his staff assembled at the vault and inspected the seal. It was still intact. Without hesitation, he ordered the tomb to be opened. Workmen broke the seal and moved the heavy slab from the entrance. Shock spread through the assembled crowd. Just as in all the previous times, the caskets were tossed all over the vault. Even more mysterious, the sand that was scattered on the floor showed no signs of human activity, nor were there signs of flood or earthquake.

The governor had had enough. He ordered the bodies to be removed and reburied elsewhere in the graveyard. The tomb was abandoned and is still empty today. No other problems were ever reported. It seems that the rest of the family is better off being separated from the likes of Thomas Chase.

AUGUST 10, 1901
PALACE OF VERSAILLES
Paris, France

In August 1901, two English women, Anne Moberly and Eleanor Jourdain, were visiting the Palace of Versailles. During the afternoon, after touring the palace, they set off to visit the Petit Trianon, another house on the property. Unfamiliar with the surroundings, they soon got lost. As they wandered about, something didn't seem right. Anne began to feel depressed. The scenery changed. Peasants, a farmhouse, a gazebo, and people in period dress appeared. Anne and Eleanor crossed a bridge, finding the house. After the tour, they returned to Paris.

Sometime later, they were discussing the trip when Anne showed Eleanor a sketch of a woman she had made at Petit Trianon. Eleanor was surprised because she had not seen the woman in the sketch. Furthermore, when they compared notes there were more discrepancies in their observations of that day. Intrigued by the mystery, they returned to Versailles. Upon their return, they found no bridge, no farmhouse, and no gazebo, at least in 1901. The women learned that they were visiting Versailles on the exact day that the palace was sacked during the French Revolution. And the woman that Anne had sketched was none other than Marie Antoinette. It appears the two women had somehow slipped back in time.

AUGUST 11, 1914
HOUGHTON MANSION
North Adams, Massachusetts

The Houghton Mansion, now a Masonic Temple, was once home to the first mayor of North Adams, Albert C. Houghton, a man who was forced to endure a series of tragic events in a span of eleven days that most people never encounter in their lifetime.

On the morning of August 1, 1914, John Widder, Houghton's chauffeur, was driving Albert and his daughter Mary and two friends, Dr. and Mrs. Sybil Hutton, to Vermont for a leisurely day. As the Pierce-Arrow rounded the mountain road, Widder came upon a work crew. He swerved around them. Unfortunately, when he did, he hit a soft shoulder, and the automobile rolled over three times. Everyone except Mrs. Hutton was thrown from the car. The men suffered minor injuries, but Mrs. Hutton died immediately from the car rolling over on her. And Mary, suffering substantial injuries, including a crushed face, died on the way to the hospital.

The day after the accident, unable to live with his guilt, John Widder committed suicide in the Houghton's barn by shooting himself in the head. Ten days after the accident, Albert C. Houghton was found dead.

Although no one is certain why Albert died, many believe his grief was so palpable he was unable to endure it any longer, and he just gave up.

Today, many visitors to the mansion have encountered the spirits of Mary, John, and Albert. Mary's presence is often felt in her bedroom. It seems she has a favorite chair that she likes to sit in. During an investigation by the New England Ghost Project, temperature gauges were placed around the room and one in her chair. And although the temperature in the room was eighty degrees, the thermometer placed in Mary's chair dropped to fifty-two. And once, during a paranormal conference held at the mansion, one man asked for proof of the spirit's presence; moments later, his more than three-hundred-pound body was lifted and glued to the wall, his toes brushing the floor, as his wife looked on in horror. It just goes to show you, when visiting a haunted location be careful what you ask for—you just might get it.

AUGUST 12, 1886
FAYETTE COUNTY COURTHOUSE
Uniontown, Pennsylvania

There is something strange about the basement of the Fayette County Courthouse. Even the bravest employees dislike the idea of going into the cellar, especially alone. "It always feels like somebody's watching you," one clerk said. Unusual noises and dim lighting is enough to give anybody the chills, but it is the reports of ghosts that send shivers up their spines. From eyewitness accounts collected through the years, three specters seem to be inhabiting the basement: an employee of the district attorney's office who was murdered there, a suspect who was allegedly beaten to death during an interrogation, and a convicted murderer named Monaghan. In 1886, Monaghan was convicted of first-degree murder in the death of his cousin, a bank robber. According to court records, he stole his cousin's loot and then murdered him. He professed his innocence, but justice prevailed. He was hanged from the clock tower.

From 1795 until 1914 many other criminals met their maker from the "gallows" of the clock tower. During one of these hangings, a convicted man was hanged five minutes early, before he could make his death statement. But with his last breath he put a curse on the tower. Since that day, no matter how many times the county has attempted to repair it, the four clocks of the tower are always five to ten minutes off. It seems that the old saying that "time waits for no man" doesn't apply to the Fayette County Courthouse.

AUGUST 13, 1831
THE MANSION OF TORTURE
New Orleans, Louisiana

The presumed epitome of high society, Lalaurie Delphine, owner of the Lalaurie mansion on Royal Street, was reputed to have an evil side. But it was her cook who would finally put an end to her cruel ways. Chained to the kitchen floor, the cook started a fire, attracting the attention of the local fire department.

When help arrived, they were horrified with what they found. The firefighters discovered punishment rooms with victims of macabre treatment still chained inside, barely alive. For her own amusement Lalaurie had cut off ears and various body parts of her slaves. Some poor souls were disemboweled. Others had their eyes and mouths sewn shut.

With the discovery of her cruelty, Lalaurie was forced to flee New Orleans.

In the years since, during renovations, workers have discovered numerous skeletal remains in the mansion's floors and walls. And these poor souls who perished at the hands of Delphine still haunt the mansion. The clanking of chains being dragged down the steps has been heard. Agonizing screams and groans radiate from the attic. And one visitor of the mansion awoke with a start to find hands encircling his throat. He claims that while he was being strangled the spirit of a black woman appeared and came to his rescue. His protector removed the offender's hands and then both spirits disappeared.

The haunting, it seems, is not confined solely within the mansion's walls. Passersby of this three-story mansion have witnessed a young black girl jump to her death. Sadly, she is believed to be the ghost of a slave who escaped her chains, choosing to end her life before her insane mistress could end it for her.

AUGUST 14, 1938
BEGGING FOR MERCY
New Orleans, Louisiana

In 1938, Reverend Howard Randle's philandering ways came back to haunt him. His wife, Lucinda, had always been a very jealous person. But then again, it appears she had reason to be. Not only had the good Reverend been spotted frequenting the local bordellos, but he apparently was deep into an affair with a young woman. His poor wife, tortured by her husband's infidelity, prayed for him to change. When he didn't, she did the only other thing she could do. She sought out the help of a local witch doctor, Dr. Rockford Lewis, who had a solution to put an end to Lucinda's anguish once and for all. She was to put a powder in his drink, and soon, her beloved would become impotent.

The next morning, Lucinda did as the doctor prescribed. However, as soon as her husband began to drink the solution, the guilt was too much for her to bear. Lucinda, uncertain how her husband's body would respond to the potion and horrified at the thought that she'd been duped by the local witch doctor and that the concoction was in fact a poison, confessed all. But not only did she confess her sins, she pleaded with her husband to end *her* life. This way they could be together forever. Hand in hand, they walked out to their favorite spot on the levee. They took a seat on a bench, where Lucinda turned her gaze to the river and laid her head upon her husband's lap. Silently, he retrieved a knife out of his coat pocket, and when Lucinda's eyes were closed, he slit her throat.

Unfortunately for the Reverend, the poison wasn't a poison after all. He later told the police the sad, sordid tale. And perhaps he prayed for his own demise, while he spent the remainder of his days behind bars.

There are many who say that even today they can still see the apparition of the poor, tortured soul of Lucinda, as she strolls the river's edge, waiting for her husband's ghost to join her.

AUGUST 15, 1693
DOG TOWN
Gloucester, Massachusetts

Dog Town, settled by sailors from Gloucester in 1693, was once a thriving town. During the War of 1812 many townsmen were killed. Since there were fewer men in town, many of the widows bought dogs for protection. Eventually they moved out, leaving the town to the dregs of society and the dogs, hence the name Dog Town. Prostitutes and witches soon inhabited it. Some wealthy men who went to Dog Town to avail themselves of its services never returned. The witches would also extort money and goods from people passing through the town, threatening them with spells if they did not pay. As the town began to decay and the houses collapsed, its inhabitants eventually took up living in the cellar holes. Finally the town was abandoned. Some years later, a wealthy businessman bought the town to preserve its remains. He researched the history of Dog Town and wrote a book. He eventually hired unemployed stonecutters to carve numbers into stones to preserve each of the cellar holes. He also had inspirational phrases, such as "kindness," "spiritual power," and others carved into the rocks. Many paranormal occurrences have been reported there. Seen by many as a dead zone, equipment fails and a deadly silence hangs heavy in the forest. With so much paranormal activity reported within Dog Town, one has to wonder if the witches still remain.

AUGUST 16, 1977
THE KING
Nashville, Tennessee

Elvis Presley, the king of rock and roll, may be gone, but he's certainly not forgotten. The king's ghostly apparition has been seen on numerous occasions. But it seems his spirit is just as busy in the afterlife as it was while he was alive. Although he's been known to frequent his beloved Memphis home, he's also been seen several times at locations he once performed at: the Las Vegas Hilton and a former RCA recording studio not far from the infamous Nashville Music Row, the same building where in 1956 Elvis recorded his hit single "Heartbreak Hotel."

TERRIFYING TIDBIT

The last book Elvis ever read, the one he died reading, was none other than *The Scientific Search for the Face of Jesus* by Frank Adams.

The building, now a television production studio, has encountered the unexplainable on several occasions. According to workers at the building, whenever Elvis's name is mentioned, things begin to go awry. Lights have blown out. Ladders have fallen over. Indescribable noises have emanated from the sound systems. Also, the ghostly image of Elvis dressed in white with sequins galore has been seen on several occasions. Elvis's ghost brings a new meaning to "the show must go on!"

AUGUST 17, 1855
WICKEN FEN
Wicken, Cambridgeshire, England

Wicken Fen is a wetland reserve near the village of Wicken. Several battles were fought near here and visitors have seen the ghostly apparitions of Normans and Romans alike. But it isn't the long-lost soldiers that strike fear into the hearts of travelers. It's the phantoms of the "lantern men." Strange lights among the tall reeds have been seen dancing and twisting in the pale moonlight. They are evil spirits intent on luring unsuspecting mortals to a hideous death and a watery grave deep within their swampy domain.

Perhaps that's how police constable Richard Peake met his demise. In 1855, while investigating a disturbance near the ruins of a nearby abbey, he disappeared, never to be seen again. Was he a victim of foul play or just another victim of the lantern men of Wicken Fen?

TERRIFYING TIDBIT

The lantern men were believed to be shadowy spirits who used their light to lure travelers from the pathways into the marshes to drown.

AUGUST 18, 2009
BROOKDALE LODGE
Santa Cruz, California

Brookdale Lodge, nestled within the Santa Cruz Mountains, is reportedly haunted by dozens of spectral visitors. The Brookdale Inn and Spa, as it's now named, has a natural brook running through the building. For its unique rustic appeal, the lodge was once featured in *Ripley's Believe It or Not*. The publicity attracted the rich and famous, bringing with it such notables as: Marilyn Monroe, Mae West, Joan Crawford, Rita Hayworth, and Herbert Hoover, to name a few.

But it was during the gangster era of the 1940s that the Brookdale Lodge became home to many unsavory characters, with rumors of bodies buried beneath the floor, tunnels erected, and secret passageways built within its walls. It was also during this period that a six-year-old girl, Sarah Logan, the niece of owner H. J. Logan, drowned in the indoor creek. It's Sarah's spirit that guests still see running through the lodge in her Sunday best. Her ghostly apparition has also been seen sitting by the fireplace, her image so clear that guests have reported approaching the crying child to offer their assistance, only to have her vanish before their eyes.

Sarah Logan is but one visitor to the lodge. The sound of big band music playing in the distance is often heard. And many visitors have reported the sighting of ethereal ballroom dancers twirling in midair, only to vanish moments later. The most active area of the lodge is said to be room 46. This room was built over a previous camping cabin. One woman while staying in the room spoke of objects flying of their own accord, followed by the ghastly image of floating spectral heads, one with a gash to his face, the other, with his eye hanging loose of its socket.

With the plethora of paranormal activity, it appears that some of the Lodge's more interesting characters have checked in, but never checked out.

AUGUST 19, 1998
THE DOPPELGANGER
Quebec, Canada

One night, a ten-year-old boy woke up to use the bathroom. He was a little scared to get up by himself in the middle of the night, but finally, gathering his courage, he left his bedroom and made his way to the bathroom. To do so, he had to walk the length of the hallway, which passed by a galley-style (long and thin) kitchen. As he did, he turned to see his mother, or so he thought, sitting at the end of the table, her back toward him as she smoked her cigarette, something she frequently did. He knew it was her by the way the moonlight filtered through the curtains, highlighting her body as the smoke curled up and over her head.

On his way back from the bathroom, he stopped at the kitchen; he was going to ask his mother to tuck him back into bed. But although he could still see the curling wisps of smoke, his mother was nowhere to be found. Believing he would catch her before she went back to bed, he ran to her bedroom. She was asleep. Confused, he shook her awake and said, "Mom, how come you're asleep already. I just saw you in the kitchen."

Surprised by her son's words, the young boy and his mother went to the kitchen to investigate. And although the ashtray on the table was empty, both mother and son could still smell the scent of tobacco lingering in the air.

TERRIFYING TIDBIT
A doppelganger is a ghost that takes on the form of a living person.

AUGUST 20, 1877
SHANGHAI TUNNELS
Portland, Oregon

Underground tunnels buried beneath the streets of Portland, Oregon, are believed to be one of the most haunted locations in America. Since it's well known that haunting and history go hand and hand, it's no surprise that these secret passageways and old holding cells would be overflowing with paranormal phenomena. According to A&E, a world of terror lay beneath the streets of Portland from the 1870s to the 1940s. The term "shanghaied" originated at this time when drunk or unsuspecting men and women fell through trap doors on the street. A crimmper (someone who abducts for profit) would then seize the victim and haul him or her away. More often than not, the prisoner was beaten, raped, and sold to the highest bidder. A special process to break the spirit of strong-willed women was created. The women were locked in a darkened four-by-four cell. Their shoes were removed and the floor of the cell was littered with crushed glass, a deterrent to escape. Once the women were made ready, they were sold as prostitutes to other countries. But that's not all. The numerous passageways and rooms in the tunnels were also opium dens, places where clients could escape the scrutinizing eye of the law.

But are these tunnels haunted? Many say yes. Today, these underground dirt channels have become a paranormal enthusiast's playground. Many who have taken the tour have reported feeling ill. Others have said they've felt an uncomfortable feeling of adrenalin coursing through their system, as they have an inexplicable desire to escape something unseen. There have also been reports that a few of the tourist guides have experienced so frightful an ordeal with the otherworldly that they've quit on the spot, refusing to return. However, if you find yourself intrigued, and plan to visit this haunted location, do not venture off on your own. The ghost of the ever vigilant crimmper may claim you as his next victim.

AUGUST 21, 1948
GOODLEBERG CEMETERY
Wales, New York

In an old house next to the cemetery lived a doctor who allegedly performed illegal abortions out of his home. According to the story, "Doctor Goodleberg," as he was called, disposed of the fetuses and the occasional mother that didn't survive within the cemetery and the creek adjoining his home. In August 1948, Helen Lindeman, the wife of a dentist, disappeared. Over the next few weeks, parts of her dissected body began showing up in a creek near the cemetery. Goodleberg's house was searched, but the results were not revealed. Soon after, and under mysterious circumstances, the doctor was found dead. Some say he died of a heart attack, while others claim he hanged himself in the cemetery. Many agree that the evil doctor and other ghastly phantoms haunt Goodleberg Cemetery.

Some have seen weeping mothers roaming the grassy knolls of the cemetery, looking for their lost children, while translucent forms of infants have been seen crawling between the gravestones, their sad cries echoing in the darkness. Even the doctor has been seen hanging there.

Many paranormal investigators have come looking for the doctor. They hear voices and cries, and catch strange lights on their cameras. One investigator reported his horror at returning to his car to find it covered with tiny handprints from some unseen children. Sadly, the abhorrent acts of the doctor linger to this day.

AUGUST 22, 1857
THE WHALEY HOUSE
San Diego, California

Entrepreneur Thomas Whaley built the Whaley House in 1857, but it was more than just the family home. At various times during its history, it has housed a granary, theater, ballroom, business parlor, courthouse, polling place, and general store. But as soon as the Whaley family moved into the home, they became haunted by a dark past. The land that the house stood on was formerly used for the town's gallows. It wasn't long before the family began hearing the sounds of disembodied footsteps. Thomas attributed them to the ghost of James "Jim Yankee" Robinson, who was hanged in 1852. But that should have come as no surprise to him, since he was a spectator at the hanging. Jim Yankee began to be a regular guest at the house and was seen or felt by most of the family members. In 1960, the house became a museum and the paranormal activity continued.

Lights flicker, sometimes turning on and off of their own accord. Faces appear in mirrors. The odor of cigar smoke and perfume permeates the air. And the cries of a baby and music can be heard. But the apparitions are what make the Whaley House truly haunted.

A little girl, believed to be a childhood friend of the Whaley children, haunts the kitchen. Jim Yankee has been seen in the hall, and Thomas Whaley appears at the top of the stairs. It is even believed that their dog Dolly Varden can be seen scampering around the building. Although the Whaley family no longer lives in the house, to most visitors to the museum it seems that they have never left.

AUGUST 23, 1976
BANFF SPRINGS HOTEL
Calgary, Alberta, Canada

Like many other Canadian hotels, the Banff Springs was constructed by the railroad, in this case the Canadian Pacific Railway. In the 1930s it became a popular destination for the rich and famous. But who haunts it now?

The most helpful ghost is that of a bellman named Sam Macauley. Macauley died in 1976, but that doesn't stop him from helping guests with their bags, opening doors, or turning the lights on for them. Any time someone tries to tip him, he vanishes.

And then there is the phantom bartender, who frequently informs customers that they've had too much to drink, and should go to bed. However, before having a chance to argue, he disappears.

But it's the rumors about the dark spirits inhabiting room 873 that will make the little hairs on your neck stand to attention. The story goes that a family was murdered there. Bloody fingerprints appear on its mirrors, and no matter how hard the staff worked to remove them, they continually returned. Finally, no longer able to endure the paranormal phenomena, the management bricked up the door.

The hotel has changed hands, and the new management doesn't like to talk about the ghosts, but of course, they cannot prevent the stories their guests carry out.

AUGUST 24, A.D. 79
POMPEII
Naples, Italy

Pompeii was a cosmopolitan port city on the Gulf of Naples. It traded in olive oil, wine, and slaves, had a community of 20,000, and stood in the shadow of the volcano Mount Vesuvius. The Roman city was home of the oldest amphitheater in the empire, where gladiators and animals died for the amusement of its citizens.

In A.D. 79, on a hot August day, a column of superheated steam and ash surged 9 miles into the sky. Ironically the city was celebrating the Festival of Vulcanalia, the Roman god of fire. The pumice from the angry volcano rained on the city like a light snowstorm. As the day grew longer the eruption grew more violent, until it was 100,000 times more powerful than the atomic bomb dropped on Hiroshima. It spewed tons of stone, magma, ash, and toxic gas on the frightened city. In twenty-four hours it was over. The city was destroyed and buried beneath ash. Ten thousand people died that day.

In 1594, an engineer constructing an aqueduct discovered one of Pompeii's buildings, thus initiating one of the world's great archaeological finds. The ash and earth were carefully carted away, revealing the terror that overtook the city that day. Men, women, and children were discovered frozen in time, their bodies petrified in their final acts. Their outer flesh had been preserved by the ash, as their internal organs had liquefied.

Today much of the city has been excavated. As you walk among the ruins, the ghosts of that day come to life. A faint wisp of sulfur, shadows darting in the corner of your eye, and the terrifying screams from disembodied victims fill the air. The dead of Pompeii are reborn.

AUGUST 25, 1862
LEMP MANSION
RESTAURANT AND INN
St. Louis, Missouri

If a recipe for hauntings includes suicides, then the Lemp Mansion in St. Louis is guaranteed to be a soufflé of the paranormal. The Lemps, who were the first Americans to brew a lager beer, have seen their share of pain and misery. The Lemp family lost four of its members to suicide, three of which took place within the mansion. Perhaps this could explain the plethora of paranormal activity that is witnessed by patrons of the restaurant and inn. Ragtime melodies play on an ethereal piano, drinks stir themselves, glasses are thrown through midair by some unseen force, and lights turn on and off by themselves.

Are the bouts of paranormal activity associated with the tragic history, or, perhaps the oddities surrounding the design of the building? When venturing into the basement of the mansion, you will find not only a swimming pool, but also an auditorium and ballroom that have been built into the structure of a natural cavern. And, although now closed due to inherent danger, a tunnel once existed that led from the mansion directly to the brewery. Regardless of the reasons why, one thing is known for sure: the Lemp Mansion has been listed as "one of the most haunted places in America."

AUGUST 26, 2009
THE VENETIAN THEATRE
Hillsboro, Oregon

In 1888, the First National Bank of Hillsboro was built. When the bank moved to another location in 1911, the mayor, Orange Phelps, purchased the building. Phelps converted the structure into the Grand Theater. However, in 1925, fire destroyed the building. Undeterred, Phelps restored it to its original beauty and gave it a new name, The Venetian Theatre.

According to an article published in the *Hillsboro Argus*, the Venetian is extremely haunted. Co-owner Saxony Peterson states when the theatre is closing down for the night, the staff is required to make rounds ensuring the building is empty. However, sometimes it's not. Sitting in the farthest back rows is the ghostly image of a gray-haired gentleman who disappears when approached. Often staff will shut off the lights and music on the upper floors for the evening, yet before they even have a chance to make it down the stairs, everything is on again. Once, workers reported that all the activity in the kitchen had to be halted due to water pouring from the ceiling. After the mess was cleaned up, they investigated further. Removing the ceiling tiles, they were astonished to find that not only were the tiles dry, but also no water pipes were in site. In fact, there was nothing that could logically explain the source of the flooding. Another employee spoke of her contact with the spirit in the auditorium. While she checked the exit doors, a blast of cold air swept past her. With it, she heard a distinct whisper in her left ear. But exactly who are the spirits that frequent the Venetian? With its lengthy history, we may never know for sure.

AUGUST 27, 1963
SHEPPTON MINE DISASTER
Hazleton, Pennsylvania

A full recount of the Sheppton mine disaster was reported in the *Hazleton Standard-Speaker* on August 27, 2002. Thirty-nine years after the incredibly tragic, yet divinely spiritual rescue. Two men had been entombed within the Sheppton mine for fourteen days. David Fellin and Hank Throne, wearing football helmets and parachute harnesses, were guided through a borehole to safety on the morning of August 27, 1963. When their fourteen-day ordeal was revealed to the public, the strange revelations of their experiences surfaced.

Fellin, who was fifty-eight at the time, recalled Throne, the twenty-four-year-old worker he'd been buried alive with, saying they ought not speak of their experiences, for fear of people thinking they were crazy. David Fellin, however, thought the world should know who had given them the strength to survive. Both men, interviewed separately, described with amazing accuracy their visitor, who had stayed with them during the last eight days of their ordeal when they'd all but given up. Who was the dedicated spirit that made its presence known? None other than Pope John XXIII, who had died just weeks before. David recalled a span of time when he left his body, saw a beautiful marble door, and witnessed scores of Egyptian men going about their work. He was in awe at the sight before him, as he studied the men building the pyramids. He went on to say that the Egyptians did not move the stones as many people over the centuries have surmised. Rather, twenty-five men carrying buckets of sand and water poured the mix into wooden forms and built each multiton block one at a time.

There may be some that think Fellin and Throne were hallucinating. Fellin swore an oath on the Bible, that everything he experienced while trapped in the mine was true. He passed at least two polygraph tests. Recently, in 2002, a researcher studying the pyramids shared his revelation that, just as David Fellin had seen, each block was created from "cement" being poured into a form.

AUGUST 28, 1837
LIBERTY HALL MUSEUM
Frankfurt, Kentucky

Senator John Brown built the hauntingly beautiful Liberty Hall in 1796. It remained in the Brown family for generations before being willed to the Colonial Dames of America in 1955. This home turned museum has since been a staple of Kentucky's history. But who is the illustrious "Lady in Gray" that so many visitors to Liberty Hall have witnessed seeing? Margaretta van Varrick, also known as Margaret, was the aunt of John Brown's wife, whose assistance was requested after a death in the family. Sadly, only days after her arrival, Margaretta died of a heart attack. Her remains were buried in a small family plot located on the property. But later when the plot was relocated, Margaretta's body was lost. Soon after, the first reports of a ghostly apparition referred to as "The Lady in Gray" began. The first to report the sighting was Rebecca, a visitor to Liberty Hall who stayed the night in Margaretta's old bedroom. She awoke with a start to find a woman standing next to the fireplace. She was so terrified she hid beneath her covers. When she regained her courage, she stole a peek, but the woman was gone. She'd vanished into thin air. Many visitors who have slept in the haunted bedroom have had similar experiences. Other visitors to the museum have reported seeing "The Lady in Gray" peering out of the upstairs windows. A skeptical college professor in search of an explanation for the odd occurrences stayed overnight. To his surprise he was awakened by a gentle touch upon his shoulder and confronted by the transparent image of a woman smiling down at him. The professor's perception of the paranormal was changed that night, by "The Lady in Gray."

AUGUST 29, 1989
U.S. COURTHOUSE
Pittsburgh, Pennsylvania

United States District Judge Gerald J. Weber was a stern man with a dry sense of humor. Many described him as a "character," larger than life. He served as chief judge for the district court from 1976 to 1982. His most notable decision was Gerald Mayo vs. Satan and His Staff. In this case, a man attempted to sue Satan and his staff for causing him "misery and unwarranted threat" and "depriving him of his constitutional rights." The case was dismissed on a technicality.

Weber died from cancer in 1989, but it appears the judge doesn't know he's dead. Workers at the Grant Street courthouse have reported the judge's presence throughout the building, especially on the fourth floor. Cleaning crews have heard their names called out, only to find no one is there.

The elevator inexplicably stops on the fourth floor. The doors open and close, then it continues on to its destination. The faint aroma of cigar smoke lingers in the air. (The judge smoked six cigars a day despite the objections of fellow passengers on the elevator.)

There have been several reports of airy figures in black robes roaming the building. But what makes people think it is Judge Weber? An electrician was on the fourth floor working on a ladder when he was approached by a man in a black robe who said, "How's it going?" When he turned around to reply, the man was gone. The worker saw the robed phantom several more times that night. Finally, he became so disturbed by it that he reported it to the security guard. He was even able to identify him as Judge Weber from his portrait. Evidently the judge's dry sense of humor fell short on the worker. The man left the building, never to return again.

AUGUST 30, 1986
THE HAUNTING OF JACK
AND JANET SMURL
West Pittston, Pennsylvania

In 1973, Jack Smurl; his wife, Janet; and their two daughters, Dawn and Hanna, decided to move into a duplex in West Pittston with Jack's parents. At first their ordinary household flourished. After renovating their new home, they finally settled in. Soon after, Janet gave birth to twin girls. Life couldn't be happier. However, things soon changed in January 1974, when, out of nowhere, the family began to experience a series of strange phenomena. Irremovable stains appeared on the carpets. New bathroom fixtures developed deep scratches. Although soldered several times, water pipes continuously leaked. And then one day the irritating events took a turn for the worse when their television spontaneously combusted. Soon after, Jack was attacked by something unseen. All this paranormal activity convinced the Smurl family that they were being plagued by a demonic presence.

Soon the word of the Smurl family haunting spread, and they were they subject of a media explosion. Some neighbors, after witnessing the phenomena for themselves, sympathized with the Smurls. Others accused them of falsifying the truth in order to make money on a book deal.

TERRIFYING TIDBIT

An exorcism is a ritual performed to drive out a demonic presence from a person, place, or thing.

One day, while in the basement, Janet heard her name called out. She responded, but no one was there. As if it had been invited in, the entity grew bolder. Dark shadows began to slither through the home. The children were tossed down the stairs. The family dog was repeatedly lifted and thrown against the wall. And loud scratching could be heard at all hours of the day and night.

No longer able to withstand the torment, in 1986, the Smurl family reached out to demonologists, Ed and Lorraine Warren. The Warrens investigated and believed the home contained four entities, one of which was pure evil. For a short period of time, holy water and prayer was the only thing that quieted the demonic presence. But soon, the Warrens realized that was not going to be nearly enough.

Evidently angered with the Smurls, the evil presence began physically attacking them. Some members of the family were bitten and their arms slashed. The Warrens called in the services of Father McKenna, who performed a total of three exorcisms. And although their torment seemed to end, it started up once again in December 1986. Finally, in 1988, the Church performed what would be the fourth and final exorcism. At last, the Smurl family was released from the darkness that had plagued them for over thirteen years.

AUGUST 31, 1888
JACK THE RIPPER'S
FIRST VICTIM
London, England

Mary Ann Nichols was the first of many to be murdered by the serial killer, Jack the Ripper.

Just after midnight on the night of her death, Mary Ann Nichols was seen at a local pub looking for lodging. However, without the funds to procure a bed for the evening, she was forced to venture out into the streets of London yet again, this time in search of customers willing to pay for her favors.

The next time Mary was seen was when her body was discovered in the entrance of a stable on Buck's Row. Constable John Neil was the man to sound the alarm of Mary's murder, and he bore witness to the horrific way in which she met her death. Found with her legs out straight and her skirt raised to her waist, Mary's abdomen had been severely slashed and ripped. Further inspection of Mary's body showed that her throat had been cut from ear to ear. The gash was so deep that vertebrae were nearly visible.

Although Buck's Row has evolved over the years, on numerous occasions, a ghostly, green apparition lying on the ground has been reported. The sightings match the exact spot at which Mary's corpse was found. As with many traumatic deaths, it seems that the soul of poor Mary Anne Nichols continues to wander this earthly plane in search of justice.

SEPTEMBER 1, 1990
THE WHITE LADY
Easton, Connecticut

According to locals as well as paranormal enthusiasts, Union Cemetery is a hot bed of paranormal activity. Reportedly, the spirit of a woman, referred to as "the White Lady of Easton," haunts this graveyard.

In fact, one night, a Connecticut fireman traveling down the road adjacent to the cemetery nearly lost control of his vehicle trying to avoid the figure in white that stood smack dab in the center of the road. He slammed on his brakes, but to no avail. He hit it. Once stopped, he jumped out of his car to see what he'd hit, but to his amazement there was no one in the road, and there was no evidence to suggest he'd actually hit anything. Rattled, he bent to look beneath the car but could see no body, human or otherwise. Whatever he'd hit left little trace behind. There were no bodily fluids to indicate anyone or anything had been harmed. Apparently, the "victim" just vanished into thin air. On another night, famed ghost hunters Ed and Lorraine Warren heard a woman weeping while they were investigating the cemetery. With his video camera rolling, Ed captured what appeared to be the apparition of the White Lady of Easton. Later, while researching the history of the cemetery, they discovered that in the 1800s, a woman's body, a murder victim, was dumped nearby. They are now convinced that she is the White Lady.

SEPTEMBER 2, 1895
BELCOURT CASTLE
Newport, Rhode Island

Eccentric Oliver Belmont finished building Belcourt Castle in 1894. He had such little regard for his neighbors that he built the estate with its back to them. This 50,000-square-foot estate had sixty rooms, one bedroom, and no kitchen. It is said that all of his meals were delivered from town. And the first floor, oddly enough, had been outfitted to house his beloved steeds.

Over the years, the mansion passed through several hands until the Tinney family purchased it in 1956. Harold Tinney and his wife, Ruth, moved into the castle with their beautiful antiques and reproductions. But are the antiques responsible for the haunting of the castle, or, is it the castle itself that is haunted?

The ballroom appears to be the heart of all the paranormal activity. Visitors have caught the movement of shadows out of the corner of their eye. Furniture has moved of its own accord. And once, when Ruth went to turn the lights on, a loud scream emanated from within the room, a scream that continued with each attempt to turn on the light. Finally, she decided to wait for her husband to arrive before trying again.

Certain items appear to be more haunted than others. Echoes of horrific screams have risen from suits of armor dating back to the 1500s. A statue of a monk has been the source of numerous sightings.

A full-bodied apparition wearing a brown robe has been seen near the statue. And two chairs once used by kings have caused quite a stir. Many a male visitor who has tried to take a seat has either felt an odd pressure preventing them from sitting fully or has been altogether shoved out of the chair. Evidently the spirits inhabiting this castle have room for only one king.

SEPTEMBER 3, 1777
COOCHES BRIDGE
Newark, Delaware

The site of the only skirmish with the British on Delaware soil took place at Cooches Bridge. Two miles south of the bridge, on August 30, 1777, the engagement between 700 colonials and the British forces that had landed at Turkey Point in Maryland ensued. Outnumbered by the Redcoats, the Americans pulled back. Under the command of General William Maxwell, 100 handpicked marksmen were tasked with lying in wait for the advancing British forces. Although horribly outnumbered, their mission was to create a diversion, buying time for George Washington's troop to flee Philadelphia. On September 3 the men waited in the dense brush for the Redcoats to advance. As they approached the bridge, the militiamen made a stance against the British on Cooches Bridge. Soon their ammunition was depleted, however, and the Americans retreated. Yet it seems that not all of the marksmen left the bridge that fateful day. Legend has it that during the battle one militiaman's head was blown off. And in the dim light of a moonless sky, he can still be seen walking the bridge in search of his head.

SEPTEMBER 4, 1840
OLD PRESQUE ISLE LIGHTHOUSE
Presque Isle, Michigan

Old Presque Isle Lighthouse is said to be haunted by the ghost of George Parris, the former property keeper. The lighthouse was in service for only thirty-one years when it was abandoned. In 1977, George and Lorraine Parris moved into the small keeper's house where they looked after the grounds and provided guided tours to vacationers. In 1979, the Coast Guard removed the wiring in the lighthouse, yet when George died in 1991, a mysterious light began to appear in the tower—or not so mysterious according to Lorraine. She believes that George is still there. Sailors, pilots, and many others have seen the eerie light in the tower of the lighthouse. The Coast Guard investigated it further and couldn't find any worldly cause for the light. George makes himself known in other ways as well, according to his wife, who continued with her duties after his death. When he was alive, he made her bacon and eggs in the morning. And after his death, there were many times she was awakened by the smell of bacon cooking, always to find that no one was there. "I knew it was him," she said.

SEPTEMBER 5, 1922
THE WINCHESTER HOUSE
San Jose, California

This Victorian mansion located in downtown Santa Clara, California, is surrounded by legends of hauntings and the results of a wealthy woman's paranoid fears of the paranormal. Sarah Winchester, the eccentric Winchester Rifle heiress, built the mansion after she'd met with Boston medium Adam Coons. During their session, the medium confirmed Sarah's worst fears. Coons told Sarah that her husband's, as well as her daughter's death from tuberculosis were in fact the result of a curse. He believed that all the souls that had been killed by a Winchester rifle were out to get revenge. And Sarah was next.

As a way to put an end to the curse, Coons directed Sarah to move out West where she should build a home for the spirits. As long as the home was being built, she would be safe. A fearful Sarah soon moved to San Jose, where she acquired an eight-room farmhouse. She then began building a mansion. Its construction went on twenty-four hours a day, seven days a week, and it would continue for thirty-eight years. Today this 160-room mansion has 40 staircases, 950 doors, 10,000 windows, and 47 fireplaces. The list of oddities for this mouse maze of construction goes on and on.

One of the most peculiar rooms is the séance room. It is in this room that Sarah is said to have held nightly séances, seeking construction advice from the spirits who lost their lives to the Winchester rifle.

Visitors and tour guides of the mansion have reported the inexplicable eerie sound of organ music. Doorknobs have turned of their own accord. Strange lights have been witnessed illuminating the darkened hallways. And along with the frequently heard unexplainable voices, some visitors have described the sudden appearance of an ectoplasmic mist. It appears that Sarah, who died at the mansion at age eighty-three, still fearing the ghosts of the victims of Winchester rifles, is afraid to leave this earthly plane.

TERRIFYING TIDBIT

Ectoplasm is believed to be caused by the manifestation of spiritual energy.

SEPTEMBER 6, 1978
THE HAUNTED MIRROR
St. Francisville, Louisiana

The most well-known ghost at Myrtle's Plantation is that of a young, blond girl named Chloe, but even more strange is the haunted mirror hanging in the hallway. According to legend, Chloe was frolicking down the stairs when she stopped to glance at her reflection. At that very instant, she was shot and killed by an unknown assailant. It is said that the mirror captured her spirit, and there it will remain until the day she looks upon the face of her killer.

TERRIFYING TIDBIT

In 1605, John Dee, a well-known alchemist, used a mirror for scrying (a method of seeing the future). He is credited with foretelling the plot to kill King James.

Today numerous visitors to the plantation have claimed to see the little girl's ghost trapped within the mirror. She has been described as being about nine years of age and having blond hair. Sometimes her reflection is seen walking or kneeling on the stairs. Yet whenever they turn around to look at the staircase, no one is there. Quite often, the sound of a young girl singing or crying emanates from the mirror. The sad truth, however, is that the tragic event occurred many years ago, so it is possible Chloe will never get to look upon her killer and will forever be stuck in the mirror.

SEPTEMBER 7, 1989
THE DECAPITATED GHOST
Paris, France

Soon after a young couple moved into their new home on the south side of Paris, a headless specter made her presence known. Standing before them with her head in her hands, with blinking eyes and a moving mouth, she screamed at them to get out. She told the young couple they didn't belong there. At first, they thought they were crazy, but when the ghost returned for the next six nights in a row, the terrified couple ran to the safety of a motel. In their interview with *Weekly World News*, Louis Gaits and his wife Belinda told the reporter they intended on hiring an attorney to nullify their mortgage agreement. Although the real estate company refused to comment, a spokesman stated that the couple was well aware of the legends surrounding the 150-year-old home and were warned to take the information seriously. But who is this ghostly phantom? As reported by historian Guy Bujon, a seventy-three-year-old spinster named Catherine Didry was the victim of a brutal attack in her home in 1898, when she was raped and decapitated. Now her restless spirit is said to roam the earthly plane looking for justice. Unfortunately for future owners of this home, the atrocities done to Catherine Didry will forever remain unsolved.

SEPTEMBER 8, 1565
OUR LADY OF LECHE CHURCH
St. Augustine, Florida

The nation's oldest city, St. Augustine, Florida, is home to Our Lady of Leche Church. This peaceful, yet haunted, Spanish-style chapel is located in an area also referred to as "America's Most Sacred Acre." In fact, on September 8, 1565, the first Catholic mass in the Americas took place at this beloved chapel.

But what of the hauntings? Many a visitor has witnessed the ghostly apparition of a nun kneeling in prayer who is said to dissolve into thin air when approached. She has also been seen walking around the mission's grounds. Could it be one of the multitude of nuns that are buried in the area surrounding the church? Many believe so. Has her devotion to God breached the barrier between life and death? No one knows for sure. One thing, however, is certain; many visitors to Our Lady of Leche Church offer up prayers of quiet reflection with the hopes that they too will be among the blessed few to be graced by her presence.

SEPTEMBER 9, 1983
THE ROCK-THROWING POLTERGEIST
Tucson, Arizona

The torment of the Berkbigler family began in September 1983 when seemingly out of nowhere rocks began to be hurled at the family of five. It all started one evening around 5:30 P.M., when they first heard the sound of the stones being thrown from the roof and ran outside to investigate. At first, they thought it was a vagrant trying to scare them out of their new home. But no one could be found.

Soon tiring of the unexplainable phenomenon, they reached out to friends and family and finally the sheriff's department. They too became increasingly frustrated with the unseen culprit, especially since they and their vehicles too were pelted by the stones when investigating. And still, no perpetrator could be apprehended.

In November, Rick, the father, intent on finding answers, gathered a group of people to search the grounds while the rock throwing was going on. That's when things went from bad to worse. During the search one of the helpers was struck in the jaw by a rock. Hearing what they thought was movement in the brush, the men ran toward it. Just then, another rock was strewn, this time striking Rick's father in the head and knocking him unconscious. Fed up, the men picked up rocks of their own and began wildly throwing the stones at the bush. But when all was over, there was still no physical person found to explain the assault.

In December, a television crew interested in the odd occurrences began to film the activity. Sure enough, out of nowhere, rocks sailed through the air. This time the Berkbiglers' twenty-one-month-old daughter, Anita, was struck. Luckily, she was unharmed.

The unexplained poltergeist activity lasted for a span of a few weeks, then it abruptly stopped. Rick's wife, Mary, speculated that the home might be built over a sacred burial ground. So far no other explanation has presented itself.

SEPTEMBER 10, 1641
THE SCREAMING SKULL
OF WARDLEY HALL
Wardley Hall, Worsley, England

There are a series of screaming skulls throughout England. Many are shrouded in mystery, but not the Screaming Skull of Wardley Hall. This skull belongs to Father Ambrose Barlow. The fourth son of a nobleman, Ambrose was born in 1585. His family reluctantly converted to Protestantism during Britain's great suppression of Catholicism. In 1605, he converted back to Catholicism and became a priest. On March 7, 1641, Charles I signed a decree, proclaiming that all priests should leave the country or face arrest for treason. Despite the urging of his congregation, Ambrose decided to remain. On Easter Sunday in 1641 he was arrested. Found guilty of treason, he was hanged and then drawn and quartered. His head was removed and placed on display at Lancaster Castle. The skull was secretly removed and taken to Wardley Hall and hidden. It was forgotten and lost for some time, until the owner of the mansion discovered it in the 1800s. It was then preserved and put in a place of honor. One day a servant who feared the skull threw it in the moat. The skies turned dark as night, and a powerful storm struck the hall. The owner, realizing what had been done, drained the moat and returned the skull to its rightful place. Stories have been told of other attempts to destroy the skull. Burning, burying, and even smashing it have failed. It seems that Father Ambrose Barlow is as stubborn in death as he was in life.

SEPTEMBER 11, 1903
TROY HILL FIREHOUSE
Pittsburg, Pennsylvania

The original firehouse on Troy Hill was built in 1874. Twenty-seven years later it was demolished and the current station, Engine House #39, was built, making it the oldest firehouse in Pittsburg. For over a hundred years it served the north side residents of Troy Hill. It was the last station to use a horse-drawn fire apparatus and the only station in the city with a named old-time fire bell: "Die Glocke Sarah," German for "The Sarah Bell." Through its long history, the community has fought several attempts to close the station. In 2005 it finally lost the battle and it was shut down.

During its time as an active firehouse, there were many accounts of supernatural activity within its venerable walls. Spectral footsteps were heard on the second floor and on the stairway. Shades went up and down of their own accord. Blankets were pulled off of sleeping firemen. And ghostly firefighters have been seen playing cards in the basement, waiting for the next alarm. Paranormal investigators believe that the building is haunted by eight firefighters, three chaplains, and a firehouse dog named Queenie. Plans are underway to convert Engine House #39 into a fire apparatus museum, which should make the spectral firefighters feel right at home. Until then, they're still on call, waiting for the next alarm.

SEPTEMBER 12, 1878
CLEOPATRA'S NEEDLE
Embankment, London

Cleopatra's Needle, named after the ship it sailed on, was gifted to the British Government in 1819. This 3,500-year-old, sixty-eight-foot monument was a tribute from the Egyptian people, commemorating the victory of Admiral Nelson at the Battle of the Nile. However, without the funds dedicated to procure the statue, the obelisk remained in Alexandria for more than fifty years, until a prestigious doctor, by the name of Sir William James Erasmus Wilson, paid for its transportation to England.

Unfortunately, *Cleopatra*, the floating pontoon being towed by the *Olga*, began to roil in the waves. The *Olga*, struggling to save the cargo, sent six volunteers on a small rescue boat to stabilize the pontoon. The boat capsized and all six men drowned.

Cleopatra's Needle has two sphinxes on either side of it. However, one cannot be sure why the Needle was installed incorrectly. The sphinxes, rather than having their back toward the obelisk, guarding it, are facing toward it. The bronze creatures are adorned with hieroglyphics that say *netjer nefer men-kheper-re di ankh* (the good god, Thuthmosis III given life). Perhaps the reversed sphinxes are having an adverse effect on the general population, as increased suicides by jumping into the River Thames have been reported in the general area of Cleopatra's Needle. Visitors taking in the grand, granite obelisk often hear mocking ethereal laughter. And the ghostly specter of a naked man plunging into the depths of the Thames is a frequent occurrence. One has to wonder if the mocking laughter and increased suicides are directly related. Maybe the suicidal, naked ghost is in search of souls to join him.

SEPTEMBER 13, 2008
NICHOLAS CAGE'S HAUNTED HOME
New Orleans, Louisiana

As reported in contactmusic.com, the actor Nicholas Cage purchased the haunted LaLaurie Mansion in 2007 for $3.5 million dollars. So far, he has stated, his family will join him for dinner, but they refuse to sleep in the home. Cage mentioned that at some point although he will more than likely be on his own, he would sleep there. He had been told that his new purchase, which is located in the Vieux Carré, the French Quarter, was rife with the spirits of slaves tortured by Lalaurie Delphine. Keeping an open mind, Cage said he was aware of the legends before buying the home and knows that at any given point there may be several spirits watching him.

He has been contacted by at least six parapsychologist groups interested in visiting his new home. However, ever mindful of the spirits, and not willing to exploit them, Cage has refused their requests. One can only imagine, what with the horrors that long-ago slaves endured at the mercy of Lalaurie Delphine, if Nicholas Cage will ever encounter a peaceful night's sleep.

SEPTEMBER 14, 1658
DUNGEON ROCK
Lynn, Massachusetts

In 1658 a pirate ship arrived in Lynn Harbor. Four passengers disembarked with a mysterious chest and headed up the Saugus River in a small boat. Learning of the pirates, the local British troops intercepted them in the woods. They quickly captured three of the four men. But the fourth, a man named Thomas Veal, escaped with the treasure. The three captured men were hanged, but although the British tried, they were never able to find Thomas Veal. He went deep into what is now called Lynn Woods until he found a natural cave in the rocks. There he took up residency, and after some time he became a member of the community. He mended shoes and lived in the cave, which came to be known as Dungeon Rock. Some time later, an earthquake hit the area causing the entrance to the cave to collapse and killing Thomas Veal. Two hundred years later, a spiritualist by the name of Hiram Marble reported that he had received a message from Thomas Veal instructing him to go to Dungeon Rock. Hiram purchased several acres of land around the rock and moved his family there. With the aid of the ghost of Thomas Veal, he and his son began to search for the treasure. He became obsessed with finding it, not only for the riches it would bring him, but also to validate his connection with the spirit world. Both Hiram and his son Edwin died without ever finding the treasure or proving that they communicated with the dead.

SEPTEMBER 15, 1907
CULP'S GHOST
Pittsburg, Pennsylvania

The Allegheny County Jail was designed by Boston architect Henry Hobson Richardson and was completed in 1888. The formidable fortress was a mix of architectural styles: Syrian arches, French Gothic dormer windows, French Renaissance roofs, and Byzantine columns, with Romanesque elements. Rising 300 feet above the massive walls, arches, and turrets is the impressive courthouse tower connected to the jail by the Renaissance footbridge known as the "Bridge of Sighs."

In 1907 W. A. Culp was awaiting trial for the murder of his brother. Overcome by guilt, he killed himself in murderer's row. But according to the *New York Times*, this isn't the end of our story. Each night after his suicide, the ghost of Culp began visiting the fourteen men awaiting trial or execution on murderer's row. The ghostly specter harassed the prisoners, keeping them awake all night and only disappearing in the dawn's light. The criminals in the cells complained so vehemently that, according to the article, Warden Lewis moved murderer's row to another part of the prison. This seemed to work because Culp's ghost left them alone. And although there were occasional reports of paranormal activity in the jail, none were as well documented as this.

SEPTEMBER 16, 1865
THE OLD COOT
North Adams, Massachusetts

An elderly man, nicknamed the "Old Coot," haunts Mt. Greylock. The tragic story begins during the Civil War, in 1861. William Saunders, a local farmer, having enlisted in the Union army, said his goodbyes to his wife, Belle, and his children, then left to join the battle. A year later, his wife received word that William had been seriously wounded and was in a military hospital. And although she prayed for his return, she never heard another word. As time went by, Belle, unable to care for the farm and her children alone, hired a local man to help out. Soon the two were wed, and the man she married had adopted William's children, taking them for his own.

In 1865, four years after William left, he returned. The second he stepped foot off the train, he raced home, only to have his excitement turn to torment, as a strange man held his wife and his children called another man "daddy."

Heartbroken, William turned his back on his old life and headed into the mountains, where he lived out the remainder of his days. From time to time, the disheveled old man would work small jobs for the locals, who nicknamed him, "Old Coot." And he was so unrecognizable from the man he used to be that he even worked his old farm a time or two, and no one was ever the wiser.

Many years later, during the winter months, a group of hunters walking through Bellow's Pipe stumbled across the old man's cold, dead body. But they were suddenly startled when the Old Coot's spirit shot from his body and soared up the mountain.

Since then, many hikers have reported seeing the spirit of a tattered old man who disappears up the mountain pass. If you're a hiker and find yourself climbing near the remote area of Bellows Pipe, keep an eye out for William Saunders's ghost.

SEPTEMBER 17, 2009
PATRICK SWAYZE
New York City, New York

As reported on deathsoup.com, rumor has it that recently deceased Patrick Swayze is revisiting his part in the movie *Ghost*, when Sam is trying to speak through Odamay. But instead of a movie, real-life Odamay—or should we say Whoopi Goldberg—is the recipient of Swayze's efforts to communicate with the living.

The story goes that when pennies began moving of their own accord in actress Whoopi Goldberg's New York apartment, she placed a 911 call for help. The pennies, she stated, began to form the word "Odamay."

Whoopi is said to have called in the ghost hunters from Penn State's Paranormal Research Society who have vouched for Whoopi's sanity, stating she wasn't crazy.

It appears that Whoopi also placed a call to Oprah, updating her on the situation. It seems that not only has Swayze visited Whoopi's apartment, but he also appears to follow her into the subway station and, once again, just as in the movie, he is moving and smashing soda cans with his mind.

Will Whoopi be able to convince Swayze that she is no longer playing the role of Odamay and movies are no replacement for real life?

SEPTEMBER 18, 1692
GILES COREY
Salem, Massachusetts

Abigail Hobbs implicated the Coreys during the witch hysteria of 1692. The Coreys were led to Ingersoll's Tavern, where they could be questioned.

According to the harsh laws of the day, if one pleaded guilty, his home and land, along with everything he'd worked for, would be awarded back to the colony. Those proclaiming their innocence, if convicted, would still lose all their holdings. Not only that, but they would be put to death. It's believed that Giles realized this, so he did not make a plea, perhaps hoping that both of his sons-in-laws would inherit everything he'd worked hard for.

As a punishment and in an attempt to make him speak, they stripped the eighty-year-old man of his clothes and laid him beneath a plank of wood. For two days he endured the torture of heavy stones being laid upon his chest and abdomen. It is said that Giles did not cry out, nor did he make a plea. Instead, when he was pressured for a response as to his innocence, he cried, "more weight!"

On September 19, 1692, with his dying breath, Giles cursed the town of Salem and the corrupt Sheriff Corwin with it.

Coincidently, every sheriff of Essex County since then has either died in office or was forced to leave due to blood-related illnesses. And Giles, well, it seems as if he's still holding a grudge. His ghostly apparition has been seen on several occasions. Each time that Giles makes a visit it is immediately after a tragedy has befallen the town of Salem. It makes one think that, just maybe, Corey is relishing the town's pain as a way to lessen his own.

TERRIFYING TIDBIT

Spectral evidence is a form of evidence based on dreams or visions that was used during the Salem Witch trials to convict the accused. When it was declared invalid, no more witches were convicted.

SEPTEMBER 19, 1936
THE BROWN LADY OF RAYNHAM HALL
Norfolk, England

Two London photographers, Mr. Indre Shira and Captain Provand, were hired by *Country Life Magazine* to take pictures of Raynham

Hall for an upcoming issue. It was about four o'clock in the afternoon when Indre exclaimed that he could see a veiled figure descending the stairs and asked Provand to take a picture. Although the Captain could not see anything himself, he did as his friend requested and took a picture of the staircase. When the plate was developed, it revealed an eerie luminescent woman descending the oak stairs. The photograph was published in *Country Life* in 1936 and since then, it has become known as the best photographic evidence of the existence of ghosts. But who was the specter in the photograph?

Most believe it is Lady Dorothy Townshend, also referred to as "The Brown Lady." She was the wife of Charles Townshend, second Viscount of Raynham. She died and was buried in 1726, but there are rumors that the coffin was empty. Some suspect that Charles, believing that his wife had been unfaithful, faked the funeral and kept her locked up in a remote corner of Raynham Hall until she died. Over the years, several prominent people have seen "The Brown Lady," including King George IV. There is even one report where two visitors to the hall were so frightened by the ghostly apparition that they fired a pistol at her—with, of course, little result.

SEPTEMBER 20, 1857
THE PHANTOM FUNERAL
PROCESSION OF RED FORT
Red Fort, India

Bahadur Shah Zafar became the last Mogul Emperor when his father died. By then, the emperor was just a figurehead and had no real power. Bahadur showed little interest in ruling and spent his time in calligraphy and poetry. In fact, some believe he is one of the greatest Urdu poets of India.

In 1857 Indian regiments under British control revolted and seized Delhi. Despite his reluctance, Indian forces proclaimed Zafar their leader. British forces crushed the revolt and captured Zafar, but not before slaughtering many of his family. He was found guilty of treason, and he and his wife were exiled to Myanmar where he died a short time later, but that was not the last time he was seen.

Since then, on Thursday nights, there have been many reports of a ghostly funeral procession led by the ghost of the dispirited Zafar and his grief-stricken wife. Some believe the procession through the streets of Red Fort is for one of Zafar's children who were butchered by the British. So although Zafar's body remains in Myanmar, it appears his spirit remains in India.

SEPTEMBER 21, 1348
THE COOK FROM HELL
Prague, Czech Republic

The church and monastery was founded by King Charles IV and consecrated by Archbishop Ocko of Vlasim. Originally known as Na Slovanech, the Emauzy, as it is now known, derives its name from the gospel in which Jesus met his disciples near the town of Emmaus. It became the home of Slavic Benedictine monks from Croatia and Dalmatia.

Through the centuries, the monastery suffered atrocities under various rulers, including the Nazis and Communists, but survived.

Today it houses some of the Czech Republic's most precious frescos and wall paintings, as well as a legend or two.

The Benedictine monks of the Emauzy lived a simple and pious life. Their virtuous lifestyle was so well known that it is said to have even reached the gates of Hell itself. Angered by their reputation, Satan sent a spy to the monastery, a cook, dubbed the "Emauz Devil." He prepared such succulent meals that the monks soon forgot their pious ways, delighting in wine and epicurean delights. Finally discovering his true nature the monks cast a spell, turning him into a black cock. The monks returned to their virtuous ways, but they remain on guard, ever vigilant for another "cook from Hell."

SEPTEMBER 22, 1913
BOGGO ROAD GAOL MUSEUM
Brisbane, Queensland

To relieve overcrowding, the Australian government opened the Boggo Road Gaol (jail) in 1883. Drunks, robbers, murderers, debtors, rapists—whatever crime you committed, you ended up in the Gaol. Its most notorious denizen was a man by the name of Ernest Austin, a wicked man who was convicted of killing an eleven-year-old girl named Ivy Mitchell. Austin showed no remorse for his dirty deed and even bragged that the girl enjoyed it. It was said that he had made a pact with the Devil. There were no tears shed on the day they hanged him at the Boggo Gaol. But there was laughter. According to accounts of that day, Austin laughed an evil laugh until the rope snapped his neck. And although he was the last man ever executed in Queensland, it seems his evil spirit still remains, harassing guards and prisoners alike. Many a poor guard ended his shift white as a ghost, some never to return again.

The prison closed in 1989. Most of the buildings were demolished, except for division two. With the help of three of the former guards, the building became the Boggo Road Gaol Museum. It was designed to give visitors a scary glimpse into the harsh prison life of the Australian penal system, but it seems it offers up a different type of fright. The museum is so haunted, that it has been added to the local ghost tour.

SEPTEMBER 23, 1919
THE LAMPLIGHT HOTEL
Truro, Nova Scotia

The Lamplight Hotel closed on July 13, 1928. It's hard to find any traces of it today, except for this story. A husband and wife were staying at the hotel when the husband noticed a man on the balcony, an old friend he knew from the war (World War I). He went out and chatted with him for a while, and his wife joined him shortly thereafter. As time went by, he decided to go to the bar for a nightcap, leaving his wife and friend on their own. Later returning to his room, he was stunned to find his wife and friend in bed together. Grabbing a pistol from the dresser drawer, he shot them both, and then jumped off the balcony to his death.

From then on, strange things began to occur in that room. Dresser drawers would open on their own, their contents flying across the room. Breakfast trolley carts would drive about violently, being pushed by some unseen entity. Phantom screams and gunshots terrified guests. And in the middle of the night the bed would sometimes levitate and spin in the air. On one occasion, a woman claimed that she was awakened by two people making love in the bed next her. She sat up and screamed, only to have a man burst through the door and shoot them. And then they all faded away.

Although terrified of the spirits, the staff continued their duties until that September night in 1928. A guest was nearly killed by "two tremendous forces that sandwiched him" in bed. The hotel reportedly closed seven hours later, never to open again.

SEPTEMBER 24, 1975
ANDREW IRVINE
Mount Everest, Himalayas

In 1924, British mountaineers George Mallory and Andrew Irvine set out to be the first to climb Mount Everest via the North Col route. They were last seen on June 8 nearing the summit, but they disappeared soon after. In 1975, fellow countrymen Douglas Scott and his climbing partner Dougal Hatson attempted to be the first to scale the southwest face of Everest. They soon ran into trouble. Despite being considered one of the greatest high-altitude mountain climbers of all time, Scott wanted to turn back. They then began to feel the presence of another. Late that night, as they slept in a snow hole, Scott swears the spirit of Andrew Irvine stayed with them and urged them on to complete their climb. They continued their ascent, and despite poor conditions they reached the summit.

Seventy-five years after Mallory and Irvine's disappearance, an expedition sponsored by the BBC and the television show *NOVA* attempted to find evidence of their ascent to the summit. On May

1, 1999, the team discovered Mallory's frozen body just below the north face of the mountain. However, neither Irvine's body nor any other evidence of the expedition was ever found. Through the years, numerous individuals have seen Irvine's ghost, especially when they found themselves in difficulty. Perhaps Andrew, in death, is helping others achieve what he couldn't in life, reaching the summit.

SEPTEMBER 25, 1978
HISTORY REPEATS ITSELF
Boxford, Massachusetts

Lorraine lived in an old Colonial home in Massachusetts overlooking a seventeenth-century cemetery. Her life was seemingly ordinary. That is, until her daughter, Maureen, turned thirteen years of age. At first she began being plagued by nightmares. And it wasn't long after that her fitful sleep ended in bloodcurdling screams. Lorraine, concerned for her daughter's well-being, asked her what was wrong. Maureen told her of voices that wouldn't stop and of ghosts in her bedroom that visited her each night.

Not sure what to believe, Lorraine took her daughter to a doctor, who scheduled a series of tests and then prescribed a heavy sedative to help drown out the unexplainable voices. That weekend, while she and her daughter were alone in the 200-year-old home, the voices began again. While Maureen lay on the couch, Lorraine went to the kitchen for a glass of water and a sedative for her "ill" daughter. But just as she walked into the kitchen, the front door swung open on its own. Bewildered, she shut the door. In an attempt to keep the door from swinging freely, Lorraine retrieved a butter knife out of the drawer and shoved it in the door jamb. Then she went and took a shower while Maureen slept. After the shower she returned to the kitchen; to her horror she found two knives jammed in the door. The next morning, she confronted Maureen. Perplexed, Maureen was at a loss for words. Lorraine continued, "I put *one* knife in the door, and when I got out of the shower, there were two—and not only that, all the gas jets were turned on. You could have killed us!"

"The ghosts must have been mad that they couldn't speak to me," Maureen replied.

As if a realization struck, Lorraine just stood there, mouth agape. The horrors of her youth suddenly resurfaced: unexplainable sounds and the disembodied voices that had called to *her* at all hours of the night. She paled. Finally, Lorraine understood. Maureen hadn't been ill at all. Unfortunately for them both, the ghosts of the past had returned.

SEPTEMBER 26, 1901
LINCOLN'S TOMB
Springfield, Illinois

Was the ghost of Lincoln guarding his own tomb? It appears so. In 1865, many visitors claimed to see Lincoln's ghostly apparition appear in and about his new grave. The sounds of unworldly weeping and disembodied footsteps were also reported.

The unexplained sounds heard were so disturbing they drew the concerns of Lincoln's friends, who requested the aid of a plumber to drill a hole through the crypt wall so they would be able to check on Lincoln and his sons as needed.

They did so but found nothing out of the ordinary.

It's been noted that the Secret Service was once credited for circumventing a plot to steal the president's remains as part of a plot to procure ransom. Although the would be criminals were stopped, the idea of it was enough to garner the attention of certain individuals who would later form a group, calling themselves the Lincoln Guard of Honor. Their duties were to repeatedly exhume the president's remains over an undisclosed period of time, ensuring all was as it should be, then rebury the president again.

It's not hard to believe that a body at such unrest might choose to make a visit now and then to keep tabs on the strange goings on. Perhaps it explains why, even today, the sound of footsteps, the shuffling of feet, and moans can be heard near his tomb.

SEPTEMBER 27, 1934
THE GHOST BUS
OF LADBROKE GROVE
London, England

The number seven double-decker bus had an established bus route that ran through Ladbroke Grove. One place along its journey, through a curvy junction of St. Mark's Road and Cambridge Gardens, was an extremely dangerous blind spot. The strange goings on along this stretch of road took place in the 1930s. Apparently, a different number seven bus was seen at all hours of the day and night. And not only was this phantom bus visible, it was reputed to cause countless motor vehicle accidents. Witnesses to the accidents always reported the same thing. Each time, the accident occurred when the driver was taking the hairpin turn and swerved to avert what would have been a head-on collision with the red, number seven, double-decker bus. Those who investigated the accidents were at a loss. It made no sense. All the accidents took place during a time when no other bus was scheduled to be on that route.

One driver, who had a near miss, told of yanking her steering wheel seconds before colliding with the bus. She stated that the bus's lights glared above and below, yet there were no passengers or driver in sight.

Finally, tragedy struck and a driver was killed. Once again, a witness described the number seven bus being the cause. The coroner, not sure what to believe, reported it as such. The public, having heard of the coroner's disbelief, wrote hundreds of letters. Each description was eerily similar. One letter was from a transportation worker who had seen the red bus pull into a local station. The bus, with engine idling, simply disappeared.

Not sure what else to do, the decision was made to straighten the road. And so far their plan has worked. Since then, the phantom double-decker that once wreaked havoc on travelers of Ladbroke Grove has never been heard of again.

SEPTEMBER 28, 2006
BOOKSTORE SPECTER
Tottenham, Ontario

One day, Leigh Ross managed her friend's used bookstore as a favor. The building, which had once housed a hardware store, was located in Tottenham, Ontario. While working by herself on the first day, she sat at the desk dusting books. But with no customers perusing the aisles and no sound of music in the air, the hundred-year-old building turned ominously quiet. Out of the stillness, a book crashed to the floor, shattering the eerie silence. Leigh quickly walked to where the sound of the crash seemed to come from, but no books were out of place. She then searched the remainder of the shop and found nothing. Shrugging it off, she headed back to the front desk.

A few minutes later, she heard a second crash. Leaving the security of her desk, she searched the store a second time. Still, there was nothing out of place. Sitting back at the desk, she wondered what made the noise. She knew the building was old and the town had its share of ghosts. Apparently, whoever the spirit was wanted to be heard, because it wasn't long before there was a third crash. And although Leigh didn't expect to find the source of the racket, she once again got up and checked the shop. Just as she had expected, she could find nothing out of place.

Moments later, as she stood behind the counter, she heard another crash. This time it was right beside her. Not sure what else to do, she turned, and said, "Hi there, I know you're here. Thanks for telling me you are here." Her words must have had a calming effect on the ghost because she finished her day in silence.

When her friend returned from vacation, she asked, "Why didn't you tell me you had a ghost?" Her friend replied, "I thought you knew! He's been here for ages!"

SEPTEMBER 29, A.D. 350
BINDON HILL
Lulworth Cove, Dorset, England

Bindon Hill is on the coast near Lulworth Cove in Dorset. The Romans landed here before obtaining a great victory at the Battle of the Drove.

They set up camp on the hill controlling the valley. One night as the fog rolled in the Romans were marching along Bindon Hill when they lost their footing and fell to their deaths on the rocks of Arish Mell below. Because they were marching in tight formation they lost a whole legion. Today, they say if you listen very carefully when the fog rolls in from the sea covering Bindon Hill, you can still hear the ghostly footsteps and the clash of armor as the Legion falls to their deaths.

SEPTEMBER 30, 2008
THE MILLIONAIRE'S GHOST
Nottinghamshire, England

A millionaire and his family living in a fifty-two-room mansion in Nottinghamshire were forced to flee their home because of ghosts. According to *XMOTU Ghost News*, eight months after purchasing the mansion, it had to be taken over by the bank. It seems the Rashid family stopped making payments and refused to live in the home a moment longer. Anwar Rashid, in an attempt to save his home and the sanity of his family, called in a team of paranormal investigators, but to no avail. The malevolent spirit had a different agenda. The eerie voices and the tapping on the walls continued. Then one night, Rashid and his wife looked in on the baby and they were aghast at what they found. There before them was their little one, draped in a blanket spotted with blood. Not willing to play victim to a spectral villain, the Rashid's moved out of their home. Anwar admitted that prior to living in the mansion, he was a nonbeliever in ghosts. But now, having lived through the ordeal, he will tell all who ask that ghosts do in fact exist.

OCTOBER 1, 1995
THE BLACK FOREST HAUNTING
El Paso County, Colorado

As viewed on the *Sightings* television show, the paranormal activity now referred to as the "Black Forest Haunting" began soon after the Lees purchased their secluded log cabin home. The Lee family began to experience a series of unexplainable phenomena: explosions of lights cascading throughout their home, undetectable chemical odors that seared their eyes and throats, and depending on the day, the sounds of chains rattling, or orchestras playing. "It was as if the gates of hell opened up," proclaimed the Lees.

Unable to attribute the anomalies to any sort of trickery, they installed cameras throughout their home and property in an attempt to capture the light forms on film. They weren't disappointed. To this day, thousands of large and small light anomalies have been captured on video and film, including outlines of faces and animals. A multitude of witnesses, including private investigators, psychics, and various paranormal researchers have experienced this oddity for themselves. Even a Colorado senator visited the Lee home and validated the unusual events by capturing the unexplainable light anomalies on his own camera. The Hopi Indians believe the paranormal events to be attributed to a "Rainbow Vortex" (a rare location where our world and the next connect). Whatever the source of the happenings, they cannot be easily explained away, even when the laws of physics are applied. Evidence concludes that the Lee home is one of the most notably haunted locations in the nation.

OCTOBER 2, 1942
THE GHOSTS OF CURACOA
Long Beach, California

When the luxury liner HMS *Queen Mary* made its maiden voyage on May 27, 1936, it was faster and more powerful than the *Titanic* and the preferred mode of transportation for the rich and famous wanting to cross the Atlantic. However, when war broke out in 1939 it was converted to a troopship and painted a military shade of gray. Nicknamed The Grey Ghost, it transported thousands of American troops across the Atlantic Ocean to join the Allied cause in Europe.

On one such journey it was involved in a tragic accident. The *Grey Ghost* was part of a convoy transporting 20,000 American troops. Cruising in an evasive zigzag pattern, it inexplicably cut into the path of its escort vessel the British light cruiser HMS *Curacoa,* striking it amidships and cutting it in half. The *Curacoa* quickly sank, and the cold waters soon became cluttered with men and debris. Fearing a German U-boat attack and with severe damage of its own to its bow, the *Grey Ghost* steamed on, leaving the ill-fated crew of the *Curacoa* in the frigid sea. Several hours later one of the escorting ships returned to the scene to rescue survivors. Of the 338 crew of the *Curacoa*, only 99 were rescued.

The *Queen Mary* was retired in 1967 and is berthed in Long Beach California. It has become a luxury hotel and is the site of countless strange happenings apparently caused by numerous spirits. Through the years, several eerie incidents have been reported near the ship's bow. Many have heard the bloodcurdling sound of disembodied voices of men screaming in fear and a strange clanking sound on the hull of the ship. Some believe these hideous noises are the ghosts of the *Curacoa* reliving that deadly accident back in 1942, never being able to rest.

OCTOBER 3, 2009
DAVID CARRADINE
Bangkok, Thailand

BIO's "Celebrity Ghost Stories" interviewed David Carradine and aired on October 3, 2009. During the interview, the actor, who played Kwai *Chang* Caine in the 1970s hit television show *Kung Fu*, said that a ghost in his closet was haunting him. He believed the ghost was Dana, his wife's deceased husband. He said the closet turned strangely cold the moment he stepped inside, and many times when he opened the closet door, Dana's tie would be turned around facing him. It read, "Grateful Dead." How did Carradine take this bizarre communication? He decided it was the ghost's way of telling David that everything was okay and he knew that David would be there for his kids.

A few months after the interview, David Carradine's body was found in a Bangkok hotel, hanging in a closet. One has to wonder if the ghost that had been stalking this late actor was actually not Dana's deceased husband but something more sinister. And what of the message "Grateful Dead"? Rather than a statement of gratitude, what if it was a preview of coming attractions?

OCTOBER 4, 1869
SAXBY'S GALE
New Brunswick, Canada

In London in 1868, Lieutenant S. M. Saxby of the Royal Navy issued a press release stating "a storm of unusual magnitude would visit the earth at 7 a.m. October 5, 1869." Eleven months later, the "perfect storm" of the nineteenth century struck. Forming off of the coast of Cape Cod, on October 4, 1869, a day later, it tore through New England and into Canada. When Saxby's Gale, as it was dubbed, ripped through the Fundy region of New Brunswick, it destroyed countless vessels, including the *Genii*. For days after the storm, the bodies of the crew of the *Genii* washed up on the shore. The townspeople dragged corpses up from the beach to the nearest building, until they could be buried. Another victim of the storm was a young woman from the village. After discovering that her true love had died in the gale, she walked into the sea to join him.

Since that day of Saxby's Gale, on nights when the moon is full, an eerie fog rolls in from the sea carrying with it the ghostly crew of the *Genii*. Objects in the buildings where their bodies had been laid out move as if by some unseen force. Pitiful moans haunt their walls, and the spectral crew wanders through the village on some unworldly mission. Cries echo from the beach where the lonely lover met her end, as she roams through the fog still looking for her long lost love.

OCTOBER 5, 2007
THE HAUNTED POLICE STATION
Ramol, India

A female ghost terrorized Ramol police officers working the nightshift. More than ten officers reported the ghostly activity. Invisible forces overturned tables and chairs and some police officers reported being strangled and pushed. In fact, some even complained of severe chest pain, as if from the pressure of a disembodied weight sitting upon their chests. The police officers became so spooked that when they arrived for work in the evening, rather than sit in their usual seats, they clustered around the front door.

After speaking with the villagers, the officers were informed that a young woman had in fact died while working in the mill, and they confirmed that her spirit was said to still roam the premises. They reported that the machines of the mill had been heard many times, even when it was empty of workers.

One local, hearing of the officer's plight, brought in a Tantrik, the Eastern equivalent of an exorcist, to rid the station of the ghostly visitor. After performing his ritual and capturing the spirit in a red pouch, he hung the picture of the deity Meldi Mata and the pouch on the wall. And although the police officers are still a bit leery, they have stated that all unusual spirit activity has come to an end. To ensure the young woman's soul stays at rest, however, the Ramol police officers continue to offer up prayers to the Meldi Mata shrine that remains on the wall.

OCTOBER 6, 1859
THE RINGING BELLS
Charlottetown, Prince Edward Island, Canada

Early one Friday morning, the residents of the small town of Charlottetown were awakened when the bell of Saint James Church rang out. It rang just once. Thinking that odd, they investigated. On the way to the church it tolled a second time, again just once. As they approached the church, again it rang just once. Entering the church grounds, they heard it toll again for the fourth time, and then again for a fifth. As they stood in front of the church, it tolled a sixth time. When the doors of the church were flung open, a powerful wind blew through the doorway and three glowing women appeared, all dressed in white. The people stood in awe as the bell tolled for the seventh time and the doors slammed shut. They tried to open them again, but the doors were locked. Peering through the windows, they saw the three women float to the bell tower steps and disappear. The minister arrived and they unlocked the doors, only to find the church empty. The bell tolled for an eighth time, as they all ran up to the belfry. There was no one there. Puzzled, they searched the entire church and could not find a living soul. The bell rang no more.

Later that evening, the *Fairie Queene*, a local passenger ferry from Nova Scotia to Prince Edward Island, failed to show. A few days later, the good people of Charlottetown learned that it had sunk on the day the church bell rang. Eight passengers—five men and three women— had drowned that day—the same number of times the bell had tolled.

TERRIFYING TIDBIT

When church bells are heard at sea, it means someone on the ship will die.

OCTOBER 7, 1849
THE GHOST OF POE
Baltimore, Maryland

Edgar Allen Poe was undoubtedly America's "Master of the Maca-bre," penning such dark works as "The Raven," "The Tell-Tale

Heart," and "The Cask of Amontillado." Even his hideous death in October 1849 seemed somehow appropriate for a man whose life was shrouded by a dark mysterious veil. He was found lying in a gutter in someone else's clothes. His death was blamed on a series of afflictions, including alcoholism, rabies, a seizure, and even murder. No matter how one believes he met his demise, one thing is for sure, many believe his spirit is not at rest. Poe's spirit has been detected in several locations that he frequented in life, including Fort Monroe, his grave at the Old Western Burial Ground, the Worthen House Café, and most notably the Edgar Allen Poe House and Museum.

The Poe House and Museum is a typical five-room row house located at 3 Amity Street in Baltimore. He lived there with his grandmother, aunt, and cousin Virginia, whom he later married. Poe had a room in the attic where he penned several works, and although he traveled, he lived there until his mysterious death in 1849. Visitors sometimes get more than they bargained for when they visit Poe's old haunt. Cold spots, eerie lights, and spectral voices have been heard. Doors and windows mysteriously open and close. And worst of all, some have reported the sensation of a cold icy hand upon their shoulder. But does Poe haunt the building? Once during a power outage in Baltimore, the neighborhood went completely dark—except for a flickering light at Poe's house. Perhaps it was the master of the macabre inking one final story by the glow of a dancing candlelight.

TERRIFYING TIDBIT

Every January 19, Poe's birthday, a mysterious man wearing a scarf and a black top hat and carrying a cane visits his grave site. Since 1949, the Poe Toaster, as he is known, has left three roses and a bottle of cognac on his grave in the early morning hours.

OCTOBER 8, 1993
FILMING AT LITTLE ROUND TOP
Gettysburg, Pennsylvania

Scores of motion pictures depicting the bloody Battle of Gettysburg have been shot on location there. During the filming of *Gettysburg* in 1993, an unexplainable phenomenon occurred.

Due to the large number of soldiers required to depict the battle, the production company hired reenactors dressed in both Union and Confederate soldiers' uniforms to play the part. While filming at Little Round Top, and as the sun had begun to set, the reenactors decided to take their break and sat down upon the hill. It was there they met a disheveled old man wearing a tattered Union uniform and smelling of gunpowder. He spoke to the men of the heinous battle. Then, without uttering another word, he passed around handfuls of ammunition and then walked away, leaving a curious group of onlookers in his wake.

At first the group of men assumed the old soldier was part of the production team staff. But they soon realized their error when they brought the fistfuls of rounds back to the man in charge of handing out the props. As it turned out, the prop man was just as confused as the reenactors. Not only had he not been responsible for the distribution of the bullets, but also the ammunition in question was not a prop at all. In fact, the men sitting on Little Round Top that day had been given genuine musket balls—the same type used during the Civil War. Evidently, the disheveled old man was not a reenactor, but the real deal.

OCTOBER 9, 1960
MACKINAC ISLAND
Mackinac Island, Michigan

Mackinac Island is rife with reports of ghost sightings. Once you've listened to the countless legends, as well as the history of the island, even if you're the staunchest of skeptics, you may have reason to think again.

One of the most haunted locations on the island is the Mission House, a building used by Christians intent on converting the Native Americans of the time. It's been said that during its history a large amount of children living in the home came down with tuberculosis. Thinking that a damp basement was the remedy to their ailment, the children were locked in and quarantined. The rampant sightings of ghost children running throughout the basement and upper floors of the Mission today are an indication of how poor a remedy it was.

Other explanations for the haunting on the island could be attributed to the nearly 1,000 bodies that were unearthed while the land was being tilled. Or, perhaps, it was the skeletal remains that were dug up during the construction of the Grand Hotel. And if that's not enough, during the War of 1812, the British slaughtered seventy-five Native Americans there. Are these men among the restless spirits that are so often seen wandering through the homes and hotels of the island?

With so many sordid tales of death, it may be difficult to pinpoint the cause. Regardless, the fact remains that Mackinac Island is indubitably flooded with paranormal phenomena.

OCTOBER 10, 2007
DAUGHTERS OF UTAH
PIONEERS MUSEUM
Salt Lake City, Utah

While monitoring the video surveillance cameras for the Daughters of Utah Pioneers Museum, the Capitol Hill police department saw more than they ever thought possible. For a period of eight straight days, random motion-sensor alarms were set off. When the officers arrived to investigate, they discovered a secured building. On several occasions, between the hours of 11:00 P.M. and 3:00 A.M., an unusual apparition of a woman's face began showing up on camera. Yet again, each time the police or staff investigated, they found no one present and the building locked up. Coincidently, during the eight days, a custodian noticed a young woman dressed all in black, sitting on a bench in the foyer. After explaining to her that the museum was closed, he walked toward her and guided her to the front door. The woman never uttered a word. The custodian opened the front door to let her out. However, rather than the woman walking down the steps, she floated above them, before vanishing. The museum has their own idea as to who the ghostly apparition is. It seems that twenty years before, a sampler (a piece of embroidered cloth) was stolen. Then one day, one of the staff recognized the item on eBay. The gracious new owners of the antique, once they realized it had been stolen, returned it to its rightful place at the museum. Perhaps this young woman had put a lot of heart and soul into her embroidered creation. Literally.

OCTOBER 11, 1780
RINGWOOD MANOR
Ringwood, New Jersey

The original manor, built in 1740, a much smaller version, was torn down in 1807 to make way for the now fifty-one-room estate. Ringwood Manor was home to numerous families prior to 1936, when it become property of the state of New Jersey. Today it is a very active museum, both paranormally and otherwise. In fact, Robert Erskine, General Washington's mapmaker, lived there during the Revolutionary War. Perhaps he took his role for Washington a little too seriously, as he's never left the manor. Well, not completely anyway. His ghostly apparition can still be seen at dusk, roaming the property, just behind the pond where his tomb lies. It is said that not far from where Erskine dwells there are unmarked graves of French soldiers. Their hushed foreign words can be heard late at night, floating atop the wind.

But what of the spirit within the walls of the manor? Curators and staff believe it to be Erskine's wife, making her rounds when the museum is closed. While locking up for the evening, staff make sure several doors are closed, yet they are wide open in the morning. But why do they suspect Mrs. Erskine? A visiting psychic informed the museum that Mrs. Erskine had become restless and unhappy with the plethora of visitors to her home. It seems that Mrs. Erskine will be eternally unhappy, since the museum is a popular site.

OCTOBER 12, 1898
LARNACH CASTLE
Dunedin, New Zealand

Constructed of the finest materials, this impressive castle was erected by businessman, banker, and politician, William James Mudie Larnach as a gift for his lovely wife, Eliza Jane. This expression of his undying love for her had all the makings of a fairy tale, but it ended more like a Greek tragedy. Eliza died alone in her bedroom of apoplexy shortly after they moved in. Grief stricken, but in need of companionship, William married Eliza's sister, Mary Alleyne. She too died tragically five years later from blood poisoning. William married again, this time to Constance, a woman twenty-one years his junior. Five months after his third marriage, his beloved daughter Kate died of typhoid at the tender age of twenty-one.

Tragedy struck again when William discovered that Constance was having an affair with his favorite son, Douglas. Guilt-ridden by what he had done, Douglas could not live with his betrayal and committed suicide. A few years later, with his business failing, William followed in his son's footsteps and shot and killed himself.

After his death, the castle and his estate were sold at auction. It became a private residence, mental asylum, and finally a world-class hotel. Sightings of the spirits of the Larnach family can be seen in many rooms of the castle, achieving in death what they could not obtain in life — togetherness.

OCTOBER 13, 1812
THE OLDE ANGEL INN
Niagara-on-the-Lake, Ontario

During the War of 1812, the inn was known as the Harmonious Coach House. Canada was in the firm hands of the British; however, in May 1813 American forces captured Fort George and Newark, as Niagara-on-the-Lake was called then. The British retreated, except for one officer by the name of Captain Swayze. He went to the coach house to bid farewell to the innkeeper's daughter, with whom he had fallen in love. As the Americans approached, he hid in the cellar. Troops searching the house found Captain Swayze in the basement and bayoneted him to death before torching the coach house.

The inn was rebuilt in 1815 and renamed the Sign of the Angel Inn. By 1820, accounts of ghostly sightings reached the local newspaper. The paper described a variety of ghostly activities including: footsteps heard in empty rooms, clinking of glasses, laughter, disembodied voices echoing throughout the inn, and the unnerving appearance of specters.

Today the inn is known as the Olde Angel Inn, and after nearly 200 years, the haunting continues. In addition to hearing the unexplainable noises, many patrons have seen dark shadows. The sighting of spectral red coats in the mirror of the women's bathroom has been frequently reported. But fear not. The innkeepers tell us that as long as the British flag flies over the door, they'll do you no harm. Then again, it seems Captain Swayze still holds a grudge. The American beer tap at the bar often malfunctions, while the British and Canadian taps work fine.

TERRIFYING TIDBIT

After a death in the family, it is believed that you should cover all the mirrors. This will keep the ghosts from using any mirror as a portal from one world to the other.

OCTOBER 14, 2009
THE SORORITY HOUSE SPIRITS
Bloomsburg, PA

According to *www.ghosttheory.com* a Bloomsburg University sorority house is plagued by spirit activity. Rumor has it that the girls of Phi Sigma Sigma are being frequented by unseen entities intent on getting their attention. The girls speak of strange occurrences ranging from faucets being turned on by themselves to all the fire alarms going off at once for no apparent reason. On numerous occasions it has been reported that the cries of children can be heard emanating from the interior walls, as if they were trying to escape. Then there's the physical contact. Several girls of Phi Sigma Sigma have reported having their hair pulled, as well as being shoved down the stairs. Coincidently, the area where they've been shoved is the same place that a dark shadow has been seen looming in the hallways and stairwell.

Numerous sororities occupying the location prior to Phi Sigma Sigma have reported similar ghostly tales. But to what do the sisters attribute all this paranormal activity? Well, one sister, having been intrigued by the paranormal all of her life, decided to take matters into her own hands. Using a Ouija board she attempted to make contact, and she received tidbits of information, the name Maggie and the year 1934 being the most prevalent. After a bit of research, she found that there had been a woman by the name of Maggie that died of natural causes back in 1934. Whatever the cause of the phenomena, they continue to this day. Perhaps Maggie is hazing her sisters from the other side.

TERRIFYING TIDBIT

Ouija boards, also known as spirit boards, are used as a method of communing with the dead. Many believe these boards should be used with extreme caution, as unsuspecting participants can inadvertently open a door allowing evil spirits to enter.

OCTOBER 15, 1999
THE GREY LIBRARY GHOST
Evansville, Indiana

The Willard Library, financed by Willard Carpenter, opened on March 28, 1885, almost two years after his death. The Victorian Gothic building is the oldest public library in the state of Indiana. According to the Willard Library website, it is thought to be haunted by the Lady in Grey, who first appeared in 1937 when she was spied by a maintenance man who went into the basement to stoke the furnace. It was 3 A.M. when the spectral figure of a veiled woman appeared to him and then faded away. He became so frightened by this image that he quit his job.

The Lady in Grey has made several appearances throughout the years. She has been seen by library workers, patrons, and even a policeman. In 1999, the Willard Library installed the world's first ghostcam, allowing millions of viewers to log in and remotely search for the Lady in Grey. But who is she?

The most accepted theory is that she is Louise Carpenter, the daughter of the library's founder. After his death, the bulk of Willard Carpenter's estate went to the library. Louise sued, and to her dismay, she lost. Embittered by her disappointment, she roams the library forever in search of her lost fortune.

OCTOBER 16, 1859
JOHN WILKES BOOTH HOUSE
Harpers Ferry, West Virginia

The John Wilkes Booth House located in Harpers Ferry is steeped in history. During the Civil War, it was the place where abolitionist John Brown attempted to start a slave revolt. In 1859, Brown, along with sixteen men, some of them freed slaves, tried to seize a U.S. arsenal at Harpers Ferry. Unfortunately for the men, Colonel Robert E. Lee thwarted their efforts.

Is the John Wilkes Booth House haunted? Just ask the locals their opinion. The "haunted cottage," as it's often referred to, has been the subject of many unexplainable ghostly sightings. Passersby have seen glowing lights in the slave quarters when no one is home. And translucent figures have been seen walking past the windows on more than one occasion.

Research into the property uncovered the fact that relatives of Booth owned the home. Booth was reported to have made a special visit to Harpers Ferry to attend the execution of John Brown. Evidently Booth had planned to return to the house and to the arms of his wife after he assassinated President Abraham Lincoln. However, that would never come to pass. Twelve days after the assassination, Booth, who had fled the scene, was tracked down by Union soldiers and killed. There are those that believe the ghost of John Wilkes Booth still roams this building, completing his journey home—an act he failed to accomplish while alive.

OCTOBER 17, 1926
WAVERLY HILLS SANITARIUM
Louisville, Kentucky

Waverly Sanitarium is reputed to be among the most haunted locations in the world. The town of Waverly Hills had a benign, even serene beginning. During an era when women were discouraged from learning, Major Thomas H. Hayes, a man way ahead of his time, purchased the property and had a one-room schoolhouse built. In 1883, Hayes hired Lizzie Harris to instruct his girls.

The Board of Tuberculosis Hospital later purchased the property in 1910, opening its doors to the sick. In 1926 a larger building was added to handle the scores of patients that were being transported from all over the country. In 1962, it stopped being a tuberculosis hospital and became a center for geriatric patients. In 1982, the state of Kentucky stepped in and closed it.

Today, paranormal investigators from all over the world visit Waverly Hills. Although the hospital is a playground to hosts of spirits, many reports of spiritual phenomena seem to center around the death tunnel, also known as the body chute. Countless patients died while undergoing treatment for tuberculosis. Rather than horrify the patients with impending doom, and to dispose of the bodies quickly, the dead were deposited in the chute, which emptied into the basement. There they were either cremated or sent to a funeral home for burial. It's near this chute that visitors have often witnessed full apparitions and heard the eerie chatter of patients of long ago, roaming the halls in search of their remains. The playful spirits of a little girl and boy have been seen wandering throughout the hospital. One investigator, Marley Gibson, captured what has come to be known as "the ball video." For more than a half hour, the spirit of a child seems to be playing tug of war with Marley over a beach ball. The floor was level. There was no breeze in sight, but on the video, one can see a playful force behind unseen hands. Skeptical? Perhaps you should visit with the many investigators who walk the halls of the old hospital in search of communing with the dead. Waverly Hills Sanitarium may make a believer out of you yet.

OCTOBER 18, 1871
THE HAUNTED MAUSOLEUM
Cleveland, Tennessee

This is not your typical ghost story with phantom specters appearing or the creepy sounds of those long deceased attempting to reconnect with the living. However, if you find yourself visiting Cleveland, Tennessee, you may want to visit the cemetery located behind St. Luke's Episcopal Church. Here you will find the crypt of the Craigmiles family.

The colossal, white marble crypt is said to bleed reddish pink splotches. The family's tragic history began with that of poor Nina, who was killed in a buggy accident in 1871. When she and her grandfather were enjoying a fast-paced buggy ride, he would often give seven-year-old Nina the reigns. Nina loved to go fast. Unfortunately, on that fateful day, little Nina, not paying attention, crossed the path of a speeding train and was killed instantly.

After her burial, red stains began appearing on the white mausoleum that was erected in her honor. The tragic deaths of the Craigmiles family continued. Nina's father died of blood poisoning in 1899 after falling on an ice-covered street. Adelia, his wife, was struck and killed by a car in 1928, and an infant child died at birth.

And with each consecutive addition to the Craigmiles family plot, the red stains only became more prominent. The locals, disturbed by this strange phenomenon, tried to scrub away the stains. When that didn't work, they replaced the discolored marble with a new block, only to have the red stains return. Maybe Nina is crying tears of blood over the deaths of those she loves. Then again, this strange phenomenon's origin may never be resolved.

OCTOBER 19, 1923
LENIN'S GHOST
Moscow, Russia

Since Lenin's death in 1924, his ghost has been sporadically spotted throughout Moscow. Soldiers guarding his former apartment have heard eerie noises, footsteps, and furniture being moved from the empty room. In fact, Sergei Filatov, chief of staff under Boris Yeltsin, retells his own experience with Lenin's ghost. According to Sergei, he was working late one night in an office under Lenin's old apartment when he heard creaking in the floorboards above. At first he ignored it, but then realized it sounded as if someone was pacing back and forth. Calling security, he asked what was going on in the apartment, which is now a museum. He was informed that there was no one there. The footsteps continued even as he spoke. Disbelieving the guards, he asked them to meet him at the apartment. They unlocked the door and thoroughly searched the museum and building. They found no one.

A few years later, a student from Moscow State University had a run in with Lenin. While walking across the cobblestones of Oktyabrskaya Square in Moscow, his path crossed that of the famous Bolshevik leader. At first he couldn't believe his eyes. As he stood there awestruck, he could clearly see Lenin's facial features right down to his signature beard. When the phantom realized that he had been spotted, he stepped into his monument and disappeared.

Perhaps the strangest sighting of Lenin's spirit happened on October 19, 1923. That night he was seen walking in and about the city without his guards. This caused great alarm to many security agents, who reported the sightings to their superiors. To this day, no one can explain the sightings that night, since Lenin was in Gorki, ill but alive.

OCTOBER 20, 2008
COUNTRY HOUSE RESTAURANT
Clarendon Hills, Illinois

As reported by the *Chicago Tribune*, the Country House Restaurant has experienced its share of paranormal phenomena. Built in 1922, the first floor of this two-story building has changed ownership several times over the years. During the 1950s, a young blond woman who was having an affair with the bartender brought her daughter in for a visit. Soon after, she and the bartender got into a heated argument. The blonde asked the man to watch the child. When he refused, she stormed out of the restaurant with her child in hand, got into the car, and crashed into a tree. Although the woman died, the child was spared.

It's the blond woman's spirit that is believed to be behind the host of paranormal events. Disembodied voices are heard. For no apparent reason, napkins have sailed across the room. During the wee hours of the night, the jukebox has repeatedly turned itself on. Once, during a period when the Country House was being renovated, a worker heard it begin to play. When he went to investigate further, he noticed the spooky image of a blond woman standing beside it. Even spookier was the fact that she had no legs. Patrons of the restaurant while waiting for a table have often heard their names called out by a woman, only to be told that they must have been mistaken; the table wasn't ready yet. It's apparent by her actions that this ghost is a bit of a prankster.

TERRIFYING TIDBIT

If you are afraid of ghosts, you are said to have phasmophobia.

OCTOBER 21, 1805
THE GHOST OF LORD HORATIO NELSON
Nova Scotia, Canada

Pleasant Point Lighthouse, or French Point Light, as it is sometimes called, was built in 1904 on a grassy knoll. The wooden eleven-meter-tall structure was built in the classic peppershaker design. Its first keeper was a seafaring man named John Kent. For almost a hundred years the Kent family members have tended to the lighthouse. Like so many other lighthouses, it has a ghost attached to it. But unlike so many others, this ghost is rather famous. According to a story told by Ivan Kent, his great grandfather was the navigator for none other than Lord Horatio Nelson. Not only that, he was with Lord Nelson when he died at Trafalgar. The admiral's body was laid to rest in London, England, but it seems the admiral's spirit had other plans.

The ghost of Nelson remained with Kent, even following him to North America when he settled in Nova Scotia. The Admiral haunted Kent's original home in Canada, and when that was destroyed it seems he immigrated to the nearby lighthouse. The ghost has been pretty benign, except for a couple of incidents with the family pet. On two separate occasions, with two different cats, the presence of Nelson has been felt. The cats each disappeared, only to be later found beneath a trap door in the floor of the lighthouse. They acted frantic, as if they were possessed. Away from the tower, they soon recovered. But after their encounter with the ghost of Nelson, they wanted no part of the lighthouse. Visitors have all felt his presence, and Ivan doesn't mind Nelson hanging around, he just wishes he'd leave his cats alone.

OCTOBER 22, 2003
TIGGER'S RETURN
Montreal, Canada

In 2003, Leigh Ross's cat Tigger passed away peacefully at the veterinarian's office. Her loveable cat slept at the foot of her bed every night. During Tigger's last days, when the cancer was taking its toll, she stayed at the end of Leigh's bed all day and night. Despite her best efforts, Tigger passed away. For weeks after, an invisible weight on the bed could still be felt, and Leigh had the sensation of a cat curling up at her feet. Since it was something Leigh had experienced every night for the past thirteen years, coupled with the fact that she was still grieving for Tigger, she pushed the odd goings-on out of her mind.

Then the unexpected happened two years later when Leigh brought two kittens home. Due to their rambunctious behavior at all hours of the night, the kittens were banned from the bedroom. One night, Leigh awoke to feel a cat jump up at the foot of her bed. Half asleep, she reached down to pet the cat and felt it purr when she did so. It took a moment for her mind to clear and realize that there were no cats in the bedroom. Once again she reached down, felt the cat, then got up out of bed. She checked the door, which was still closed. Quickly she turned on the light. To her amazement, Tigger's ghostly apparition jumped off the bed! And although Leigh hasn't seen the spirit of her beloved cat since, on several occasions she has felt her astral presence as she curls up beside her. Tigger may be gone, but she's certainly not forgotten.

TERRIFYING TIDBIT

Animals are thought to be sensitive to paranormal activity, which is why they can often be seen staring intently off into the distance.

OCTOBER 23, 1642
THE SPECTRAL BATTLE OF EDGEHILL
Edgehill, England

The Battle of Edgehill was the first major armed conflict of the English Civil War. On October 23, 1642, approximately 1,400 royal troops under the command of the Earl of Forth met slightly smaller forces of parliamentary troops under the Earl of Essex. The fierce battle raged back and forth with more than 1,500 men losing their lives. At the height of the battle, the Roundheads captured the flag and killed its bearer, Sir Edmund Verney. Spying the loss, Captain John Smith, a Royal Calvary officer, charged the group and retrieved the royal standard and returned it to the king. Verney's detached hand was still tightly clasped around the pole. The battle was indecisive, with both sides claiming victory.

A couple of months later, several shepherds were tending their flocks when they heard the distant sound of drums. As they drew closer, the drums were accompanied by the sounds of horses, clashing steel, and moaning men. To the shepherds' amazement, the sky above the original battlefield lit up with spectral armies refighting the battle. After the battle was over the shepherds rushed to the nearby town of Kineton, where they reported what they saw to local officials. The spectral battle took place several days in a row. The king, hearing of the event, dispatched several men to investigate the claims. Just as the shepherds had seen, they too witnessed the ethereal conflict. Several of the men who had fought in the original battle themselves were stunned as they recognized some of their fallen comrades.

Eventually the vision of the ghostly battle faded away. But some say that even today, if you listen, you still can hear echoes of the phantom Battle of Edgehill.

OCTOBER 24, 1980
TOYS "R" US
Sunnyvale, California

The haunted Toys "R" Us in Sunnyvale is a prime example that shows that even the newest of buildings can be haunted. In this case the paranormal phenomenon originates from a period in history when the majority of the area around Sunnyvale was farmland. One farmer in particular was Johnny Johnson. In 1884, he was a young man rejected by his love. One day, while cutting wood, he slipped with the axe and drove it into his leg. Refusing to quit his chores, he cinched up his leg with a piece of cloth and continued working. And that's where he was eventually found, having bled to death of his wound.

But what does Johnny's death have to do with a toy store? Soon after being built on the same land in 1970, employees of the Toys "R" Us began to encounter an onslaught of paranormal experiences. Faucets began turning on by themselves. Previously stacked toys were found scattered in the aisles. Sealed boxes of mechanical dolls reportedly became activated and began to speak of their own accord. Toys flew off the shelves, and disembodied voices were heard. Among the creepiest occurrences to afflict the help have been those reported by the female employees, who have felt invisible hands brush back their hair as someone unseen whispers in their ear. Perhaps Johnny is still pining for his lost love, Beth.

In October of 1980, renowned psychic Sylvia Brown was called in to investigate the odd goings-on and was permitted to perform a séance. During the séance she attempted to communicate with Johnny Johnson, convince him of his demise, and help him to move on to a better place. A photo taken during the séance later revealed a dark figure leaning against the wall. The curious Johnny had no intention of leaving.

OCTOBER 25, 1829
EASTERN STATE PENITENTIARY
Philadelphia, Pennsylvania

Eastern State Penitentiary opened on October 25, 1829, and was designed for incorrigible prisoners to be kept in forced solitude. The austere cells contained nothing more than a bunk and a Bible. The only light that entered the cells came from a small glass window referred to as "the Eye of God." Each prisoner was given one hour a day of exercise, and a black hood was placed over their heads as they were led from their cells. Under these conditions, even a sane prisoner could go mad. Desperate for human interaction, many men would tap on pipes and whisper through the walls. If caught, they were severely punished. There were several horrific tortures that had been carried out, but the most deadly of the tortures was saved for the repeat offender who continually broke the enforced vow of silence. An iron clamp was secured to the tongue. With the prisoner's hands behind his back, a set of chains was then attached to the device. Any movement by the prisoner resulted in the tearing of his tongue leading to an abundance of blood loss and finally death. Due to overcrowding and harsh conditions, the penitentiary was forced to close its doors in 1971. However, the penitentiary's walls were so stained by misery and torture that today countless reports of paranormal activity have been made, and Eastern State Penitentiary has become one of the most haunted locations in the country. One paranormal report came from a locksmith doing restoration work on cellblock four. He states that just as he removed the 140-year-old lock, he was assailed by a blast of energy so powerful that he couldn't move. As if he'd released the Devil himself, the surge of energy tore past him and out of the cell. There before him were the hideous ghostly faces of tormented souls swirling and morphing into shapes. Tourists still report the sound of whispering and weeping emanating through the prisons walls. It seems these souls have finally found their voices. Evidently, they were dying to speak.

TERRIFYING TIDBIT

Poltergeists are noisy ghosts. Sometimes they are malicious and destructive entities known to display aggressive behavior. Among some of their disturbances are loud banging, thumping noises, moving and levitating objects, and setting fires.

OCTOBER 26, 2007
THE HAUNTED SWING
Firmat, Argentina

Through the years people have been frightened by many possessed or haunted items, but never a playground swing. Until now! The citizens of Firmat, Argentina, became spooked when a playground swing began to move on its own. The middle swing of three would move back and forth by itself, while the other two remained still. "It was like some invisible child was on it," one parent said. After a couple of months, anxious parents informed the police. Its movements even baffled them. They, in turn, contacted a physics professor for an explanation. After investigating, the professor ruled out environmental causes such as wind, vibrations, and electromagnetic forces. The swing continued to move. At one point it moved for ten days straight while the other two swings remained still.

Teacher Maria de Silva Augustina told reporters that one scared child had nicknamed the area the "Blair Witch Playground." When asked her opinion, she said, "We believe it is haunted."

OCTOBER 27, 2006
PORSGRUNN NURSING HOME
Porsgrunn, Norway

According to the Norwegian newspaper *Telemarksavisa*, staff and patients at the aging Porsgrunn Nursing Home experienced so much unexplained activity that they summoned a priest. The nursing home had attempted to keep the haunting quiet until the newspaper got wind of it.

The building was erected in 1932 as a modern Lutheran Hospital. In 1971, it was converted to the nursing home, but it appears that not all of the hospital staff has left. The identity of the ghost is believed to be that of an "oversykepleier" (head nurse), a past employee of the hospital. Her presence not only can be felt but smelled, as it is accompanied by the odor of an old perfume, eau de Cologne 4711. Although the spirit has never harmed anyone, some of the staff have become uncomfortable with her presence, so much so that some have refused to work at night. To remedy the situation a priest was called. In a quiet ceremony, the priest blessed the home in an attempt to rid it of its spirit. Administrators feel that they have taken the correct action and have not reported the nurse's presence since the blessing.

OCTOBER 28, 2004
THE CANMORE OPERA HOUSE
Alberta, Canada

According to an October 28th article in the *Gauntlet*, prior to its move, the 1800s Heritage House was once The Canmore Opera House located in Canmore, Alberta. History has it that somewhere around the nineteenth century, while it was used as a concert hall, its walls reeked of death. When the Canmore mine disaster struck killing seven hundred people, the Opera House, due to its size, was used as a morgue.

The building changed hands several times, until it was donated to Heritage Park in the 1960s. Currently it sits upon a parcel of land that was once a farm. However, no one is certain if the resident ghost, "Sam," as he's been lovingly named, once lived on the farm or was perhaps one of the poor souls lost in the mine tragedy.

Where Sam came from matters little. What is known is that Sam is not afraid to show himself. On numerous occasions, during rehearsals, he's been seen sitting in the third seat of the third row. He must be an admirer of the fine arts because he merely sits and watches in appreciation, then vanishes when the rehearsal is done. But it's doubtful that Sam is alone. One witness swears he heard an awe-inspiring voice of a female opera singer reverberating from the main stage. However, when he entered the hall, there was not a soul to be found. Or was there?

OCTOBER 29, 1867
RMS *RHONE*
British Virgin Islands

The RMS (Royal Mail Ship) *Rhone* was built in South Hampton, England, in 1865 for the Royal Mail Packet Company. Both sail and a powerful steam engine propelled its iron hull measuring 310 feet through the seas. It was considered one of the fastest ships of its time. Because of its speed and elegant cabins, it was also a popular mode of transportation between England and the Caribbean.

In 1867, while refueling off the coast of Great Harbour, the skies grew dark and the barometer plunged, signaling an impending storm. The *Rhone* and the *Conway*, another ship anchored there, weathered the storm with little damage. When the seas grew calm again and the skies cleared, both captains realized that they were now in the middle of a late-season hurricane.

They decided to transfer the passengers from the *Conway* to the "unsinkable" *Rhone*. The *Rhone* headed for open seas, while the *Conway* made its way toward the safety of the harbor. It didn't get far. The *Conway* couldn't escape the rear of the storm, and it was lost with all hands on board.

Meanwhile Captain Robert F. Wooley of the *Rhone* ordered that the passengers be lashed to their bunks to prevent injury. As the *Rhone* headed to open seas, a giant wave swept across its deck, washing the captain away. The violent hurricane drove the ship into the rocks off of Salt Island, breaching its hull. When the cold seawater made contact with the red-hot boilers, there was a violent explosion splitting the *Rhone* in two. There were only twenty-three survivors.

In 1967, the area surrounding the wreck was turned into the Rhone Marine Park. Guided scuba diving tours take tourists into the wreck, which is littered with artifacts. But even underwater they are not free from the ghosts of the *Rhone*. Divers have reported being tugged on the shoulder, only to find that they are alone. And even the most seasoned diver cannot explain the eerie sounds. Screams and groans can be heard beneath eighty feet of water, making the wreck of the *Rhone* not only the most popular dive site in the Caribbean, but also the most haunted.

TERRIFYING TIDBIT

The wreck of the RMS *Rhone* was used in the opening scene of the 1977 movie *The Deep*, with Jacqueline Bisset and her infamous wet T-shirt dive.

OCTOBER 30, 2001
PHANTOM LIGHTS
Saskatchewan, Canada

Have you ever considered a train to be haunted? Why not ask the people of Saskatchewan, Canada. As legend has it, late one night during the 1920s, while checking the track, a railway engineer working for the Canadian National Railway was hit by a train and decapitated. Today, a strange light, like that of a lantern is seen at all hours of the night. Skeptics believe it to be the headlights from passing cars on a nearby highway causing the anomaly. However the town's mayor pointed out that the highway can't be viewed at the location where the paranormal activity is spotted.

A CBC television crew visited the site to investigate further. To their surprise they did collect film footage of the traveling cascading lights. However, they cannot give a definite cause for the light phenomenon.

Could it be the lights of passing cars? Or, possibly a long-lost train engineer, roaming the tracks in search of his head?

OCTOBER 31, 1936
HOUDINI'S GHOST
Hollywood, California

Houdini was born Ehrich Weiss in Budapest, Hungary, in 1874. His family moved to America and he grew up in Appleton, Wisconsin, where his interest soon turned to magic. Taking the name Houdini after a famous French magician, he soon performed to sold-out shows, becoming one of the greatest magicians of all time.

After his mother died he became interested in the Spiritualist movement. He soon discovered that many of the mediums involved were fakes, employing simple magic tricks. He became disillusioned with the movement and took on a crusade to expose as many of the frauds as he could. Despite his crusade, he became obsessed with death and the afterlife, telling his faithful wife, Bess, that if anybody could come back from the other side, he would. They devised a plan with a code phrase that he would convey from death to let her know that he was there.

In 1926, on Halloween, Houdini died at the age of fifty-two under mysterious circumstances. The official cause of death was peritonitis from a ruptured appendix, but some say he was murdered by members of the Spiritualist movement. After his death, Bess Houdini began holding séances in hopes of communicating with her late husband. The last official séance was held on the roof of the Knickerbocker Hotel on Halloween night, 1936. An hour passed with no contact. Just as they gave up, a violent storm struck with driving rain and intense thunder and lightning. The mysterious storm appeared nowhere else in Hollywood, except for over the Knickerbocker, and although Bess never heard the code word, many are certain this was Houdini's last attempt to make contact from beyond the grave.

TERRIFYING TIDBIT

Physical mediums of the late nineteenth century claimed they communicated with spirits by luminous clouds and ectoplasm that would emanate from them and harden to the touch. Most were considered frauds, while others could not be debunked.

NOVEMBER 1, 2006
THE HAUNTED HIGHWAY
Britain

The Britain Tourist Board calculates there are over 10,000 haunted locations in Great Britain, which is why it is thought by some to be the most haunted country in the world. With its long history, it's no surprise to hear of the strange goings-on and the plethora of alleged ghostly sightings. However, one might think these paranormal experiences would take place on a dimly lit street at the wee hours of the morning or perhaps while sitting in a historic inn or pub. Think again. Motorists traveling down the M6, one of Britain's longest and busiest highways, have reported seeing eyes peering out from the bushes, a phantom woman hitchhiker, and a truck driving down the wrong way.

Most compelling have been the reports of seeing Roman soldiers. One such report told of seeing about twenty soldiers. The woman was quoted as saying; "They were more like upright shadows than men, walking through the tarmac as you would through water."

It is believed that these ghostly sightings have been the cause of numerous accidents on the M6. So if you find yourself traveling on one of the most haunted roads in Britain, be prepared for the unexpected!

NOVEMBER 2, 2009
LAKE COUNTY CORONER'S OFFICE
Waukegan, Illinois

Employees working late nights at the Lake County coroner's office tell a series of eerie tales: strange knocking sounds coming from the inside of coolers and swinging doors that have stayed open as if some unseen force were holding them. And out of the corner of your eye, you can sometimes see people wandering about an otherwise empty autopsy room.

And to what does the staff attribute all the paranormal events? A woman scorned. Apparently, in the late 1990s, the body of an elderly woman by the name of Anna died in a nursing home. Her body, retrieved by a deputy coroner, was then inadvertently left unattended in a cooler. Several months later, when her body was discovered, she was finally identified. Soon after, unexplainable paranormal phenomena began to plague the Lake County coroner's office. During the transport of her body to the funeral home, the deputy reported that the controls of the car went on the fritz. When he retrieved Anna's body out of the hearse, the windows repeatedly went up and down of their own accord, and then it locked by itself. But the really odd thing was that the car was turned off.

It appears that Anna had become so accustomed to her surroundings, she demonstrated her displeasure at leaving.

NOVEMBER 3, 1948
THE *OVEREXPOSED*
Glossop, England

The *Overexposed* was a specially modified B-29 airplane assigned to the USAF's Sixteenth Photographic Reconnaissance Squadron. It was on a routine flight from RAF Base Scampton to AFB Burtonwood when for some unknown reason it slammed into the moors killing all on board. The bodies of the thirteen crewmen were never found. Since that time the *Overexposed* and its Captain Landon P. Tanner have been seen several times.

In 1997, several local residents witnessed a low-flying plane that eventually crashed into the upper moors, or so they thought. An RAF helicopter and several rescue teams were dispatched to the area to look for survivors. Not only were no survivors found, but no wreckage was either, except of course the old wreckage of the *Overexposed*. This was just another case of the phantom bomber.

Several years later, two history buffs were inspecting the wreckage of the aircraft when one of them found a ring among the debris. As he turned to show his companion what he had found, he saw the ghost of Captain Landon P. Tanner. Startled by what had happened, he sent the ring to Tanner's family in the United States. Another time, a group of investigators used a Ouija board to contact the captain. The Ouija board spelled out the name of the crew, along with the message that all thirteen souls were not at rest where they lay. Legend says the moors never give up their dead, so it seems the captain and his phantom bomber crew are doomed to walk the moors for all eternity.

NOVEMBER 4, 1953
THE BOATHOUSE
Laugharne, Carmarthenshire, England

In the spring of 1949, playwright and poet Dylan Thomas and his wife moved into a quaint cottage overlooking the sea. The Boathouse provided Thomas with a workshop where he composed his best-known poem, "Do Not Go Gentle into That Good Night," and other well-known works. One night, while staying in New York, he retuned from a night of heavy drinking. A "bit" inebriated, he said, "I've had eighteen strait whiskeys. I think that's a record." Six days later he slipped into a coma and died. Dylan Thomas's body was brought home and buried at a local cemetery, but it seems he haunts the Boathouse. Cold spots abound, lights go on and off of their own accord, and the sound of a chair scraping across the floor can be heard. Paintings are even removed from the walls and placed in a different area. It seems it is not only his work that is living on after his death.

NOVEMBER 5, 1883
RAM ISLAND LIGHTHOUSE
Boothbay Harbor, Maine

The entrance to Boothbay Harbor was a treacherous place, where many a boat met its demise on the rocky shoals. But the woman in white has saved many others. Sea captains and sailors have all reported seeing the spectral guardian waving a torch, warning of impending danger. Whether she is in a flaming boat, or standing on the reef, she has always been described as a luminous figure frantically waving her arms to boats in danger. Sometimes she is even accompanied by lightning, but no matter how she appears, those who heed her warning are saved from the dangerous rocks.

In the early 1800s, fishermen would put a lighted lantern on the rocks at night or hang one from their dories to warn others of the lurking ledge. It wasn't much help to larger ships, but it did help the smaller boats of the lobstermen and fishermen. In 1883, the government finally built a lighthouse there, marking the way to "Fisherman's Passage." But even today, there are those who report seeing the mysterious woman in white standing guard over the harbor.

NOVEMBER 6, 2009
THE BONES IN THE WALL
Wellsburg, West Virginia

According to the information shared with the Steubenville news station WTOV9, members from the Brooke County Paranormal Society, while on a hunt for ghosts, stumbled across skeletal remains.

It appears that during an investigation of Aspen Manor, built in 1895, one member of the paranormal investigative team found more than she bargained for. Kathy Larntz sensed that someone was buried in the basement, so she followed the voice and her intuition. Upon entering, she and her team walked to the back of the cellar where she spotted a bone on the floor. Thinking it was that of an animal, she picked it up and began digging with it. Soon after, skeletal remains (chopped bones), hair, reading glasses, and other items were discovered behind a crumbling brick wall.

The sheriff's department was called in to investigate, and the bones were collected and shipped off to the medical examiner's office.

But it seems that this was not the only evidence the paranormal team discovered. While capturing EVPs (electronic voice phenomena), or voices of the dead on playback, they heard the distinctive sound of clicking. For verification, Rick, the founder of the team, brought the recording to a local church. Upon hearing the recording, it was confirmed that the distinct sound did resemble that of a "clicker," a device nuns often used to keep students in line. Interestingly enough, during a spell of the mansion's history, it was owned by the Catholic Church and once was a home to numerous priests and nuns.

NOVEMBER 7, 2008
FULL MOON
Connecticut

As reported by Ryan Dube on paranormal.lovetoknow.com, a Connecticut family requested the service of a paranormal investigative team to verify the especially evil entity that was taunting them. The lead investigator of the group invited along a physicist and amateur paranormal investigator from Massachusetts whom the others referred to as "Doc." Doc did not believe in ghosts. He felt that all so -called "paranormal events" could easily be explained.

Soon after arriving at the site, Doc was given a tour by the homeowner while the remaining team of paranormal investigators began setting up their equipment. At one point the owner, Doc, and another member of the investigative team were standing at the bottom of the staircase when they began to hear loud footsteps on the floor above. Doc asked the owner whether there was someone else in the home. The homeowner replied, "My wife is at work and we don't have any children."

Eager to find out more, Doc challenged the spirit to show him what else he could do. The owner cautioned Doc to be careful how he spoke to the ghost. Not easily swayed, Doc yelled up the stairs once again, this time provoking the spirit even more by calling the ghost a lousy prankster. Suddenly, by some invisible force, Doc's pants were pulled down around his ankles. While everyone else burst out in uproarious laughter, Doc struggled with his pants and made a hasty retreat for the door. Is Doc now a believer? That's hard to say. However, it is reported that he has since refused to re-enter the home or talk about his experiences ever again.

NOVEMBER 8, 1848
STREEPERS TAVERN
Merion, Pennsylvania

The original inn and tavern was built in 1704 on land first owned by William Penn, the founder of Pennsylvania. It changed hands and names several times through the years. During the Revolutionary War, Streepers Tavern, as it was then called, was frequented and eventually occupied by British and Hessian soldiers (German mercenaries in employment of the king). Under the direction of Hannah Streeper, whose husband had gone off to serve with the colonials, it became a hotbed of spy activity. After the war ended, the inn was renamed the General Wayne Inn after American general Mad Anthony Wayne.

The inn continued to thrive and became a popular stopover for such notables as Ben Franklin, George Washington, and even Edgar Allen Poe. In the 1800s it was used as a polling place for Lower Merion Township. One election day, a female poll worker went into the cellar to retrieve some ballots, when a soldier confronted her. The young soldier, wearing a green uniform, seemed confused and frightened and to her surprise simply faded away. She reported this incident to her supervisor, who included it in an official report to the election board. The soldier in the green uniform has been seen several times through the years, but who was he?

During the Revolutionary War, a Hessian soldier, who wore a green uniform, went into the basement to get some wine. He never returned. While he was in the cellar, he discovered a secret tunnel. Patriots, hiding there, killed the soldier to prevent discovery and hid the body. Since then, it seems that he roams the inn hoping that his body will be discovered, looking for a proper burial.

NOVEMBER 9, 1929
THE BAKER HOTEL
Mineral Wells, Texas

The Baker Hotel opened in 1929. Although now closed, in its heyday the hotel in Mineral Wells, Texas, was a celebrity magnet, attracting clientele such as Judy Garland, Jean Harlow, Will Rogers, and Marlene Dietrich to name a few. At one time this fourteen-story, 460-room building was an impressive sight to behold. Now, all that remains is a decaying structure, overlaid with a long, rich history of visitors both living and deceased.

But who are among the spirits that are believed to roam the halls of the Baker Hotel? The story goes that one of the many spirits can be attributed to the gruesome death of an elevator operator in 1948. Playing a game of chance, he would often leap into the elevator while it was moving. One day he failed to jump all of the way in. A coworker, trying to help, grabbed on to the young man's legs in an attempt to pull him free. Unfortunately, he was too late. The elevator operator was crushed at the waist. It's been said that the ghost of the elevator operator has shown himself in the basement of the Baker on more than one occasion. Well, actually, he's only shown half of himself, since all that can be seen is his head and upper torso.

NOVEMBER 10, 1836
THE WALKER HOUSE
Mineral Point, Wisconsin

One of the oldest inns in all of Wisconsin, the Walker House, built in 1836, flourished as a meetinghouse where men from all over the region could gather. In November 1836, a man named William Caffee was executed by public hanging for shooting another man in an argument. But this would not be the last anyone saw of William Caffee. From the mid-1950s the inn stood vacant, until Ted Landon purchased it in 1964. While abandoned, it was the target of vandals and was in desperate need of repair. But soon after Langdon began renovating the building, he began to experience the unexplainable. Disembodied footsteps along with the sound of heavy breathing were heard. It's not known whether the spirits had anything to do with Ted's decision to sell, but once again, the inn would change hands. This time, only four years later, the inn came under new ownership by Dr. David Ruf. The new manager of the building was Walker Calvert. It was Calvert who first reported the ethereal voices arising from thin air and the shocking ghostly image of a headless specter wearing a tattered gray suit. Not long after seeing the torso of a ghost, Calvert spied the full-bodied apparition roaming about the second floor of the inn. Although the Walker House is no longer open to the general public, the owners of the structure are pretty sure that the spirit of William Caffee is still hanging around.

NOVEMBER 11, 1920
TOMB OF THE
UNKNOWN WARRIOR
London, England

Westminster Abbey, said to be consecrated by Saint Peter himself, is known for the elaborate coronations of English kings and queens. But it is also the home of the Tomb of the Unknown Warrior. During World War I, over 116,000 soldiers lost their lives on foreign soil.

Since it was impossible to bring all of the bodies home, and identification of all was near impossible, it was decided to build a monument to the brave lads who gave up so much for their country.

On the night of November 7, 1920, six bodies were exhumed from battlefields in France and brought to the church at St. Pol, each draped with the Union Jack. The British Commander, Brigadier General Wyatt, selected one of the bodies which was transported to England aboard the HMS *Verdun*. The others were reburied.

On November 11, 1920, the casket of the unknown warrior was honored by King George V and given a royal funeral. It was laid to rest in soil brought from the French battlefields and under a marble slab quarried in Belgium. The text on the tomb reads: "They buried him among the kings, because he had done good toward God and toward his house." After the funeral, over a million people visited the tomb. Today it is one of the world's most visited graves, but it seems that not all of the visitors are among the living. When the crowds thin and a deadly silence settles over the tomb, the ghostly apparition of a sullen soldier appears next to the grave. He stands in silence, head bowed, and then simply fades away. Is he the ghost of the unknown warrior or perhaps just the dead honoring the dead?

NOVEMBER 12, 1912
THE HAUNTING OF CROOKED CREEK
Harrison, Arkansas

The devastating murder of Ella Barham lives on in the memories of the townspeople of Harrison, Arkansas. Sadly, it was in November, 1912 when she would become the victim of a gruesome murder.

Ella was last seen when she left her home to go horseback riding, but the horse returned alone. Later that same evening, her corpse was found near an old mine shaft. The hunters who found her stated that they'd spotted a curious pile of stones, and upon removing them, located the remains of Ella. Her body had been dismembered by a saw.

Not long before she was murdered, Ella had refused the unwanted advances of a man named Odus Davidson. Naturally, Odus became the prime suspect. Terrified of being blamed for Ella's murder, Odus, in an attempt to confuse the scent of the bloodhounds, peppered his socks and fled into the woods. His effort proved to be futile because soon after, the posse found him.

Although he did not confess to her murder, he did admit to cutting wood that day close to where poor Ella's remains were found. Odus was tried, found guilty, and hanged for his crime.

It appears Ella's spirit has not left this earthly plane. Today, numerous visitors to the mineshaft have reported seeing the ghostly apparition of a woman in white.

NOVEMBER 13, 1974
AMITYVILLE HOUSE
Amityville, New York

The haunting of the Amityville house: fact or fiction? You decide. At approximately 1:00 A.M. on the morning of November 13, 1974, all hell broke loose. Butch DeFeo murdered his whole family in cold blood. Among the six to die were his father, mother, two brothers, and two sisters. One of them was named Dawn, whom he later branded an accomplice. But what could possibly drive a son to murder his parents and siblings? If one is to believe Butch, the plan was concocted after years of abuse at his father's hands. In fact, Butch, who never admitted to killing his siblings, stated that it was Dawn who first approached him with the heinous request of murdering their parents in cold blood. Butch refused, until the night of the thirteenth that is, when under the influence of drugs and alcohol, he finally caved in to Dawn's abhorrent requests. Since Butch was the only member of the DeFeo family to survive, it's difficult to say exactly what took place during that murderous night. However, it has been discovered that more than one gun was used, and gunpowder was in fact found on Dawn's nightgown, so perhaps there is some truth to Butch's tales. But what of the supposed haunting?

Tales of the haunting began thirteen months after the murders, when the Lutz family moved in. A priest named Father Mancusco blessed the home on December 18, 1975. During his blessing of the home, he allegedly heard, "Get out!" in one room in particular. Keeping the strange experience to himself, he recommended the Lutzes not use the room for a bedroom. Apparently they listened, and the room was converted into a sewing room, a room that later become the focus of unexplainable phenomena.

As reported by the Lutzes, supernatural events began to escalate in the next few weeks. The personalities of those living in the home changed. The children became so unruly that the Lutzes were forced to punish them severely, beating them with straps. The walls dripped green slime, and the sewing room became infested with large black flies, despite it being winter. On numerous occasions, George awoke to find his wife had turned into a ninety-year-old hag. Another time, he witnessed her body levitate off of their bed. Through the many supernatural tortures, the Lutzes became increasingly agitated. Finally, when a crucifix was found hanging upside down, George called in the priest once again. But when he refused to return, the family blessed the home themselves. Not long after, the Lutzes, taking minimal belongings with them, left the home, never to return. They lived in the reportedly haunted Amityville house for only twenty-eight days.

But are the tales of the Lutz family true or nothing more than a hoax for Hollywood to hype numerous books and movies? That's for you to decide.

NOVEMBER 14, 2007
BLUE MIST
Parma, Ohio

As reported in *Associated Content*, a surveillance camera at a Marathon gas station in Parma, Ohio, captured what appears to be a floating blue mist or blob circling around the gas pumps and finally coming to land atop a customer's windshield.

One baffled worker stated that the phenomenon lasted for approximately thirty minutes before finally vanishing.

Curious onlookers, attracted by all of the media attention, flocked to the gas station for a closer look. When interviewed by local media, it was apparent that opinions of the cause of the blue cloud varied. There were those that believed it to be nothing more than a blue plastic bag caught in the wind. However, when the surveillance video was replayed, even the most stringent nonbelievers were left scratching their heads.

One person believed the property to have once been inhabited by Native Americans and perhaps the gas station stood atop their burial grounds. Others believed the oddity to be an angelic presence or a spirit. It appears the floating blue blob is one sighting that may forever remain unexplainable.

NOVEMBER 15, 1910
HARRY'S ROAD HOUSE
Ashbury Park, New Jersey

Ever since Harry's opened, something hasn't been quite right, especially in the basement. One night, the manager closed the basement door only to have it swing back open as if pushed by an unseen hand. Another time, he observed a ghostly old woman traverse the cellar stairs and pass into the kitchen. But he's not the only person to see the glowing figure. On another occasion, the manager and two chefs went into the basement of the closed restaurant. They were startled when they witnessed an old lady across the room. The manager called out to her, informing her that they were closed and that she would have to leave. She didn't respond. Once again, he addressed her. Still there was no response. Finally as he approached her, she simply faded away. A garbage collector who she even called by name has also seen her. And on numerous occasions, the sobbing of a female can be heard in the women's bathroom. But who is this mysterious sullen woman?

She may have something to do with what happened in 1910. In November of that year, the mutilated body of a young girl was found near Harry's. And although a man was convicted of her murder, perhaps this apparition is that of the young girl's mother, still looking for her missing daughter.

NOVEMBER 16, 1919
SUICIDE BRIDGE
Pasadena, California

With much fanfare, the Colorado Street Bridge was dedicated on December 13, 1913. The nearly 1,500-foot concrete structure snakes its way across the Arroyo Seco in Pasadena. Like many major construction projects, there is a legend associated with it. During its construction, a worker tumbled to his death into a vat of quick-drying cement. Unable to retrieve the body, he became a permanent part of the bridge. This may be only a legend, yet it does reveal the bridge's darker side.

On November 16, 1919, the first of many suicides occurred. A man jumped from the bridge, falling 150 feet to the riverbed below. Since then, over a hundred suicides have been recorded, earning it the name Suicide Bridge. One of the most notable was that of a young mother, who on May 1, 1937, threw her baby over the rail and then jumped after her. Ironically they were not united in death as the mother had hoped. The baby landed in the trees below and survived.

In 1993 major renovations of the bridge were completed, including a new suicide fence, making it much more difficult to add to the bridge's checkered past. Yet, the great number of suicides continues to haunt the bridge, at least in spirit. Several ghosts have been associated with the bridge and the riverbed below. Motorists and pedestrians have spotted numerous spirits, including a man with wire-rim glasses and a woman in a long flowing robe who appears to jump from the bridge. The woman who threw her baby off the bridge is seen wandering the structure looking for her child. Below, the spirits walk aimlessly about and there are reports that strange sounds and crying can be heard. No one knows why there are so many suicides, but some say it is the construction worker who feeds people's depression, urging them to jump so that he may never have to roam alone.

NOVEMBER 17, 1896
OHIO STATE REFORMATORY
Mansfield, Ohio

Built in the late 1800s, the Ohio State Reformatory became home to more than 150,000 inmates in its ninety-four-year reign. Troublemakers were tossed into solitary confinement, also called the "hole." Some were never seen again. The others were executed, murdered, tortured, and forced to endure grueling mental and physical abuse day in and day out.

At first Ohio State Reformatory had good intentions. It would be a place where prisoners could be reformed for their reentrance into society. Just like anything else, the best-laid plans sometimes go awry. As the Gothic-style building aged, so did the ideals of the institution. In 1990, the building's state of disrepair, coupled with the torturous conditions, led to its demise.

With its turbulent history and the horrors meted out within its walls, it's no wonder that the Reformatory is reportedly haunted. Much of the activity takes place at the chapel. A chapel? Ah, but if you look deeper, it begins to make an eerie sense. You see, the chapel is located on the same spot where the executions were once carried out. It's here where many visitors have seen full apparitions of those they believe to be among the prisoners hanged in this room. But the chapel is not the only paranormally active place. The cells are alive with ethereal chatter, and the "hole," where many men suffered their last breaths has made many a visitor physically ill. And if nausea isn't enough to deter thrill seekers from entering the "hole," perhaps the report of glowing red eyes peering out of the threatening darkness will do the trick.

NOVEMBER 18, 1926
HAUNTED ROUTE 66
Catoosa, Oklahoma

If you're planning a road trip and you're not sure where you want to go, keep the "Mother Road" in mind. Route 66 is the road that cuts across eight states, running from California to Chicago. There are numerous ghost sightings along this roadway. And if you happen to find yourself in the vicinity of Catoosa, Oklahoma, it's been recommend by many a motorist that you stay on Route 66, and keep driving. If you don't, you may find yourself in the same predicament as other road warriors and come face-to-face with the ghost of a little boy. It seems that at some point in history, a young Native American boy was struck and killed just outside of Timber Ridge Cemetery, which is where he's now buried. It's this little boy's apparition that is sometimes seen kneeling on the side of the road by passersby. Others have stated that when driving down Highway 412, they've hit the ghostly apparition, only to see him vanish moments later. When they step out of their car to investigate further, they find no body, just a dented bumper smeared with bloody handprints.

NOVEMBER 19, 1797
HICKORY HILL
Gallatin County, Illinois

It is rumored that the former slave house in Hickory Hill is alive with torturous moans and whispers of days gone by. As retold by his descendants, John Crenshaw was a salt miner who was known to kidnap and lease slaves for mining. He was also a man who took great pleasure in torturing the slaves for the smallest of transgressions. However, once Crenshaw's tactics of procuring slaves became public knowledge, he was forced to change his ways and leave behind his mining of salt for a career in farming.

It wasn't until after 1920, when the slave house was converted into a tourist attraction, that strange occurrences were reported. On their walk through the attic (where the slaves had been shackled), visitors began to report unexplainable cold air and the eerie sounds of people crying and moaning, which appeared to arise out of nowhere.

In fact, it is said that one intrigued local ghost hunter, touched by the ghostly tales, declared that he would put the ghosts to rest. Rather, it turned out *he* was put to rest. Although he was in good health, not more than a few hours after venturing into the attic of Hickory Hill he dropped dead.

TERRIFYING TIDBIT

A recent Gallup poll revealed that 45 percent of Americans believe in ghosts.

NOVEMBER 20, 1734
AMERICA'S STONEHENGE
Salem, New Hampshire

America's Stonehenge, located deep in the woods near Salem, New Hampshire, has always been shrouded in mystery. This 4,000-year-old megalith site is a maze of stonewalls and trails punctuated with stone chambers. The main site contains a sacrificial alter, working observatory, burial chamber, and oracle hole. Little is known about the site or why it was abandoned.

The property is open to the public, and many visitors have witnessed their share of paranormal activity. Some have felt as if they were being watched, while others have spoken of a pair of red eyes watching them from the forest. Batteries in electronic devices become drained, and even hot coffee goes cold quickly. There have also been reports that one of the larger stones in the parking lot has morphed into the shape of a little old lady. Stones taken from the area have been quickly returned by frightened visitors, who claim that they had been transformed into nine-foot-tall Native Americans.

Many feel that Mystery Hill, as it is sometimes called, holds the secrets to America's past buried beneath its rock formations. But up to now it has yet to reveal them.

TERRIFYING TIDBIT
Smudging is a ceremony in which a bundle of herbs, most commonly sage, cedar, and sweetgrass, is burned to drive out a negative energy or entity from entering a space.

NOVEMBER 21, 2001
WINDHAM RESTAURANT
Windham, New Hampshire

In 1812, the Dinsmore family built the house where the Windham Restaurant is now located. Through the years it has seen its share of owners, and each time there have been reports of surreal goings-on.

Staff frequently experience the antics of spirits that wander around this New Hampshire restaurant. One waitress described feeling a cold chill, and an invisible hand brush back her blond hair as her unclasped necklace fell to the floor. Quite often the owners, Vess and Lula, have found place settings rearranged and chairs turned, facing the window, when they open in the morning, as if the spirits had been watching a parade.

Batteries continually drain from the air fresheners in the women's restroom. Much to their surprise, guests have also experienced paranormal activity. Female guests have had their dangle earrings toyed with. One gentleman, after asking his waitress about the ghosts, had his wine glass neatly fracture in his hand. The owners, rather than fearing their invisible guests, have embraced them. So much so that there have been numerous paranormal investigative teams, along with television crews, that have documented the strange occurrences. But who are the ghosts that inhabit this establishment? The spirit of a young girl has been seen, as well as a little boy, referred to as William. And on more than one occasion, staff members have run to the rescue of a man tumbling down the stairs, only to find that when he reaches the bottom, he vanishes. No matter when you make a visit to this haunted restaurant, it's doubtful you'll be disappointed. The sign over the door at the Windham Restaurant reads, "Food and Spirits," a phrase that is truer than you think.

TERRIFYING TIDBIT
Batteries are often drained in haunted locations. Paranormal investigators believe that spirits consume the batteries' energy to manifest.

NOVEMBER 22, 1904
THE FOX SISTERS
Hydesville, New York

The "Spook House," as it was so aptly named, was the location where the Fox sisters first realized their abilities to communicate with the dead.

Although the disturbing sounds had been heard prior, on March 31, 1848, the spirit of a man reached out to the Fox sisters by rapping on the walls. As if the spirit could hear and see all, it accurately answered a series of questions for both family and neighbors alike. Through a succession of beats, the Fox sisters learned that the spirit was that of a peddler. He'd been murdered, his throat slashed for a sum of $500. He stated that he was hidden, buried in the basement, ten feet below ground.

On April 1, 1848, an attempt to dig for the remains was halted due to flooding. It wasn't until November 22, 1904, when school children were playing in the cellar of the old Hydesville building, that the discovery would be made. The children found skeletal remains, along with a peddler's tin, beneath the dirt in the crumbling cellar. For a period of fifty-six years, the Fox sisters had been the subjects of ridicule and scorn. Finally, their claims of communicating with the deceased peddler were validated.

TERRIFYING TIDBIT

The Hydesville house, along with the peddler's remains and his tin, can be viewed at the central headquarters of American Spiritualists in Lilydale, New York—a true testament to the Fox sisters' ability to communicate with the dead.

NOVEMBER 23, 1924
SANTORIO CARLOS DURAN
Cartago, Costa Rica

Named after its founder, Dr. Duran, the old tuberculosis hospital built in 1915 is thought to be among the most haunted buildings in Costa Rica. Back in the days when it was a hospital, it had become home to tuberculosis patients, lepers, and the mentally insane, among others.

The building is abandoned now and under constant guard—during the day that is. There are not too many people who would willingly subject themselves to the haunted complex in the evening hours.

Stories prevail of the inhumane treatment of patients, who found themselves imprisoned in the facility. Perhaps their torment and suffering continues today, because numerous ghostly apparitions have been sighted. The echoes of voices have often been heard. And coins have mysteriously appeared out of thin air, thrown from what were previously patients' rooms. One repeatedly encountered specter is that of a nun. Many visitors to Santorio Carlos Duran have witnessed her presence. In fact, it's been said that one time a journalist doing an article on the old hospital spotted the nun upon her arrival and began interviewing her. Later, when she was discussing the interview she'd had with the old nun, the journalist was informed that the nun she had been interviewing was no longer among the living.

NOVEMBER 24, 1854
SACHS BRIDGE
Gettysburg, Pennsylvania

The Battle of Gettysburg raged for three days, killing over 50,000 Americans and wounding thousands more. The entire town and almost all of its buildings were involved in one way or another. The Sachs covered Bridge, which was built in 1854, was no exception. Like many of the buildings, the bridge too served as a field hospital for the troops, where doctors, under the poorest conditions, treated the wounded and the dying.

Now the bridge is a historical landmark and a hotbed of paranormal activity. Pictures taken from the bridge at night have shown strange glowing orbs and streaks of light. Visitors have heard the painful moans of the long-passed soldiers, while others have been overcome with grief, sensing the soldiers' unyielding pain. Full apparitions of men in uniform, both Union and Confederate, have been seen from time to time, bearing witness to the horror they witnessed those days in July of 1865.

NOVEMBER 25, 1758
POINT STATE PARK
Pittsburgh, Pennsylvania

The thirty-six-acre Point State Park opened in 1974 in downtown Pittsburgh. The park was built on the site of the old Fort Pitt, which played a vital role during the French and Indian War. Its key position at the point where the Allegheny and Monongahela Rivers meet to form the Ohio River helped make Pittsburgh the gateway to the west. And according to *www.hauntsandhistory.blogspot.com*, police and security guards have been reliving the park's past since it opened.

Police patrols have spotted the frightening apparitions of British and French soldiers and their Indian allies. Others have reported strange mists, undistinguishable voices, and even phantom battles, all occurring within the boundaries of the park. Despite heightened security, objects have disappeared from the park's museum, never to be seen again. Men in uniform have appeared on security monitors, but when guards go to investigate, they can't be found. And even America's great general, George Washington, has graced the park with his presence. Recently human bones were uncovered within its grounds, and a French reenactor was murdered. It appears to those working there that the park's past has come back to haunt them.

NOVEMBER 26, 1983
HUMMEL PARK
Omaha, Nebraska

The 200-acre Hummel Park was named after J. B. Hummel, a long-time superintendent of Omaha's Parks and Recreation. The park is on the site of an old fur trading post and may even include an Indian burial ground within its borders. Rumors of evil doings have been associated with it, including unsolved murders, lynchings, and animal sacrifice. In 1983, a prostitute was sexually assaulted and bludgeoned to death in the park. The vestiges of satanic rituals and the carcasses of dead animals have been found by the Morphing Stairs. They are called this because if the stairs are counted on the way up, there is a different number on the way down.

Visitors to the park have an uneasy feeling of being watched. And screams can be heard at night, although few dare to venture into the park after dark for fear of attack from the albino entities living in its trees.

TERRIFYING TIDBIT

If you're afraid of being in total darkness, you are said to have lygophobia.

NOVEMBER 27, 1944
11:11
Staffordshire, England

On a cool November morning, at 11:11 A.M., a horrific explosion ripped through what used to be the old Fauld gypsum mines. Thirty-five hundred tons of stored munitions exploded, creating a crater one-quarter mile wide and 300 feet deep. Over eighty people were killed in the explosion at the site and at a nearby plaster mill. It was the largest explosion of World War II before the dropping of the atomic bombs on Japan. It burst a nearby reservoir dam sending a wave of destruction upon the village below. The crater is still there today as a desolate reminder of the past, and it appears that some of its victims remain as well. Visitors to the site overcome by grief, disembodied screams and moans reverberating from the ground, and echoes of the victims below are all reminders of the tragedy that occurred at 11:11 that day.

NOVEMBER 28, 1700
FIVE-TO-FOUR FRED
Newton Burgoland, Leicestershire, England

The Belper Arms has been one of the most popular pubs in this region for centuries. Visitors come to enjoy good food and spirits. Every day at five minutes to four, just like clockwork, Freddy arrives. He always has a cold air about him as he makes himself known by stroking unsuspecting women's faces and giving the men a good squeeze with his cold clammy hands. And not being a politically correct type of guy, he often gives the lasses a good pat on the bottom. "Five-to-Four Fred," as the locals call him, certainly is a character, even if he is dead.

NOVEMBER 29, 1892
HOTEL DEL CORONADO
San Diego, California

Built in 1888, Hotel Del Coronado, designated a national historic landmark, is located at the water's edge on Coronado Island. This Victorian era building is legendary for its superb atmosphere. Or is that ethereal atmosphere? It appears that the Del Coronado is home to an eternal guest. Although rumors of murder abound, the sad tale goes that back in 1892, a young woman by the name of Kate Morgan, grief stricken and jilted by her lover, committed suicide.

So naturally, when guests report seeing the wispy image of a beautiful young woman walking through bedrooms, hallways, and gardens, it's Kate that immediately comes to mind.

In fact, there have been so many reports of strange occurrences that Christine Donovan, the Del Coronado's historian, has been recording visitors' ghostly experiences and has also written a book called *Beautiful Stranger: The Ghost of Kate Morgan and the Hotel del Coronado.*

Christine believes Kate to be relatively harmless, as the majority of the reported sightings include televisions and lights being turned on and off, glassware flying from gift shop shelves, and the feeling of being brushed up against by someone walking past. However, there have been more dramatic stories involving Kate. One guest wrote that during the night the ceiling fan above his head turned on for a short period of time, and then turned itself off. Upon waking, he found that all of his pillows had been removed from his bed and stacked atop his computer pyramid style. And just when you think it can't get any stranger, another couple, enjoying a romantic Valentine weekend away, had the scare of their lives when their bedding was ripped off their bodies by some unseen force. That story leads one to think that even in death, poor Kate is having difficulty bearing witness to passionate love.

NOVEMBER 30, 2003
NAM KOO TERRACE
Hong Kong, China

The two-story red brick house was built in 1915 by a prominent Chinese businessman. Today it is sometimes referred to as The Wan Chai Haunted House, after the district it is in. Because of its history, Nam

Koo Terrace is considered one of the most dangerous haunted houses in Hong Kong. Since the early 1900s it has been the stage for countless acts of violence, including rapes, suicides, and murders, the latest in 2009 when a man was found hanging from a tree outside the building. During the Japanese occupation, it was used as a brothel by the military. Numerous local Chinese women were raped and tortured by their captors.

The supernatural activity associated with the house has grown over the years. Citizens have reported hearing bone-chilling screams and seeing spectral fires, headless bodies, and acrid green smoke emanating from the building.

Thinking of visiting the building? Think again. In 2003 the *Oriental Daily*, a local newspaper, reported that a group of eight teenage ghost hunters attempted to investigate the haunting there. During the night, a ghostly assailant assaulted three female members, an experience so frightening that all three were hospitalized. It seems that, once again, Nam Koo Terrace has lived up to its reputation as Hong Kong's most dangerous haunted house.

DECEMBER 1, 2009
THE SCREAMING WOMAN
London, England

Filmmaker Peter Jackson has made a number of ghost movies, such as *The Frighteners*, a movie cowritten in 1996 with his wife, Fran Walsh, and *The Lovely Bones*, written by Alice Sebold. When asked by Britain's Channel 4 TV about the spiritual accuracy of *The Lovely Bones*, he said he couldn't be certain what a real soul was like.

He could, however, tell of his own supernatural encounter. Evidently, twenty years prior, when he lived with his wife across from the Thames Theatre, he found out firsthand what a ghostly apparition looked like. One morning Jackson awoke to the screaming face of a fiftyish-looking woman—a dead fiftyish-looking woman. Terrified, Jackson watched as her ghostly form glided down the end of his bed and disappeared into the wall. Unsure of what he'd just seen, he relayed his experience to Fran, who replied, "Was it the woman with the screaming face?" Fran, it seems, had seen her two years earlier.

Legend has it that the Thames Theatre is haunted. During the Vaudeville days, it was said that a woman, after having been booed off the stage, committed suicide. She is known to materialize in the theatre quite often. Perhaps her visit across the street to Jackson's apartment was due to the reported restoration, or maybe this screaming lady was only in search of an audition.

TERRIFYING TIDBIT

When a spirit materializes, it is said that it gains physical substance, as if suddenly appearing out of thin air.

DECEMBER 2, 1931
THE GURDON LIGHT
Gurdon, Arkansas

On cloudy and moonless nights, strange lights appear by a section of railroad tracks near Gurdon, Arkansas. The lights move from side to side, appearing and disappearing at will, casting no reflection, with no rational explanation. If you ask the locals, they'll tell you all about it.

Most believe the phenomenon involves a murder that took place on the railroad tracks back in 1931. Louis McBride worked for the Missouri-Pacific Railroad during the Great Depression. Because of the economic conditions of the time, there was a limit on how much time employees could work. Will McClain was McBride's foreman, and it wasn't long before the two got into a heated discussion about McBride's hours. The exchange turned violent, and in a fit of rage, McBride struck McClain with a railroad hammer, knocking him to the railroad bed. He continued to strike him until he severed his head.

The Gurdon Light started to appear shortly after McClain's murder. Most believe that it is the headless McClain wandering the tracks with a swinging railroad lantern searching for his severed head.

TERRIFYING TIDBIT

Phantom lights are considered to be a paranormal phenomenon when the floating lights cannot be explained by ordinary means.

DECEMBER 3, 2009
THE DISNEY WORLD GHOST
Orlando, Florida

The Haunted Mansion at Walt Disney World is haunted by more than just props and visual effects. As reported in the *McDowell News*, the mansion was built beside a lake that in the 1940s was the sight of a fatal plane crash. And it's believed that the man piloting the small-engine plane is the ghostly apparition that now inhabits the building.

One employee, who reported the sighting, said that he'd been working in the empty load area of one of the rides when all of a sudden he looked up to see an elderly man sitting in one of the "doom buggies." The young man approached the well-dressed gentleman and tried to get his attention, but the man refused to respond. Concerned, he spoke to other members of the staff and asked them to keep their eyes out for the phantom rider. But the man never appeared again.

Background music is often heard in the séance area, even when the attraction is turned off. And the mysterious sound of music playing from behind the walls is often heard. So the next time you pass through the Haunted Mansion, be aware that the ghosts floating before you may not all be holographic images.

DECEMBER 4, 1924
FACES IN THE WAVES
Gulf of Mexico

The oil tanker, S.S. *Watertown*, was sailing through the sea on its way to the Panama Canal when tragedy struck. Two crewmembers, Michael Meehan and James Courtney, were overcome by fumes while cleaning the cargo hold and suffocated. They were buried at sea off the Mexican coast. The following day, shortly before sunset, the first mate screamed in surprise as the faces of the dead men appeared in the water off the portside of the ship. Ten seconds later, they disappeared. But this was not the last time the two unfortunate souls were seen. For the next few days, they were spotted in the water by several members of the crew. The captain, Keith Tracey, reported this phenomenon to his employer, Cities Service Company, who suggested that he attempt to take a picture of the lost souls. He complied and then locked the camera in the ship's safe until he returned to port. When the film was developed, the faces did in fact appear in one of the six photographs he took. When a new replacement crew boarded the ship, all sightings of the phantom crewmen ended. The negatives were turned over to the Burns Detective Agency for authentication. They found no fakery. Even today, this photograph stands as one of the most amazing ghost photos ever taken.

DECEMBER 5, 1851
CAPTAIN TONY'S SALOON
Key West, Florida

Captain Tony's Saloon, previously named Sloppy Joe's, opened in 1851. Visitors to the saloon may be surprised to find that beneath the concrete floor lay numerous bodies. The story goes that, years prior, a hurricane tore through the island and destroyed the morgue, which was originally located in part of the building that the saloon now occupies. The destruction from the storm was so complete and the bodies of the morgue's inhabitants so unrecognizable that the decision was made to dig through the floor of the old building and bury the dead where they lay. They resealed the area and built walls up around it. But perhaps there were some who were a little unnerved with the way they buried their dead. Soon after, the top of the wall was lined with empty beer bottles filled with holy water, bottles that still can be found sitting on the saloon's shelf. But wait, there's more.

While enjoying a drink at Tony's, you can also take in the sight of the island's first hanging tree, which grows through the roof of the building. The island saw its share of murderous buccaneers, and what better place to execute them than a tree which stood in such close proximity to the morgue? At least eighteen people were hanged from its limbs. One of them, a woman who reportedly murdered her husband and children, is the spirit that is believed to haunt the bar. A ghostly apparition of a woman wearing a flowing nightgown has been spotted on numerous occasions. But then again, with the unusually macabre history of the building, how can anyone be sure?

TERRIFYING TIDBIT

An apparition is a physical manifestation of a spirit or entity. It can take many forms: transparent, mist-like, or even as solid as a living person. However, it often disappears quickly when being viewed.

DECEMBER 6, 1889
HOLLYWOOD CEMETERY
Richmond, Virginia

Named after the grove of holly trees on the grounds, this cemetery dating back to 1849 is reportedly alive with paranormal activity. Among its more famous residents are James Monroe, John Tyler, and Jefferson Davis. However, it's not the presidents who are said to haunt this cemetery, but the 18,000 Civil War veterans that are buried beneath the ninety-foot-tall pyramid of granite. Eleven thousand of those soldiers from the Battle of Gettysburg are interred in a mass grave. Many people who have visited the landmark at night have heard the soft moans of men floating atop the breeze. But the unknown soldiers are not the only ghosts that walk the grounds. Not too far from the pyramid is the cast iron statue of a dog. The dog had been moved from its original location, a storefront in downtown Richmond. It is said that a little girl would visit the shop every day to pet the statue. During an epidemic in 1892 she died. When she was buried at the cemetery, the owners of the cast iron dog placed it by her grave. Visitors today have sworn the dog has all but come to life, clenching its teeth and growling. So if you find yourself visiting the graves of the unknown soldiers, and you step too close to the statue of the dog, take heed; he just may come to life.

TERRIFYING TIDBIT

In Greek mythology, Galatea is a statue that comes to life. Perhaps the cast iron statue guarding the little girl in Hollywood Cemetery is of Greek descent?

DECEMBER 7, 2004
SELLING GRANDPA'S GHOST
Indianapolis, Indiana

Mary Anderson's six-year-old son, Collin, began to behave differently soon after his grandfather died. Terrified to roam around the house alone, he refused to go to the bathroom on his own. Soon after his grandfather died, he began seeing his ghost. Afraid to see his ghost again, he would even sit outside the bathroom door while his mother bathed. That's when Collin suggested to his mother that she sell grandpa on eBay.

Mary, stressed out by Collin's behavior, toyed with the idea. How could she convince Collin that his grandfather's ghost would leave? Sell him on eBay of all places? After doing some research, she realized that eBay does not allow sellers to offer intangible items such as spirits or souls where delivery cannot be confirmed. That was when a thought occurred to her: Her father's cane, the one item he was never without—why couldn't she sell it? In Collin's eyes, his grandfather and his cane were inseparable. As a ploy to ease her son's fears, Mary posted the cane for a seven-day sale. Her only request was that the buyer send a letter to Collin explaining that they'd received the cane along with the grandfather and both were doing well.

To her surprise, the cane with grandfather attached garnered 137 bids. The winning bid of $65,000 went to an online casino called the GoldenPalace.com. The cane with attached ghost was just one more item this Antigua-based casino added to their collection of oddities. What else did they purchase off eBay? How about a $25,000 grilled cheese sandwich displaying the image of the Virgin Mary. The above sales may have one pondering: Has eBay become a paranormal bazaar for unwanted souls?

DECEMBER 8, 1980
THE DAKOTA
New York, New York

This majestic apartment building, built in the Upper West Side in 1884, has been home to scores of the rich and famous: Judy Garland,

Lauren Bacall, and Boris Karloff, to name a few. Its Gothic styling is so spooky it was chosen for the filming of Roman Polanski's 1968 horror flick, *Rosemary's Baby*.

Rumors of hauntings prevail. The most notable is of its former tenant John Lennon. Tragically, John met his demise on December 8, 1980, when the former Beatle was gunned down in front of the Dakota apartment building. His ghostly apparition has been seen frequenting the building and also appeared during a televised séance held there.

But what other supernatural occurrences have taken place at the Dakota? A translucent image of young blond girl bouncing a ball was witnessed by tenants and painting contractors. The little girl walked into a closet and vanished. Other paranormal phenomena have included rugs and chairs sliding of their own accord and trash bags and tools being thrown haphazardly around the basement. In fact, one man who was about to accuse someone of making the mess stopped short when a metal bar slid across the basement floor. Upon bending to retrieve it, he realized it was too heavy for him to lift. A young boy wearing knickers has been spotted as well. The list goes on. Among other spectral visitors, a man with a black top hat has appeared. Those who have witnessed the ghostly apparition believe it to be none other than the man who built the Dakota but died before it opened, Edward Severin Clark.

TERRIFYING TIDBIT

A séance is a meeting in which a group of people gather to communicate with the dead.

DECEMBER 9, 1913
FORT GARRY HOTEL
Winnipeg, Manitoba, Canada

To take advantage of the business generated by its own trains, the Grand Trunk Pacific Railway commissioned the building of the Fort Garry Hotel. However, tragedy struck even before it was completed. During its construction, a worker fell to his death down an open elevator shaft. When the hotel was finally completed in 1913, the elegant 340-room building was the jewel of Winnipeg, but once again, tragedy struck. A young bride committed suicide in room 202 after she was informed that her new husband was killed in an automobile accident. Although she died, she has never checked out.

Patrons staying in this room have experienced the most dramatic paranormal activity in the hotel. Some maids avoid this room, complaining that sometimes blood seeps from the walls. Guests have heard a woman weeping. And often they have been startled when a shadowy figure appears at the foot of their bed. Not all of the supernatural activity is confined to this room. Unexplained glowing orbs have been seen in the halls. Eerie noises and disembodied moaning are heard in other areas of the hotel. And in the dining room, a phantom diner has been spotted enjoying a meal, apparently oblivious to his supernatural state. It appears that even in death, "life" goes on at the Fort Garry Hotel.

TERRIFYING TIDBIT

The elevator in the Hotel Chelsea in New York City is said to be home to one of the more famous ghosts. Sid Vicious, a deceased member of the band the Sex Pistols, has been seen lingering on the lift a time or two.

DECEMBER 10, 1997
THE SILVERPILEN
Stockholm, Sweden

Built in the 1960s as a prototype, this eight-car silver aluminum subway train was featured on the Swedish television program *Det spökar*, a popular show that deals with allegedly true hauntings, and rightfully so, because since the Silverpilen (Silver Arrow in English) was taken out of service, the gleaming phantasm has been seen by many. Subway employees and commuters have all witnessed the flash of the Silverpilen zipping through abandoned tunnels and unused lines, and even stopping to pick up unfortunate passengers. Those unlucky enough to board the glowing specter receive more than they bargained for. Once the train door closes, they become lost in time and space, arriving at their destination, hours, days, and even months later. The less fortunate ones, it is said, get off at the abandoned Kymlinge station and disappear, never to be seen again.

So if you ever go to Sweden, for either business or pleasure, and you decide to venture onto its subway system, beware of the Silverpilen. And remember this: *"Bara de döda stiger av i Kymlinge"* (only the dead get off at Kymlinge).

DECEMBER 11, 1849
ST. ANDREWS ON THE RED CHURCH
Selkirk, Manitoba, Canada

This Gothic Revival church was built between 1845 and 1849 and was consecrated in December 1849. It is the oldest Anglican Church outside of the British Isles and perhaps the most haunted. The church's organ is known to play of its own accord, and a woman in white appears in the balcony at services. In the graveyard behind the church, a man in black has made his presence known. A phantom automobile appears out of nowhere. And a pair of red disembodied eyes follows your every move. Rumors say that the woman in white may have died when the church was under construction and became entombed within its foundations.

Those unlucky enough to spy the spirits of St. Andrews on the Red Church are said to suffer hideous nightmares involving the rattling of the church's gates. Is it the spirits of the church warning curious visitors to keep away? Or is it a plea from the ghosts to unravel their mysterious appearance?

TERRIFYING TIDBITS

Many religions and cultures believe dreams to be a way to connect the physical world with the ethereal world, or the supernatural.

DECEMBER 12, 1986
THE WHITNEY RESTAURANT
Detroit, Michigan

A massive three-story mansion was built in 1894 for lumber baron David Whitney Jr. The Romanesque Revival house contained 52 rooms, 20 fireplaces, 218 windows, and a secret vault. The building remained in the Whitney family until the 1920s, when it became the home of the Wayne County Medical Society. In 1980 Richard Kughn purchased the building and opened a restaurant. In 2007, former Chrysler executive, Bud Liebler, purchased the restaurant.

Reports of paranormal activity began surfacing in the mid-1980s during its restoration. The ghosts of both David Whitney Jr. and his wife have appeared within its venerable walls. Dark shadows and the apparition of a man dressed in a tuxedo have been witnessed on the third floor. Ghostly activity has also been reported on the elevator. As if summoned by some unseen force, the elevator moves on its own, mysteriously stopping between floors. When the doors finally open, no one is there. Repair technicians have found no logical explanation for the elevator's behavior. Then there are the reports of dishes and place setting rearranging themselves in the dining room and cold spots being felt throughout the restaurant. The staff has learned to live with the unworldly activity, and the owners seem to embrace it; otherwise, why would they have a Ghost Bar?

DECEMBER 13, 1870
THE LOST VIKING SHIP
California Desert

Bizarre things happen to those who visit the desert, especially those brave enough to venture into it at night. Eerie sounds that grate on your ears, indistinguishable voices carried by the wind, and strange lights and shadows dancing in front of your eyes have been reported. Most frightening of all are the ghostly images of those who have died. Native Americans, prospectors, conquistadors, soldiers, pioneers, and Vikings have all been seen. Vikings in the desert?

Believe it or not, there have been numerous accounts of a Viking longboat submerged deep in the desert sands. Within its rotting hull lies a fortune in pearls and other valuables. Several Native American legends support these tales. They tell of a long boat with a serpent head and round shields on its sides being manned by men with blond hair and blue eyes.

Prospectors talk about finding such a vessel, and according to Julian librarian Myrtle Botts, one old man even had photographs. Under the direction of the mysterious prospector, Myrtle and her husband went in search of the vessel, but were thwarted by the earthquake of 1933. Perhaps the timing of the earthquake and the shifting of the desert's sand was no accident, but was nature's way of preserving the ghosts of the longboat's treasure for eternity.

TERRIFYING TIDBIT

The Vikings, like the Egyptians, were buried with their treasures, carrying everything they would need from this world to the next. The wealthy were put to sea on their ships, which were set ablaze.

DECEMBER 14, 1799
GEORGE WASHINGTON
Gettysburg, Pennsylvania

George Washington's ghost is said to have been sighted in numerous locations: the Hiawassee woods and at the Hotel Chamberlain to name just two. In fact, one of the more compelling stories of Washington's appearance comes from a group of Union soldiers.

It is said that Washington appeared before the soldiers while they struggled to keep the Confederates from advancing on Little Round Top at the Battle of Gettysburg. There he sat, sword drawn, atop a fluorescent white stallion. In a commanding voice he ordered them to fix their bayonets and charge. The Union soldiers obeyed the order, forcing the Confederate soldiers into a full retreat. Had they not listened to the General's ghost, they would surely have been slaughtered.

But that was not the last report of his appearance at Gettysburg. It seems that many of the residents have seen the luminescent spirit of George Washington as he and his ghostly steed gallop across a moonlit battlefield.

DECEMBER 15, A.D. 37
SANTA MARIA DEL POPOLO CHURCH
Rome, Italy

Santa Maria del Popolo Church was built upon the former grave of the Roman Emperor Nero who was born on December 15, A.D. 37 and ruled during the time of the great fire. The fire that burned for six days, destroying two-thirds of the city of Rome, was blamed on Nero's slaves. A brutal tyrant, Nero deflected the charge, pointing his finger back on the populace, proclaiming the Christians were at fault. Four years later, on June 9, A.D. 68, while facing his own execution, Nero committed suicide. His body was entombed. Legend has it that out of his grave grew a mighty walnut tree that attracted multitudes of ravens. Superstitious Roman citizens proclaimed Nero's soul was being tormented by the Devil himself. And the tree and its flock of birds was what grounded Nero's restless soul to earth. In 1099, the people of Rome had so tired of dealing with his malevolent ghost that they petitioned the Pope to resolve the situation. It is said that Pope Pascal II fasted in prayer and was soon visited by the Virgin Mary. She told the Pope how to put an end to Nero's ghost. Following the Virgin Mary's instructions, the Pope ordered the tree cut down. Then, Nero's tomb was dug up, and it was thrown into the Tiber River. To consecrate the exorcised ground, a church was built on the site. In 1472, Pope Sixtus IV rebuilt and named the church Santa Maria del Popolo. And as for Nero, there are some who believe he still wanders this earth, his soul still at unrest. But perhaps this theory is just for the birds.

DECEMBER 16, 1820
THE BELL WITCH
Adams, Tennessee

The beginning of the end for John Bell began in 1817. It all started one day when John, who was tending his crops, spotted a strange-looking creature that he described as a mix between a rabbit and a dog. The second Bell opened fire on the beast it vanished before him.

The Bells' torment had only just begun, however. First they heard the sound of loud knocking and banging against their home. The entity grew in strength with each passing day. What had started with the sound of banging, progressed to gurgling noises, animals fighting, the scraping of chains being dragged upon the floor, and physical attacks. It seems that not only did the entity loathe John Bell, it also took a dislike to his daughter, Betsy. Poor Betsy was scratched, spit at, had her hair pulled, and was forced to endure nightly beatings. Finally after a year of torment, John Bell told all.

A neighbor, James Johnston, brought in a close friend, a Methodist minister, with the intent to rid the Bell family's home of the evil presence. They failed miserably. The entity had become so powerful that it had begun to have full conversations with people, at times quoting scripture. When the presence was asked when it would leave, it replied that it would not leave until John Bell was dead and buried.

President Andrew Jackson and his men, having heard of the activity made a visit to the Bell farm. Upon arriving, one of Jackson's men boasted of his ability to destroy the spirit. No sooner had the words left his mouth than the carriage stopped in its tracks, refusing to roll forward any farther. Then suddenly, after hearing the entity's words telling it to move, the carriage began to roll. The spirit tortured Jackson and his men throughout the night. Horrified, they left as soon as they could and never returned.

John Bell, no longer able to withstand the torment, took to his bed, where he soon died. A mysterious vial of liquid (poison) was found beside his body.

At John Bell's funeral, the entity was heard merrily singing and celebrating. With its mission accomplished, it left, never to be heard from again.

TERRIFYING TIDBIT

Many people believe that the entity that tormented John Bell kept its word and left. However, did it really? Or has the malevolent spirit returned from whence it came . . . residing in a cave on the former Bell property, adeptly named, the Bell Witch Cave.

DECEMBER 17, 1886
THE DRISKILL HOTEL
Austin, Texas

Colonel Jesse Lincoln Driskill, the original owner of the haunted Driskill hotel in Austin, Texas, was said to have made his fortune through the sale of longhorns. In search of a change of careers, Jesse purchased a plot of land. His intention was to build one of the finest hotels the city of Austin had ever seen. He succeeded, and soon after it opened in December of 1886, the Driskill Hotel quickly became all the rage for Austin's high society. In fact, during Prohibition, it housed one of the finest speakeasies.

And although it has changed hands more than twenty-five times, many believe the wafting scent of cigar smoke belongs to none other than the ghost of Jesse, the original owner. But he's not the only ghost that remains at the Driskill. Among other spirits to frequent the hotel is the spirit of a little girl who, along with bouncing a ball, can be heard in the first floor lobby, the women's bathroom, and the stairs leading up to the mezzanine. But who is she? In 1887, while the Capitol building underwent construction, the Senate used the mezzanine of the hotel to host their meetings. One day, while in session, the daughter of a senator fell to her death while chasing a ball down the mezzanine steps.

Unfortunately for the Driskill, it has certainly seen its share of ill luck. The most recent fatality to stain the walls of this national landmark was in the 1990s when a young woman, who, after being jilted by her fiancé, took his credit cards and went on a spending spree. Not long after, she was found in the bathtub of her room, bleeding from what appeared to be a self-inflicted bullet wound to her abdomen.

Since then, visitors have reported seeing a young woman walking to room 29, her arms overflowing with packages. One visitor, confused as to why someone would be staying in an area that was being renovated, informed the front desk. Together they went to the room, but found only plastic sheeting. The room was completely empty. Unbeknownst to the guest, it was the same room in which the young woman had committed suicide.

DECEMBER 18, 2008
FAMILY PLAGUED BY SPIRITS
Kolkata, India

According to the *Times of India*, a frantic Ratan Das called the Khardah police station for help. It appears that a ghost had targeted him and his family. At first, the family watched as household goods began to fall from the shelves. Soon after, the refrigerator door cracked and then fell off the hinges. Flower vases vibrated, then crashed to the floor. Das began to understand the seriousness of the haunting when his daughter Rima fell to the floor after being shoved from behind by an invisible force. And the girl's books were set ablaze.

Then the Dases walked into a bedroom and watched in horror as the corner of the bed ignited into flames and the almirah doors on the clothing cabinet opened wide. Inside were saris, shirts, and the like, what was left of them anyway. All the garments had been cut up and tossed haphazardly around the room. Ratan's wife and daughter were so terrified by the ghost attacks that they pleaded with Das to leave the home immediately. Word of the paranormal phenomena spread throughout the neighborhood. The police, along with scores of curious onlookers, arrived at their home to find it in shambles. The police offered the family moral support. They were hopeful that they would find the culprit behind the mischievous acts. Let's hope for the sake of the Das family that the ghostly specter moved on. Because unfortunately for the Khardah police department, the chances of detaining a ghost are slim to none.

TERRIFYING TIDBIT

In India, an Ukobach or a Urobach (Unk) is also known as a fire demon.

DECEMBER 19, 2003
HENRY THE VIII'S GHOST CAUGHT ON CCTV
Herefordshire, United Kingdom

Alarms sounded at Hampton Court Castle in the United Kingdom. As guards rushed to the scene, they found, nothing. The heavy doors that they thought had triggered the alarm were closed and no one could be found. Perplexed by the situation, they decided to review the footage captured by a nearby closed circuit television camera. To their astonishment, the camera had captured the doors being flung open by themselves. Perhaps even stranger, they were then closed by what appeared to be a figure in a heavy robe or coat. Footage from other cameras in the area was reviewed, but it revealed no one else was in that part of the building. The next day, at approximately the same time, one o'clock in the afternoon, the door alarm went off again. This time the camera failed to pick up the image of the ghostly figure affectionately nicknamed "Skeletor" by the guards. Further review revealed that this incident had occurred three days in a row. At first they thought it was one of the guides working at the castle. However, this theory has been ruled out. Guides do not work in that part of the castle.

The press picked up on the story of the medieval specter, and they had their own take on the story. It was soon reported that Henry the VIII's ghost had been captured on CCTV at Hampton Court Castle.

DECEMBER 20, 2009
THE ENFIELD DEMON
Enfield, Connecticut

A local family living in a 200-year-old home is being tormented by an elemental, a small demon, recognized by the Native Americans as a "soul stealer," or, more formally, "Windago."

The Yaples' story was aired on national television, as part of Animal Planet's new series, *The Haunted*. But what sort of paranormal phenomenon has the Yaple family encountered that would garner national attention? Although Jay and Elke Yaple have endured a multitude of horrors at the hands of this entity, it was the Yaples' concern for the safety of their children that had them reaching out for help. The abhorrent event attracted the attention of the media as well.

One evening, while listening to the soft crackle of their baby monitor, the Yaples' heard a guttural voice say, "You're all going to die." Terrified, they ran to their children's bedroom. Then looked on in horror at the scatter of bloody handprints on the crib. Thankfully, their children were unharmed.

That's when they called the Connecticut Paranormal Investigators for help. It took nearly two hours for Jay to relate the lengthy list of paranormal afflictions the Yaple family had been forced to endure. Bob Baker, the team leader, put a plan in motion. The team, along with Father Bob Bailey, a veteran demonologist, set about to rid the family of the demonic presence. Their plan was to start the blessing at the uppermost level of the home, sequentially visiting each room. During their investigation they noted the oppressive atmosphere when they walked into the home, a feeling that for some on the team lingered on for several days. While the team was in the attic, unexplainable footsteps were heard climbing the attic steps. Then there was the slow creaking sound moments later as the team stood in the master bedroom and the invisible presence walked back down the attic steps, stopping between two members of the group. Later review of the camera footage revealed an orb exit a closet, make a right, and head toward the attic. Upon completion of the investigation and the blessing by Father Bob, the Yaple family has reported that at the time of this printing, the demonic presence wreaking havoc in their lives has dissipated.

DECEMBER 21, 1843
SPRAGUE MANSION
Cranston, Rhode Island

Rhode Island businessman William Sprague built the Sprague Mansion in 1790. Through the years it has seen its share of tragedy, mystery, and murder. In 1843, Amasa Spague left the mansion and never returned. His body was discovered the next morning by the road. He had been bludgeoned to death, shot, and bitten by a dog. John Gordon, an employee of the mansion, was arrested and on circumstantial evidence convicted of his murder. Hanged in 1845, Gordon was the last person executed in the state of Rhode Island. Sometime after his death, evidence came to light as to his innocence in the murder. This led to a public outcry, which eventually resulted in the abolishment of the death penalty in Rhode Island. Although Gordon was hanged, it seems that he may be one of the many spirits still roaming the mansion. Keeping Gordon's ghost company are Kate Chase Sprague, who has been seen on the staircase; Amasa Sprague; William Sprague II; Amasa's wife, who went insane; and "Charlie the Butler."

The mansion has many paranormal hot spots as well. Photographs of strange light anomalies have been captured in the dank wine cellar. The creepy doll room with its odd collection of porcelain dolls is known to unnerve the most seasoned paranormal investigator. And the carriage house, where dark creatures move among the shadows, has added to the mansion's reputation as the most haunted place in all of Cranston.

DECEMBER 22, 1973
THE STAGECOACH TAVERN
Gloucester, Rhode Island

The Stagecoach Tavern, now called Tavern on Main, is arguably the most haunted building in the small Rhode Island town of Chepachet. During the eighteenth century, it was a stopover for coach passengers on their way to and from Hartford and Providence. In 1842, it became a staging area for the Doer Rebellion, nearly bankrupting owner Jedediah Sprague. Through the years, the tavern has had different owners, but one thing they all agreed upon is that it is haunted.

In 1973, a woman was murdered by her jealous lover as she sat on a bar stool in the tavern. Her spirit remains there today. Employees as well as patrons have seen a wispy woman, thought to be the murder victim, sitting in a corner booth. Other times she has been spied by the kitchen, checking in on the cook. One paranormal investigator, Thomas D'Agostino, recorded strange electromagnetic fluxes near the bar stool where she was shot, revealing her invisible presence.

The ghost of a little boy haunts the women's room, kind of a spectral peeping Tom. He has also been seen in the dining room and is thought to be responsible for the mysterious moving of the place settings there. Orbs constantly show up in photographs, glasses break, coasters fly off the shelves, and employees are startled by disembodied voices, testifying that the Stagecoach Tavern is the most haunted building in Gloucester.

TERRIFYING TIDBIT

An electromagnetic field meter (EMF) is used to measure fluctuations in the magnetic fields. Many believe that ghosts cause a disturbance in the field.

DECEMBER 23, 1843
THE DEER PARK TAVERN
Newark, Delaware

In the 1700s the Saint Patrick's Inn was a popular stopping place for travelers. In 1764 Charles Mason and Jeremiah Dixon spent some time at the inn with their pet bear. They were described as a jolly bunch that consumed large portions of brandy. Of course they are most noted for their work in creating the Mason-Dixon Line, separating free states and slave states. During the American Revolution, General George Washington and other members of the Colonial Army stayed there as well. In 1843, Edgar Allen Poe made a visit to the area. When he attempted to get out of his carriage, it is reputed that he fell in the mud. He became so angry that he put a curse on the inn. The inn burned down shortly thereafter. In 1851, the Deer Park Hotel was built on the land once occupied by the St. Patrick's Inn. It was reported to be one of the finest hotels on the east coast. Now it is named the Deer Park Tavern, but if you ask the staff, some of the hotel's former residents have never left. The front door opens as if someone's walking in, but nobody is there. Employees have heard soft whispers and sometimes get the feeling that someone is behind them even though they know the tavern is empty. And the bar's security cameras once captured the most compelling evidence, as the bar stools were tossed about by an unworldly force.

TERRIFYING TIDBIT

During its active years, Fort Delaware was home to 40,000 prisoners. And with the highest mortality rate of any Union prison, it claimed over 2,500 deaths. It's no wonder why it's considered by many to be one of the more haunted forts in the nation.

DECEMBER 24, 1548
WAWEL CASTLE
Krakow, Poland

Wawel Royal Castle was erected on Wawel Hill in 1548 by King Sigismund the Old. It has been the seat of Polish royalty for hundreds of years. Kings were crowned and laid to rest in its vaults. In the hill is a deep cave known as the Smocza Jama, the "Dragon's Den." According to legend, there was a dragon that dwelled within and that ventured out to cause great harm to the people of Poland, devouring livestock and virgins alike. Prince Krak finally slew the dragon and saved the land. Today the cave contains a statue of the dragon, reminding all of his feat. But deep within, it houses a chamber of the conference of kings. Every December 24, there is a council of all the dead Polish kings. The ghosts of the kings roam the castle as well, looking after their beloved land. It is also said that when Stancyk the king's jester appears, Poland is in peril.

DECEMBER 25, 1727
MISTLETOE BOUGH GHOST
Hampshire, England

The last place you would expect to see a ghost would be Britain's Police College. Yet there have been sightings of no less than fourteen ghosts there. The Jacobean building, known as Bramshill House, has its roots back to the 1600s. Baron Zouche built the current building, but it is the next owner, Sir John Cope, or to be more precise, his daughter Anne, who is the most famous ghost associated with the property.

Anne was married on Christmas. During the wedding feast, Anne suggested a game of hide and seek. The guests and wedding party immediately dispersed throughout the mansion. The young bride soon found herself in a little-used part of the house where she came upon an oak chest. She opened it and climbed inside. It was a perfect but deadly hiding place. For little did she know, as the lid snapped shut, that she would be entombed in the ornate box for fifty years. When her hiding place was finally uncovered they found her decayed remains still in her wedding dress, her mummified hands still clutching her mistletoe bouquet. Scratch marks on the lid were silent testimony of her desperate fight for her life.

In 1953, Bramshill House became a police college; the oak chest and Anne still remain. Although the chief superintendent laughs at the reports, many of the cadets have admitted seeing Anne, the lady in white, and more notably, catching the sweet aroma of her Christmas bouquet.

There have been so many reports of Anne and the other ghosts at the college that the administration keeps a detailed record of all of the sightings associated with the mansion. If you happen to visit the college and you see Anne or one of the other spirits, don't forget to report it to the secretary so they can update the "ghost file."

DECEMBER 26, 2004
GHOSTLY TOURISTS
Ao Nang, Thailand

Four days after the Thai tsunami took its deadly toll, reports of the sounds of laughter and cries along with sightings of ghostly apparitions frolicking through the waves began to surface from the Phi Phi and Khoa Lak islands. Yet when volunteers who were brave enough ventured a look, the only thing they found was darkness and sand.

Taxi drivers have reported picking up customers and their luggage, yet moments later they glance into their rearview mirror and find that their backseat is empty of passengers.

Although mental health workers attribute these paranormal experiences to mass hysteria, the Thai people are steadfast in their beliefs. Thai custom dictates that a friend or loved one must cremate and bless the deceased or else they will continue to be at unrest. This is why many of the locals are certain that it's the foreigners who still haunt the island. They are tourists who, due to their sudden death in the tsunami, are eternally vacationing, unaware of their demise.

TERRIFYING TIDBIT

In an attempt to alleviate the worry of the deceased spirit, Thai custom discourages family members from crying at the funerals. And monks are asked to chant prayers to prevent the dead from rising and returning as a malicious spirit.

DECEMBER 27, 1972
LORD CALVERT'S MANSION
Riverdale, Maryland

In 1972, Mr. Smith, a seventy-five-year-old gentleman, afraid to live alone in Lord Calvert's mansion, asked Rick, a deputy sheriff in Prince George's County, Maryland, to be his live-in companion. The mansion was rumored to be haunted by the son-in-law of Lord Calvert, who hanged himself from a tree in the front yard. But did Rick believe it was haunted? He can't say for sure. However, one night, while the elderly man was away, Rick was out tending to the horses. Afterward, when he started back toward the house, he noticed the light in the attic. For a moment he just stood and stared. The attic had no electricity. How was this possible? He knew by the clarity of the rafters that the light source had to come from inside the house. To be certain his eyes weren't playing tricks on him, Rick looked around for an alternate light source, but found none.

Since Mr. Smith was away visiting someone for Christmas and no one else should have been in the house, Rick's police training kicked in, and he became concerned with the possibility of an intruder. He rushed back into the house and searched the three lower floors, verifying that all entrances were secured, before finally making his way up to the attic. He slowly opened the attic door. But there was nothing but darkness.

This didn't make a whole lot of sense. He knew he'd seen the light only moments before, and although there was a lamp stored in the attic for emergencies, the bulb was completely cold. In Rick's profession he has seen a lot of strange happenings, but a light coming from an attic without electricity topped his list for unexplainable events. Did he see the spirit of Lord Calvert? Rick will forever wonder.

DECEMBER 28, 1879
THE DIVER
Tay Rail Bridge, Scotland

Despite the foul December weather, the powerful locomotive NBR (Northern British Railway) 224 steamed through the raging winter winds on rain-swept tracks. By the time it reached the Tay Bridge between Dundee and Wormit, Scotland, gale-force winds were howling across the firth. As 224 reached the center of the bridge, aptly referred to as the High Girders, the center span began to creak and moan with the violent winds. Then the unthinkable happened. The bridge began to collapse, sending the NBR 224 and it's carriages into the frigid waters of the estuary.

Seventy-five poor souls lost their lives that night, including the son-in-law of the designer of the bridge. Some of the bodies were never recovered. But they managed to raise the NBR 224 from the bottom of the firth and salvage it. The bridge was rebuilt using some of the girders from the original bridge, and the 224 was reconditioned and put back into service. Nicknamed the Diver, the engine had many engineers spooked, and they were deathly afraid to drive it, especially over the newly constructed Tay Bridge. Despite its reputation, however, the locomotive remained in service until 1919, but that's not the end of our story or of the Diver.

For years, folks have reported that if you stand on the shore at 7:15 P.M. on the anniversary of the accident, you can see ghostly lights and hear ghastly screams and the screeching of the 224's brakes, as the spectral locomotive replays that dreadful night.

DECEMBER 29, 1972
FLIGHT 401
Miami, Florida

At 9:20 P.M. on a dark Friday night, Eastern Airline Flight 401 embarked from New York's JFK en route to Miami International Airport. The Lockheed L-1011 Tristar was piloted by Captain Bob Loft, copilot Donald Repo, and flight engineer Albert Stockstill. While attempting to investigate a malfunctioning landing gear lamp the airplane lost altitude and crashed into the Florida Everglades.

Of the 163 passengers and 13 crew members, 101 died in the crash, including Captain Loft and Donald Repo.

In the following months, Captain Loft and Donald Repo began appearing on other Eastern Airline flights, or at least their ghosts did. They were reportedly seen by many crew and passengers in the cockpit, galley, and first-class sections of the 401's sister ships. The ghosts seemed to be concerned about the safety of the airplanes in which they had been spotted. Reportedly, one flight was even cancelled after Captain Loft materialized in the cockpit and spoke to the crew. Although the airline denied it, it was later alleged that salvaged parts from the ill-fated flight 401 had been used in these planes. Were the ghosts of Loft and Repo trying to save others from their disastrous fate? Many who have experienced this firsthand believe they were.

DECEMBER 30, 2006
SADDAM'S GHOST
Baghdad, Iraq

Saddam Hussein was a brutal dictator who thought he was the reincarnation of the great Babylonian King Nebuchadnezzar II. His power over his people was godlike and his ability to escape death legendary. Therefore it is not surprising that even after his death some refuse to believe he is gone. He was hanged, and his body was buried with his sons in his hometown of Awja, which should have ended his reign of terror, but some believe he is still reaching out from the other side.

In life, Saddam was a mysterious man. Rumors abound about his relationship with the supernatural. Some say he made a pact with aliens, giving them and their ships safe harbor for genetically engineered demon hounds with the killing abilities of scorpions. Others say he found a mystical blue stone with the power of bestowing immortality, which he had implanted in his forearm. Supposedly, he tested by implanting it in a chicken and then shooting the chicken with a gun. The chicken lived, protected by the stone.

Whether his ghost is real or not, we cannot be sure. But it is clear that Saddam still haunts the people of Iraq, even from beyond the grave.

TERRIFYING TIDBIT

The late president of Iraq, Saddam Hussein wrote four romance novels—some written by himself, others by ghostwriters.

DECEMBER 31, 1890
JOESEFA'S HEAD
Gasparilla Island State Park, Florida

Although the legend begins some ninety years before the lighthouse was built, it is believed that one of the ghosts to frequent the Old Port Boca Grande Lighthouse is the spirit of a beautiful Spanish princess named Josefa. Jose Gaspar, a Spanish pirate, captured the princess. It is said that Gaspar was so in love with the princess that when she rejected him, in his fury, he drew his sword and, with one fatal blow, removed her head.

Apparently Jose was so remorseful that he picked up Josefa's lifeless body and buried her in the sands of Gasparilla Island. But not wanting to be without her, he kept Josefa's head and carried it with him wherever he went. Allegedly, it is the headless specter of Josefa that is seen wandering around the island, in search of her head.

TERRIFYING TIDBIT

The legend of Jose Gaspar is celebrated yearly in Tampa, Florida, at the Gasparilla Pirate Festival.

RESOURCES

About.com *www.about.com*

BBC News. *http://news.bbc.co.uk*

Belanger, Jeff. *The World's Most Haunted Places 2004.* Franklin Lakes, NJ: Career Press, 2004.

Belanger, Jeff. *Encyclopedia of Hunted Places 2005.* Franklin Lakes, NJ: New Page Books, 2005.

Brooks, Marla. *Ghosts of Hollywood 2008.* Atglen, PA: Schiffer Publishing Ltd., 2008.

Cahill, Robert Ellis. *New England's Things That Go Bump in the Night.* Peabody, MA: Chandler-Smith Publishing House, Inc., 1989.

Cohen, Daniel. *Real Ghosts 1977.* New York: Pocket Books, 1977.

Coulombe, Charles A. *Haunted Places in America 2004.* Guilford, CT: The Lyons Press, 2004.

Coulombe, Charles A. *Haunted Castles of the World 2004.* Guilford, CT: The Lyons Press, 2004.

D'Agostino, Thomas. *Haunted New Hampshire 2006.* Atglen, PA: Schiffer Publishing Ltd., 2006.

D'Agostino, Thomas. *Haunted Rhode Island 2006.* Atglen, PA: Schiffer Publishing Ltd., 2006.

D'Entremont, Jeremy. *The Lighthouse Handbook New England 2008*. Kennebunkport, ME: Cider Mill Press Book Publishers, 2008.

Everything Creepy. *www.everythingcreepy.com*

Examiner.com. *www.examiner.com*

GhostTheory.com *www.ghosttheory.com*

Jackson, Robert. *Great Mysteries Ghosts 1992*. New York: Smithmark Publishers Inc., 1992.

Jones, Richard. *Haunted Britain and Ireland 2003*. New York: Barnes & Noble, 2003.

Legends of America. *www.legendsofamerica.com*

New England Lighthouses. *www.lighthouse.cc*

O'Connor, Marianne. *Haunted Hikes of New Hampshire 2008*. Exeter, NH: Publishing Works, Inc., 2008.

Paranormaltoknow. *http://paranormal.lovetoknow.com/Main_Page*

Taylor, Troy. *www.prairieghosts.com*

The Cabinet. *www.thecabinet.com*

Unsolved Mysteries. *www.unsolvedmysteries.com*

Wood, Maureen, and Ron Kolek. *The Ghost Chronicles 2009.* Naperville, IL: Source Books, 2009.

Zwicker, Roxie J. *Haunted Portsmouth 2007.* Charleston, SC: The History Press, 2007.

ABOUT THE AUTHORS

RON KOLEK

Ron Kolek is the Emmy-winning founder and lead investigator of *The New England Ghost Project*. With a degree in environmental science from Nathaniel Hawthorne College, he was the ultimate skeptic. However, a near death experience changed all that. No longer blinded by his skepticism, he now uses his scientific background to seek the truth about the paranormal. In addition to producing and hosting *Ghost Chronicles* on Ghostvillage Radio, iTunes, and PodCast Alley, he also produces and hosts two weekly, one-hour live radio shows, *Ghost Chronicles Live* and *Ghost Chronicles International* on *www.toginet.com*, Para-X, and Ghost Channel and Beyond. *Ghost Chronicles* previously aired live for three years on WCCM, 1490 AM in Lawrence, Massachusetts. Ron was also a contributor to Jeff Belanger's *Encyclopedia of Haunted Places* (2005), Thomas D'Agostino's *Haunted New Hampshire* (2007), Jeff Belanger's *The Ghost Files* (2007) and *Weird Massachusetts* (2008), Kalyomi's *Ghosts from Coast to Coast* (2007), Richard Felix's *What Is a Ghost* (2009), Chris Balzano's *Picture Yourself Ghost Hunting* (2008), and Lesley Bannatyne's *Halloween* (2010). He is also coauthor of *Ghost Chronicles: A Medium and a Paranormal Scientist Investigate 17 True Hauntings* (2009).

MAUREEN WOOD

Maureen Wood is a fifth-generation psychic/trance-medium. For as far back as she can remember, she has communicated with the dead. At the age of fifteen, she was introduced to a woman who studied with Laurie Cabot, the official Witch of Salem, Massachusetts. This mentor took Maureen under her wing and taught her to not only understand but also to control her gifts. At this same age, she also served as a medium for adult séances. She has practiced, studied, and instructed metaphysical studies for more than twenty-five years. Maureen is currently the lead psychic/medium for *The New England Ghost Project* and co-host of the popular *Ghost Chronicles* radio show. Maureen also starred in the Emmy-winning *American Builder* Halloween special. She was a contributor to Jeff Belanger's *Communicating with the Dead* (2005) and *Weird Massachusetts* (2008), Roxie Zwicker's *Haunted Portland* (2007), Chris Balzano's *Picture Yourself Ghost Hunting* (2008), and Lesley Bannatyne's *Halloween* (2010). Maureen also cowrote, with Ron Kolek, *Ghost Chronicles: A Medium and a Paranormal Scientist Investigate 17 True Hauntings* (2009).